DELIVERED

from

DISTRACTION

DELIVERED

from

DISTRACTION

◆

Getting the Most out of Life with
Attention Deficit Disorder

EDWARD M. HALLOWELL, M.D.

JOHN J. RATEY, M.D.

BALLANTINE BOOKS

NEW YORK

A BALLANTINE BOOK

PUBLISHED BY THE RANDOM HOUSE PUBLISHING GROUP

COPYRIGHT © 2005 BY EDWARD M. HALLOWELL, M.D., AND JOHN J. RATEY, M.D.

WWW.BALLANTINEBOOKS.COM

LIBRARY OF CONGRESS CATALOGING-IN-PUBLICATION DATA

HALLOWELL, EDWARD M.

DELIVERED FROM DISTRACTION : GETTING THE MOST OUT OF LIFE WITH ATTENTION DEFICIT DISORDER / EDWARD M. HALLOWELL AND JOHN J. RATEY.

P. CM.

INCLUDES BIBLIOGRAPHICAL REFERENCES AND INDEX.

ISBN 0-345-44230-X

1. ATTENTION-DEFICIT HYPERACTIVITY DISORDER—POPULAR WORKS   2. ATTENTION-DEFICIT DISORDER IN ADULTS—POPULAR WORKS.   I. RATEY, JOHN J.   II. TITLE.

RC394.A85H349 2004

616.85'89—DC22

2004052815

MANUFACTURED IN THE UNITED STATES OF AMERICA

FIRST EDITION: JANUARY 2005

10 9 8 7 6 5

BOOK DESIGN BY MERYL SUSSMAN LEVAVI

Since this book is about hope and the power of positive human energies, we dedicate it to the memory of two women who radiated those qualities in their lives:

Josseyln Hallowell Bliss
and
Priscilla Luke Vail

and to one team that never gives up:

The Boston Red Sox

Boy, what ever you is

and where ever you is,

don't be what you ain't,

because when you is

what you ain't, you *isn't*.

—UNCLE REMUS

ACKNOWLEDGMENTS

Many people helped to create this book.

Above all, John and I would like to thank our patients who contributed their stories, as well as the people who were not patients but contacted us and shared episodes from their lives. Although their names have been changed, all the stories are true; we never could have given this book the power that true stories pack were it not for the courageous cooperation of the dozens of people you find in these pages.

Many other people supported this work. Ginny Grenham, dear friend and creative genius, was most helpful, as always. It was she who urged that a chapter be included on making the transition to college, and she who suggested the chapter on explaining ADD to children. A devoted advocate of all who live with ADD, she always finds the best in people and helps them reach and grasp higher than they think they can.

We also thank Kay Murray and Roxie Nickerson for their painstaking work on the final section of the book, the resource section.

A great number of top experts helped us in our research. We especially want to thank Janet Wozniak for her help on the chapter on bipolar disorder and Demitri Papolos for his comments on that topic.

Mel Levine was, as ever, generous, brilliant, and provocative in sharing his thoughts about attention. Ellen Braaten was most helpful in discussing psychological and neuropsychological testing. Sue Smalley was a great help in giving us information for the chapter on genetics. Stacy Bell and Helen Rasmussen shared their expert knowledge about nutrition, and Eugene Arnold helped in the evaluation of alternative or complementary treatments. Len Adler advised us about the most current data on the new medication Strattera. Ross Greene helped with his innovative ideas on untangling struggles in families. Susan Cole Ross taught me about educational therapy, and, a fine writer herself, she also helped to edit the manuscript. Peter Jensen offered encouragement and knowledge whenever we turned to him, which was often. Peter Metz, one of the best psychiatrists in the land, was a great help all along the way. Michael Thompson offered encouragement and wisdom at many junctures, as he always has.

Diane Santangelo, Peter Mustich, and others from the Rye Union Free School District gave of their time and experience in showing me the details of a school system that does it right.

Sam Goldstein, Sally Shaywitz, Clarke Ross, Bob Brooks, Kathleen Hopkins, Michele Novotni, Sari Solden, Kathleen Nadeau, Patty Quinn, Joe Biederman, Tom Spencer, Tim Willens, Larry Silver, Rick Lavoie, Russ Barkley, Kevin Murphy, Kitty McEaddy, Alice Thomas, Thom Hartmann, Theresa Citro, Lynn Meltzer, Daniel Amen, Jonathan Mooney, and many others from disparate domains of the ADD and LD communities have always encouraged us and shared their experiences enthusiastically. Thanks to the efforts of these people and many others, a community that used to be weakened by division and dissension now gains strength and even glee from discussion and cooperation.

We also thank our teachers from years ago, men and women at the Massachusetts Mental Health Center in Boston who helped us learn to listen, to observe, and to believe in what John Keats called "the holiness of the heart's affections." Many of our best teachers were our patients. And many were faculty who gave of their hearts and minds tirelessly and enthusiastically. Among the faculty, Doris Menzer Benaron, Jules Bemporad, William Beuscher, Thomas Gutheil, Leston Havens, Allan Hobson, Elvin Semrad, and Irvin Taube all instilled in John and me, as well as hundreds of others in training, a habitual curiosity and open-mindedness. With their encouragement, we didn't just study psychiatry—we studied life.

We thank our agent, Jill Kneerim, for her many years of care and help, and the team at Ballantine, led by the warm-hearted and astute editorial guidance of Nancy Miller and her assistant, Deirdre Lanning. Writers often have good reason to complain about publishers; in this instance, we have reason not only to give thanks but to feel uplifted by a sense of teamwork and kinship with the publishers. The team at Ballantine believed in this book from the outset and did all they could, every step of the way, to make it as good as it could be.

Finally, and most personally, we thank our families. John thanks his wife, Nancy, and his children, Jessica and Kathryn, for their support, loyalty, and love. And I thank my wife, Sue, and our children, Lucy, Jack, and Tucker, for making me the luckiest man on the face of the earth.

CONTENTS

◆ Part One ◆

WHAT'S IT LIKE TO HAVE ADD?

• Part Two •

THREE STORIES THAT TELL *THE* STORY

• Part Three •

MAKING THE DIAGNOSIS OF ADD

• Part Four •
MASTERING THE POWER AND AVOIDING
THE PITFALLS: THE TREATMENT OF ADD

A NOTE ON AUTHORSHIP

Edward (Ned) Hallowell wrote this book. Hence, throughout the book, the pronoun *I* refers to Ned (me). *We* refers to both John Ratey and me. When John is to be singled out, I refer to him by name.

Although I did all the writing, the project was very much a shared one, its roots extending back to 1978, when John and I first met. Indeed, this collaboration serves as an excellent example of the five-step process we recommend in our discussion of the treatment for ADD: connect; play; practice; achieve mastery; gain recognition. We drew more out of each other than either of us could have delivered alone. Collaborating wasn't easy, but it was, in the best and deepest sense of this word, a joy.

As we contemplated writing this new book, we asked ourselves, "Can two men who have ADD themselves get their acts together well enough to write a book about ADD . . . *again*?" What you hold in your hands right now is the answer to that question.

This book emerges from the twenty-five years John and I have worked and played together. I say "played" because even though we're now in our fifties, there's a lot of play in what we do, from working out to brainstorming. This is one of the many advantages of having ADD as an adult: you are less likely than other adults to lose your enthusiasm for play, or your ability to do it!

John majored in philosophy in college, and I majored in English. Then we both headed off to science and medical school. We both wanted to combine the tradition of the old-fashioned, humanistic doctor with the new wave of medical science and technology, taking the best from both.

We first met in 1979 when John was chief resident at the Massachusetts Mental Health Center and I was a first-year resident in psychiatry. Back then, your chief resident was your teacher, guru, parent, and friend rolled into one. Your chief was supposed to make sure you ripened from a sleep-deprived novice fresh from the boot camp called internship into the sort of doctor people in emotional distress could take comfort from. That was—and is—like transfusing blood into a patient who is as dry as dust and has no visible veins. John found veins.

He found more in us than we knew we had. If you ask me, he was the best chief resident in the history of psychiatry. We've been friends now for almost half of our lives. John is godfather to one of my children, and I was best man at John's second wedding.

When we first met, neither of us knew we had ADD. In fact, we didn't even know what ADD was! But we knew we liked the way each other thought, and we also knew that we went through life differently from most other people. We began to explore what we would later learn is called ADD simply by talking with each other and comparing notes on what we observed in our patients, in ourselves, and in what was emerging from psychiatry and neuroscience. It made for one of the most exciting extended discussions I've ever had, and it's still going on.

After I completed my residency I went into training in child psychiatry, while John began his career as a teacher, researcher, and clinician. We remained close friends, meeting regularly to play squash.

We talked about cases and about brain science all the time. Our discussions led us all over, one of our favorite places being the world of ADD. Before we knew it, we were diagnosed with ADD ourselves. The more we learned, the more we realized how common this little-known condition was. So we decided to write a book. It took a while to get it done because folks with ADD tend to procrastinate.

But it got done. In 1994, fifteen years after we met, *Driven to Distraction* was published: one of the first books to introduce the general public to the world of attention deficit disorder.

Since that time, brain science has so taken off that the 1990s was dubbed "the decade of the brain." As the passing years brought new knowledge, they also gave John and me time to develop and test our ideas and learn from the thousands of new patients we treated.

Because of all that we had learned since 1994, we decided in 2002 that it was time for a new book. But, we wondered, would it be possible for us to collaborate a *second* time? Once was tough enough, but *twice*? Being dreamers and risk-takers (two of the attributes often found in adults who have ADD), and also drawing upon the faith in difficult projects John had developed on the tennis courts of Pittsburgh and I had developed at Exeter, we decided to give it a go.

The last time we collaborated, we had been able to rely on squash to bring us together regularly. But age had hit us both. John hurt his shoulder, so he could no longer play squash. Then I developed such severe osteoarthritis that I had to have a total hip replacement at the tender age of fifty-two. No more squash for me, either. Since exercise had always been a key to our collaboration, we began our meetings for the new book in a gym. After working out on the StairMaster or stationary bike, we would sit down at the juice bar to develop our new book.

Gradually, *Delivered from Distraction* climbed hand over hand out of the neural networks where it took shape deep within our brains.

Never in this book do we contend that it is easy to live life with ADD. If you don't get help, ADD can curse you and make you wretched. But if you work it right, ADD can enhance your life and make you sparkle. Sometimes it seems all but impossible to scratch your way out of the mess this complex condition with such a simple name can turn your life into. But there is always, always hope.

Consider the story of the Harvard medical student who had been languishing in high school until his ADD was diagnosed. "After that, I discovered I had a brain," he told me. His life totally changed once the diagnosis was made. He got into college, which he *never* thought he could do. Not only did he get in, he excelled. He did so well in college that he won a Rhodes Scholarship. Following the Rhodes, he was admitted to Harvard Medical School.

When I discussed this book with him he responded eagerly, "Oh, good. You gave ADD its coming-out party with *Driven to Distraction.* Now it is time to give ADD its citizenship in the world. That diagnosis saved my life, and it could save millions more if people really understood it for what it is."

HOW TO READ THIS BOOK

This is not a textbook. It is a special kind of storybook in which the stories depict the charms and dilemmas of a unique place: the world of attention deficit disorder. All the stories in this storybook are true, and include bits of scientific information as well as suggestions on how to solve the dilemmas the stories illustrate.

I hope you'll read this book the way you'd have a conversation with a close friend over lunch. I hope you will enjoy yourself as you entertain new ideas and reconsider old ones. Skip around in your mind as you read, get up and go to the restroom, order another glass of wine, and settle in for an intimate couple of hours.

There is no surprise ending that you'll ruin by reading ahead, so feel free to skip around. That's the ADD way, after all.

The first chapter has "the skinny," so you might want to read it right away if that's all you think you have time for. Or you might be inclined to read it last as a kind of summing up. Or you could skip it altogether because you don't like "skinnies."

If you never finish the book, don't dismay. As Samuel Johnson said, "There are so few books one reads all the way through." Just take what you want, enjoy it, and put it to good use.

When you finish reading—or when our conversation comes to a

pause—I hope you will contact me if you have comments or questions. I love to hear from readers. You can reach me by e-mail through my website, www.DrHallowell.com.

Now, please join me in a conversation about the wonderful world of attention deficit disorder, a world where I live, which I invite you to explore and enjoy with me.

WELCOME TO THE WORLD OF ADD,

WHERE LANDING IS LEARNED IN MIDAIR

Good news. That's what is in this book. The diagnosis and treatment of ADD can change your life dramatically for the better.

Owing to the nature of ADD, it may take you a little while to find out about the good news, though. Let me tell you the story of a man named Paul, who sent me the following e-mail some time ago:

On August 5, 2003, I had the good fortune to listen to you on a radio program. I say good fortune because what you said almost made me drive off the road. Allow me to explain. Your review of ADD and its symptoms fit me to a tee. I would like to outline my history and set up an appointment for an immediate evaluation.

- I am a 47-year-old male, 5 feet 9 inches, of Irish decent and in reasonably good health.
- I am a recovering alcoholic with seven and a half years' sobriety.
- I have been told I am very bright and very creative in my thinking.
- I have had trouble all my life completing tasks and struggled in school.
- Teachers said I was lazy, disruptive, and had the ability to achieve at a much higher level.

- I have never been truly happy in my life and have always felt like a square peg in a round hole.

I know that there is much more to tell in my story and maybe after reading this you may say that it is not ADD. I still think based on what I heard yesterday that I really want you to evaluate my situation.

I am very interested in a reply, and would do anything to get an appointment.

Paul closed his e-mail by identifying himself as holding a senior management position in the Hartford area. I called him up, using the work number I was glad he'd remembered to give me in his e-mail. (I get many messages from people with ADD asking me to call them back, and they often forget to provide me with a telephone number.) Paul answered his own phone. Just as I expected, he sounded intelligent. But, just as I expected, he sounded frustrated. "Why didn't someone pick up on this when I was in school?" he asked. "And why didn't my doctor catch it?"

I gave him the answer I have given many times. "It's not anybody's fault. Most doctors don't know much about ADD, and few teachers knew about it when you were in school. Back then, people dismissed you as stupid or just bad."

I heard him grunt in recognition. "I know I could have done much better. I know I could be doing better now. Is it too late?"

"It is never too late. Absolutely never."

"Do you really think I have ADD?" he asked.

I laughed. He was eager and impatient, like most of us who have ADD. "I wish I could diagnose you here on the telephone. But just from your e-mail and this conversation, I can't do that. However, I can say for sure that it's worth looking into further."

"So what's the next step?" he asked eagerly. I could almost see him drumming his pencil or tapping his fingers as we talked.

"Well, if I may peddle my wares," I replied, "you could try reading my book *Driven to Distraction,* and if you see yourself in it, then make an appointment with a specialist and get a proper evaluation."

"What's a proper evaluation?" he asked.

"You go see a doctor, preferably one who has special training in learning differences and ADD. But make sure you see someone who has broad experience, so he or she can identify what else could be going on, maybe some undiagnosed medical condition, like hypothyroidism. That actually happened with one of my patients just the other day. Anyway, you should see a doctor. Child psychiatrists probably have the most training."

"But I am not a child," Paul protested.

"I know that," I said with a laugh. "Child psychiatrists also see adults."

"I don't know any child psychiatrists," he replied.

I asked him where he lived. Since it was only a couple of hours from my office, I volunteered my services. He gratefully accepted.

I was pretty sure I could help him. People who say, as Paul did, that they "have never been truly happy" in their lives and "have always felt like a square peg in a round hole" are the people whom mental-health professionals help every day.

Several months passed. I assumed Paul had found another doctor, maybe someone closer to his home. But three months after his initial e-mail, I received another. It began with a copy of the first e-mail he had sent months before to which he added this:

Dr. Hallowell,

As you can see, I sent you the above e-mail on August 5, 2003. You advised me to schedule an appointment with your office and purchase the book.

I thought I would give you an update.

I did purchase the book, and like most books I purchase, I've read approximately two-thirds of it. I pick it up and put it down, I pick it up and put it down . . . and so the story goes.

After we spoke, I had every intention of calling your office right then and there to schedule an appointment, but I always just seem to get involved in something else!

I think you know what the hell I'm going through. I just can't complete most things, yet I'm not unsuccessful. I really think I'm losing it and need an evaluation.

Please forward me the number at your office and I'll schedule an appointment immediately!

I want to find the answer to what holds me back in life!

Thanks.

Paul

Paul's delay in getting to me is common. One of the many traps ADD can set is that of procrastination. But, finally, we set up an appointment, and we met.

As I took Paul's history, it became clear that he did have ADD. His mind was always on the go, and ever since childhood, distractibility had been a problem for him. He had spent years in school being reprimanded, and when he wasn't being reprimanded in school he was being ridiculed by his father, a man he both worshipped and feared. Gradually, due to the mistreatment at school and the put-downs at home, Paul began to give up on himself. He didn't drop out; he was too tenacious for that. But he started to sell himself short.

He went into a career that didn't truly interest him and he married a woman he didn't truly love—both to appease his father and because he didn't think he could do any better. Settling for what he had, he tried to make the best of it, and the best of it he did make. He became financially successful at a job he didn't much like and he raised three wonderful children, being a world-class dad. He treated his wife well and was faithful to her, doing his best to love her.

His one stumbling block was alcohol, with which he self-medicated on a daily basis. However, he caught himself before it was too late, joined AA, and had been sober for almost eight years when we met.

I diagnosed his ADD, which in itself was a relief and a revelation to him. "My dad just told me I was a loser. Told me I needed a kick in the pants, which he often gave me. He'll think this diagnosis is just another excuse."

"But it's not, Paul," I replied. "It is a medical fact." I could see him sitting up straighter in his chair. "You have struggled heroically your whole life. Now it is time for you to receive the medical treatment you should have received many years ago."

I started Paul on a stimulant medication—Adderall—and I also referred him for a specialized nonmedication treatment called the Interactive Metronome, which is a type of brain-training many athletes use to improve timing and coordination. For example, the professional golfer Vijay Singh has improved his game with the Interactive Metronome exercises. In addition, I referred Paul to a support group for adults with ADD that I run with a psychologist.

I also took stock with Paul of what he really wanted to do in life. I asked him what dreams he had, dreams that perhaps he had given up on.

Usually, adults who have undiagnosed ADD have some dream, some forgotten hope, that treatment can revive and help turn into a reality.

Sure enough, Paul had a dream, but on the face of it, Paul's dream was a tremendous long shot. He wanted to become a professional golfer. Now forty-seven years old, he would become eligible to join the Senior Professional Golfers Association Tour in three years, when he turned fifty. Legions of middle-aged men all over America share the dream of turning pro at age fifty. But most of the players who actually do make it to the senior tour have already been on the regular PGA tour for many years. Very few are able to qualify to join the tour with no prior professional experience at age fifty.

On the other hand, Paul was what is called a scratch golfer. His handicap was zero, meaning his average score for eighteen holes of golf was par, which, depending on the course, is around 72. For readers who do not know golf, that is outstanding. Professionals are glad to shoot 72. One or two shots below that can win tournaments. Being a scratch golfer, Paul had a shot—still a long shot, but a shot—at making the senior tour when he turned fifty. I encouraged him to take his dream seriously.

As treatment of his ADD began, Paul got good news. The medication helped him. It does not help everyone, but it did help Paul. With Adderall he could focus more clearly, and it did not cause side effects.

Paul began to talk in the group therapy about his new life, what it felt like to have ADD, and how good it felt to give it a name. He talked about his abusive father, how he had held Paul down for so many years. He still loved his dad, but he knew it was time to rise up and be his own man, to take charge of his own life, at last. It was clear that powerful forces of change were stirring inside Paul.

Within a couple of months he had made an appointment to meet with one of the country's leading golf instructors, a man who might just be able to get his game in good enough shape for the senior tour. No guarantee, of course, but Paul resolved to give it his best shot.

He also sat down with his wife and said what he knew he needed to say: "Now that the kids are grown up, wouldn't it be best for both of us to go our separate ways?" To his surprise and relief, she agreed. The marriage had not be satisfying to her, either.

As of this writing, that's where life stands with Paul. He is on the precipice of a new life. Of course, he has not quit his job—he still needs to pay the bills—but he is doing his best to pursue his dream job and become a pro golfer. And, after he goes through what appears will be an amicable divorce, he will also consider trying to find true love for the first time in his life.

This is the kind of change that the diagnosis and treatment of ADD can bring about in a person's life. It offers hope, but, more than hope, it offers practical methods for achieving dramatic growth.

A DISTINCTIVE COLLECTION OF TRAITS

The best way to think of ADD is not as a mental disorder but as a collection of traits and tendencies that define a way of being in the world. There is some positive to it and some negative, some glory and some pain. If the negative becomes disabling, then this way of being in the world can become a disorder. The point of diagnosis and treatment is to transform the disorder into an asset.

The world of ADD baffles the uninformed with its complications and contradictions. As John Ratey's high school tennis coach used to tell John, "You are the most consistently inconsistent player I've ever seen!" Having ADD makes life paradoxical. You can superfocus sometimes, but also space out when you least mean to. You can radiate confidence and also feel as insecure as a cat in a kennel. You can perform at the highest level, feeling incompetent as you do so. You can be loved by many, but feel as if no one really likes you. You can absolutely, totally, intend to do something, then forget to do it. You can have the greatest ideas in the world, but feel as if you can't accomplish a thing.

Your typical report card—in childhood or adulthood—states that you are not performing up to your potential; constantly struggling to get organized; always waiting until the last minute—or later—to get things done; but also blessed with great creativity, originality, energy, wit, and drive. Teachers lament that you are unable to put those qualities to their best use. Welcome to the world of ADD—at its most frustrating.

But there is more to this world than frustration.

Most people regard ADD as a problem, which it can indeed be. The prisons are full of people with undiagnosed ADD. But I look at

ADD as a potential blessing—with emphasis on the word *potential*. The goal is to sculpt ADD into a blessing. You can do this by accentuating what's useful and paring back on what's not. Usually, that's not easy to do.

For a few lucky people, it happens easily, but for most people such life-sculpting takes pains. Sometimes it seems futile. But I have seen too many people with ADD prevail over their problems ever to believe it's impossible. *Everyone* who has ADD can sculpt a fulfilling, joyful life out of what they've been born with.

Doing so starts in your head and in your heart: you need knowledge and you need hope. Most people do not know much about their minds or about ADD. They believe bad report cards from years ago. They believe their past frustrations define who they will continue to be. They carry jagged bits of broken hopes that shred their confidence.

But knowledge of what is truly going on can restore confidence and inspire hope. Learning not just about the mind in general but about your own particular mind excites almost anyone who does it. We live in an era when the ancient advice "Know thyself" has taken on a biological meaning beyond its traditional psychological one. It is possible now for everyone not only to learn useful facts about their brains but also to devise practical techniques for using their brains more effectively based on those facts. Learning about ADD is one strong example.

For all the hoopla you read and hear about the overdiagnosis of ADD and the overuse of medication—indeed, serious problems in certain places—the more costly problem is the opposite: millions of people, *especially adults,* have ADD but don't know about it and therefore get no help at all.

With guidance, they could dramatically improve their lives. But they need more sophisticated help than a quick fix. Too often, a person's interest is piqued by an interview on TV or a newspaper or magazine column only to see a doctor and be given a prescription for a medication with no additional guidance or more comprehensive treatment plan. This is like buying an oxygen tank, then heading off to the Great Barrier Reef.

However, with proper preparation, you can dive the Great Barrier Reef, or do just about anything you want. You can thrive if you have ADD.

WHAT'S NEW IN THE WORLD OF ADD?

In 1994 attention deficit disorder was an obscure medical term, understood only by a small number of specialists. Now the problem has changed. In 1994 we had to introduce readers to a condition most people had never heard of. Now that ADD is almost a household term, we need to dispel myths and supply facts. We need to help people understand what ADD is, what it isn't, what we know about it, and what we don't know. We need to share the new research findings and the insights they have led to. We need also to acknowledge the many areas in which experts disagree.

True stories—which comprise the heart of this book—show ADD in many different settings, age groups, and levels of severity. This book also discusses new methods of diagnosis, new kinds of treatment, and also provides a comprehensive listing of referrals and resources. It devotes a great deal of attention to ADD in adults, and also explores the growing research into alternative or complementary treatments.

Let me preview some of what's new in the world of ADD that you will find in this book:

Advances in Treatment

- New medications for the treatment of ADD, along with their advantages and disadvantages
- Specific dietary and nutritional suggestions, including the use of fish oil, which is rich in omega-3 fatty acids, to supplement the treatment of ADD
- New information on the use of physical exercise to treat ADD
- A New Application of the 12-step program to treat ADD
- Evidence that exercises that stimulate the cerebellum may be a potential adjunct to standard treatment for ADD
- A five-step program designed to identify and promote talents in people who have ADD
- New approaches to organization and time management
- A special section on how to make the transition to college
- New research showing that reducing how much television a child watches reduces the risk of developing ADD
- A completely new, updated listing of resources

Research into Diagnosis

- New approaches to diagnosis
- A new diagnostic screening questionnaire for ADD in adults, which was recently developed by leaders in research in conjunction with the World Health Organization
- Our recommendation of the quantitative electroencephalogram, or qEEG, as a diagnostic tool
- Our critical appraisal of the SPECT scan in the diagnostic workup and in treatment planning for ADD and related conditions
- A new self-assessment quiz

New Understanding of the Characteristics of Attention Deficit Disorder

- New material on ADD in adults
- Emphasis on talents and strengths
- Core cases illustrating more complex situations than those in *Driven to Distraction,* while other stories fill out the picture of ADD in ways that John and I have learned about since 1994
- New evidence from brain scans, particularly MRIs, that ADD is associated with slight but significant anatomical differences in specific regions of the brain
- New evidence from genetics showing how highly heritable ADD is
- A model that explains the "itch" at the core of ADD, what to do about it, and what to beware of

ADD OR ADHD?

In this book we use the old term, attention deficit disorder, or ADD, because that is the term most people are familiar with. Although the condition has officially been renamed ADHD, for attention deficit hyperactivity disorder, most people still refer to it as ADD. As we use it, the term ADD includes the symptoms of both ADD and ADHD, i.e., people who do *not* have symptoms of hyperactivity as well as people who do.

PART ONE

◆

What's It Like to Have ADD?

CHAPTER 1

THE SKINNY ON ADD:

READ THIS IF YOU CAN'T READ

THE WHOLE BOOK

Most people who have ADD don't read books all the way through. It's not because they don't want to; it's because reading entire books is very difficult—sort of like singing an entire song in just one breath.

We want to make this book accessible to people who don't read books all the way through. For those people, our most dear and treasured brothers and sisters in ADD, we offer this first chapter, set off from the rest of the book. Reading this will give you a good idea of what ADD is all about. If you want to learn more, ask someone who loves you to read the whole book and tell you about it. Or you can listen to it on a tape or CD.

We offer this chapter in the ADD-friendly format of Q&A. You can get the skinny on ADD in these thirty questions and answers. For more detail and research-based answers, you can refer to the chapters of particular interest.

For those blessed readers who intend to read the entire book, some of what's in this Q&A will appear again, but some of it won't, so you too should read this section.

Q&A ON ADD

Q: What is ADD?

A: Attention deficit disorder, or ADD, is a misleading name for an intriguing kind of mind. ADD is a name for a collection of symptoms, some positive, some negative. For many people, ADD is not a disorder but a trait, a way of being in the world. When it impairs their lives, then it becomes a disorder. But once they learn to manage its disorderly aspects, they can take full advantage of the many talents and gifts embedded in this sparkling kind of mind.

Having ADD is like having a turbocharged race-car brain. If you take certain specific steps, then you can take advantage of the benefits ADD conveys—while avoiding the disasters it can create.

The diagnostic manual of mental problems, called the DSM-IV, defines ADD by a set of eighteen symptoms. To qualify for the diagnosis you need six. These diagnostic criteria are listed in chapter 12. But be careful when you read them. They describe only the downside of ADD. The more you emphasize the downside, the more you create additional pathology: a nasty set of avoidable, secondary problems, like shame, fear, and a sharply diminished sense of what's possible in life.

The pathology of ADD—its disorderly side—represents only one part of the total picture.

The other part, the part that the DSM-IV and other catalogs of pathology leave out, is the zesty side of ADD. People with ADD have special gifts, even if they are hidden. The most common include originality, creativity, charisma, energy, liveliness, an unusual sense of humor, areas of intellectual brilliance, and spunk. Some of our most successful entrepreneurs have ADD, as do some of our most creative actors, writers, doctors, scientists, attorneys, architects, athletes, and dynamic people in all walks of life.

Q: What is the difference between ADHD and ADD?

A: It's just a matter of nosology, the classification of disorders. There is an arbitrariness to it all. By the current DSM-IV definition, ADD technically does not exist. By the DSM-IV definition, the term ADHD includes both ADHD *with* hyperactivity (the *H* in ADHD) and ADHD *without* hyperactivity. Technically, this means you can have ADHD with no symptoms of *H,* hence there is no need for the term ADD. But ADD, the old term, is still used by many clinicians, including the authors of this book. Whichever term you use, the important point to know is that you can have ADHD (or ADD) without showing any signs of hyperactivity or impulsivity whatsoever. ADHD without hyperactivity or impulsivity is more common among females.

Q: What is the typical profile of a person who has ADD?
A: The core symptoms of ADD are excessive distractibility, impulsivity, and restlessness. These can lead both children and adults to underachieve at school, at work, in relationships and marriage, and in all other settings.

In addition, people who have ADD often also exhibit:

Advantageous characteristics:
- Many creative talents, usually underdeveloped until the diagnosis is made
- Original, out-of-the-box thinking
- Tendency toward an unusual way of looking at life, a zany sense of humor, an unpredictable approach to anything and everything
- Remarkable persistence and resilience, if not stubbornness
- Warm-hearted and generous behavior
- Highly intuitive style

Disadvantageous characteristics:
- Difficulty in turning their great ideas into significant actions
- Difficulty in explaining themselves to others
- Chronic underachievement. They may be floundering in school or at work, or they may achieve at a high level (getting good grades or being president of the company does not rule out the diagnosis of ADHD), but they know they could be achieving at a higher level if only they could "find the key."
- Mood often angry or down in the dumps due to frustration
- Major problems in handling money and making sensible financial plans
- Poor tolerance of frustration
- Inconsistent performance despite great effort. People with

ADHD do great one hour and lousy the next, or great one day and lousy the next, regardless of effort and time in preparation. They go from the penthouse to the outhouse in no time at all!

- History of being labeled "lazy" or "a spaceshot" or "an attitude problem" by teachers or employers who do not understand what is really going on (i.e., having ADD)
- Trouble with organization. Kids with ADD organize by stuffing book bags and closets. Adults organize by putting everything into piles. The piles metastasize, soon covering most available space.
- Trouble with time management. People with ADD are terrible at estimating in advance how long a task will take. They typically procrastinate and develop a pattern of getting things done at the last minute.
- Search for high stimulation. People with ADD often are drawn to danger or excitement as a means of focusing. They will drive 100 mph in order to think clearly, for example.
- Tendency to be a maverick (This can be an advantage or a disadvantage!)
- Impatience. People with ADD can't stand waiting in lines or waiting for others to get to the point.
- Chronic wandering of the mind, or what is called distractibility. Tendency to tune out or drift away in the middle of a page or a conversation. Tendency to change subjects abruptly.
- Alternately highly empathic and highly unempathic, depending upon the level of attention and engagement
- Poor ability to appreciate own strengths or perceive own shortcomings
- Tendency to self-medicate with alcohol or other drugs, or with addictive activities such as gambling, shopping, sexualizing, eating, or risk-taking
- Trouble staying put with one activity until it is done
- Tendency to change channels, change plans, change direction, for no apparent reason
- Failure to learn from mistakes. People with ADD will often use the same strategy that failed them before.
- Easily forgetful of their own failings and those of others. They are quick to forgive, in part because they are quick to forget.

- Difficulty in reading social cues, which can lead to difficulty in making and keeping friends
- Tendency to get lost in own thoughts, no matter what else might be going on

Q: Aren't most people somewhat like this?

A: The diagnosis of ADD is based not upon the presence of these symptoms—which most people have now and then—but upon the intensity and duration of the symptoms. If you have the symptoms intensely, as compared to a group of your peers, and if you have had them all your life, you may have ADD. An apt comparison can be made with depression. While everyone has been sad, not everyone has been depressed. The difference lies in the intensity and the duration of the sadness. So it is with ADD. If you are intensely distractible, and have been forever, you may have ADD.

Q: What causes ADD? Is it inherited?

A: We don't know exactly what causes ADD, but we do know it runs in families. Like many traits of behavior and temperament, ADD is genetically *influenced,* but not genetically determined. Environment combines with genetics to create ADD. Environmental toxins may play a role, watching too much television may play a role, and excessive stimulation may play a role.

You can see the role of genetics just by glancing at basic numbers. We estimate that about 5 to 8 percent of a random sample of children have ADD. But if one parent has it, the chances of a child developing it shoot up to about 30 percent; if both parents have it, the chances leap to more than 50 percent. But genetics don't tell the whole story. You can also acquire ADD through a lack of oxygen at birth; or from a head injury; or if your mother drank too much alcohol during pregnancy; or from elevated lead levels; perhaps from food allergies and environmental or chemical sensitivities; from too much television, video games, and the like; and in other ways we don't yet understand.

Q: Other than its being heritable, is there any other evidence that ADD has a biological, physical basis to it, as opposed to psychological or environmental?

A: Brain scans of various kinds have shown differences between the

ADD and the non-ADD brain. Four different studies done in the past decade using MRI (magnetic resonance imaging) all found a slight reduction in the size of four regions of the brain: the corpus callosum, the basal ganglia, the frontal lobes, and the cerebellar vermis. While the differences are not consistent enough to provide a diagnostic test for ADD, they do correlate with the symptoms we see in ADD. For example, the frontal lobes help with organization, time management, and decision-making, all areas that people with ADD struggle with. The basal ganglia help to regulate moods and to control impulsive outbursts, which people with ADD also struggle with. And the cerebellum helps with balance, rhythm, coordinated movements, language, and other as yet to be proven functions. It may be that the cerebellum is far more important in regulating attention than we realize today.

Q: How many people have ADD?
A: Roughly 5 to 8 percent (many experts would put that figure much higher, some lower) of the American population has ADD. The majority of adults who have it don't know it because people used to think ADD was only a children's condition. We now know that adults have it too. Of the roughly 10 million adults in the United States who have ADD, only about 15 percent have been diagnosed and treated. Until we have a precise diagnostic test for ADD, however, it will be impossible to give truly accurate figures. Studies around the world—in China, Japan, India, Germany, Puerto Rico, and New Zealand—show comparable figures.

Q: Does ADD ever go away on its own?
A: Yes. The symptoms of ADD disappear during puberty in 30 to 40 percent of children, and the symptoms stay gone. ADD therefore persists into adulthood 60 to 70 percent of the time. As the brain matures, it changes in ways that may cause the negative symptoms to abate. Then ADD becomes a trait rather than a disorder. In addition, sometimes the child learns how to compensate so well for his ADD during puberty that it looks as if the ADD has gone away. However, if you interview that child closely, you will discover the symptoms are still there, but the child is struggling mightily—and successfully—to control them. These people still have ADD and would benefit from treatment.

Q: Is ADD overdiagnosed among children?

A: Yes, but also no. It is overdiagnosed in some places, underdiagnosed in others. There are schools and regions where every child who blinks fast seems to get diagnosed with ADD. At the same time, there are places around the country where doctors refuse to make the diagnosis at all because they "don't believe in ADD." ADD is not a religious principle; it is a medical diagnosis derived from such solid evidence as genetic studies, brain scans, and worldwide epidemiological surveys.

It is important that we educate doctors, as well as teachers, parents, and school officials, about ADD, so that we can solve the problems of both overdiagnosis and underdiagnosis.

Q: What is the proper procedure to diagnose ADD?

A: There is no surefire test. The best way to diagnose ADD is to combine several tests. The most powerful "test" is your own story, which doctors call your history. As you tell your story, your doctor will be listening for how your attention has varied in different settings throughout your life. In the case of ADD it is important that the history be taken from at least two people, such as parent, teacher, and child, or adult and spouse, since people with ADD are not good at observing themselves.

To supplement the history, there is a relatively new physical test called the quantitative electroencephalogram, or qEEG, that is quite reliable in helping to diagnose ADD. It is a simple, painless brainwave test, and it is about 90 percent accurate. Though well worth getting, it is not definitive by itself.

In complex cases where the diagnosis is unclear or there is a suspicion of coexisting conditions, especially if there is a history of head injury or other brain trauma, a SPECT scan can help. The SPECT brain scan is not widely available, though we believe it could help a great deal in psychiatry if it were.

In addition to the history, which should include questions based upon the DSM-IV diagnostic criteria, and the qEEG and sometimes the SPECT, other standardized sets of questions, such as the ADHD Rating Scale or the Brown scale, add confidence to the diagnosis. Your doctor can tell you about these tests. None are necessary, but all are helpful.

Finally, neuropsychological testing can help pin down the diagnosis as well as expose associated problems—such as hidden learning disabilities, anxiety, depression, and other potential problems.

Practically speaking, if you are going to see a busy primary-care doctor for your evaluation, the time available to take a history may be brief, and access to neuropsychological testing nonexistent. In these instances, the qEEG becomes even more valuable, as well as the standardized rating scales, especially the DSM-IV criteria.

The best diagnostic procedures also include a search for talents and strengths, as these are the key to the most successful treatments.

Q: Should you always order the qEEG, neuropsychological testing, or a SPECT scan?
A: All three can be helpful, but no, none is absolutely necessary, unless the diagnosis is in doubt, or you suspect associated learning disabilities such as dyslexia, or other coexisting conditions, like brain damage due to an old head injury, or bipolar disorder, or hidden substance abuse. In such cases, you might encourage your doctor to consider getting you neuropsychological testing, a qEEG, or a SPECT scan.

Q: Whom should I see to get a diagnosis?
A: The best way to find a doctor who knows what he is doing is to get a referral from someone you know who has had a good experience with that doctor. (We have provided a list of specialists at the end of this book.)

The degree the person has is much less important than his experience. People from diverse disciplines may be capable of helping you. Child psychiatrists have the most training in ADD, and keep in mind that most child psychiatrists also treat adults. However, child psychiatry is an underpopulated specialty; therefore, child psychiatrists are hard to find. Developmental pediatricians are also good with ADD, but, of course, they do not treat adults and they are also in short supply. Some regular pediatricians are excellent at diagnosing and treating ADD, while others—those who have not had much experience with ADD—are understandably less skilled. Some family practitioners and some internists are good. Adult psychiatrists tend not to have training in ADD. However, most psychologists do.

If you cannot get a referral from someone you know, ask your primary-care doctor if she is expert in ADD, and if not, to whom would she recommend that you go.

It is worth the hassle to look around. I see patients every day who wasted years because they went to see the wrong person.

Q: What are the most common conditions that may occur along with ADD?

A: Dyslexia and other learning differences, depression, oppositional defiant disorder, conduct disorder, antisocial personality disorder, substance abuse, post-traumatic stress disorder, anxiety disorders, bipolar disorder.

Q: What other problems should one be on the lookout for?

A: Trouble in school, at work, or at home. Underachievement, even if there are no signs of what others consider to be trouble. Sometimes when the ADD is diagnosed and treated, the trouble, whatever it is, or the underachievement remit. But often they need special attention in their own right. Tutoring, career counseling, family therapy, couples therapy, individual therapy, or coaching can all help.

Q: What else should one watch out for regarding the diagnosis of ADD and getting treatment?

A: Many people in the United States today—including those who have ADD and those who do not—suffer from what I call disconnectedness. They do not have the close, sustaining relationships that they need. While we are elaborately connected electronically in modern life, we are poorly connected interpersonally. Studies have shown that such disconnectedness leads not only to anxiety, depression, and underachievement but also to substance abuse, disruptive behavior, and a host of medical problems in both children and adults. Try to develop a connected interpersonal life for you and your family as seriously as you strive to maintain a proper diet or an exercise program.

Q: What about bipolar disorder in children? Does it look like ADD? How do you tell them apart?

A: It is important to keep bipolar disorder in mind whenever the possibility of ADD arises in a child. Some experts believe that if you give a child who has bipolar disorder stimulant medication, you run the risk of doing serious harm. These children can become violent, depressed, even suicidal. This is just another reason why you must see a well-trained professional for a proper diagnostic evaluation.

Several items help distinguish between ADD and bipolar disorder. First of all, in bipolar disorder there is usually a family history on both parents' sides of bipolar disorder, alcoholism, major depression, or all of these. Second, in bipolar disorder the leading symptom is rapidly fluctuating moods independent of what is going on in the environment. In ADD the leading symptom is fluctuating attention. Third, the child with bipolar disorder often has a daily variation: he becomes highly active at night and in the morning he is like a hibernating bear, all but impossible to get out of bed. You can see this in ADD too, but it is more accentuated in bipolar disorder.

Q: What is the best treatment for ADD?
A: It varies. The best approach to treating ADD is to follow an individualized, comprehensive plan specifically designed for you, based upon your particular situation and needs. One size does not fit all. Work with your doctor to create the best approach for you (or for your child, or for whomever has the ADD). This plan should always be open to revision. If it doesn't work, change it.

Q: What are the most common, key ingredients of such a comprehensive plan?
A: I divide the best plan into eight areas, as follows:

1. Diagnosis, as well as identification of talents and strengths
2. Implementation of a five-step plan that promotes talents and strengths (detailed in chapter 22)
3. Education
4. Changes in lifestyle (e.g., reduce TV and other electronics, increase time with family and friends, increase physical exercise)
5. Structure
6. Counseling of some kind, such as coaching, psychotherapy, career counseling, couples therapy, family therapy
7. Various other therapies that can augment the effectiveness of medication or replace the use of medication altogether, such as an exercise program that stimulates the cerebellum, targeted tutoring,

general physical exercise, occupational therapy, and nutritional interventions

8. Medication

Q: In what ways are diagnosis, identification of talents and strengths, and implementation of a plan that promotes talents and strengths part of the treatment?

A: Getting a name for what's been going on with you usually brings relief. When you get the ADD diagnosis, you can finally shed all those
accusatory, "moral" diagnoses, like lazy, weak, undisciplined, or, simply, bad.

The identification of talents and strengths is one of the most important parts of the treatment. People with ADD usually know their
shortcomings all too well, while their talents and strengths have been
camouflaged by what's been going wrong.

The moment of diagnosis provides a spectacular opportunity to
change that. The best way to change a life of frustration into a life of
mastery is by developing talents and strengths, not just shoring up
weaknesses. Keep the focus on what you are, rather than what you are
not. The older you get, the more time you should spend developing
what you're good at. Work with someone who can help identify what
you're good at. In the long run that's where you will find fulfillment.

Q: What is the five-step plan that promotes talents and strengths?

A: The first step is to connect—with a teacher, a coach, a mentor, a supervisor, a lover, a friend (and don't forget God or whatever your spiritual life leads you toward). Once you feel connected, you will feel safe
enough to go to step 2, which is to play. In play, you discover your talents and strengths. Play includes any activity in which your brain lights
up and you get imaginatively involved. When you find some form of
play you like, you do it over and over again; this is step 3, practice. As
you practice, you get better; this is step 4, mastery. When you achieve
mastery, other people notice and give you recognition; this is step 5.
Recognition in turn connects you with the people who recognize and
value you, which brings you back to step 1, connect, and deepens the
connection.

No matter what your age, you can use this five-step process to promote talents and strengths. Beware, however, of jumping in at step 3.

That's the mistake many parents, teachers, coaches, and managers in the workplace make: they demand practice and offer recognition as the reward. This leads to short-term achievement but fatigue and burnout in the long run.

For the cycle to run indefinitely and passionately, it must generate its own enthusiasm and energy, not be prodded by external motivators. To do that, the cycle must start in connection and play.

Q: Why is education part of the treatment?

A: Treatment really means learning how to fit the brain you have into the world most enthusiastically and constructively. The diagnosis becomes therapeutic through education—learning what ADD is in *your* case. Diagnosis means "to know through." As you learn about your mind, and as you learn how ADD has affected your life, you gradually "know through" this condition, how it lives in you. The more you know about the kind of mind you have—whether or not you call it ADD—the better able you will be to improve your life.

Furthermore, the process of education will help identify your talents and strengths, or your potential talents and strengths. Take time, look hard, and get help in identifying these. You may not be able to see them yourself. People who have ADD often don't think they have any talents or strengths.

If there were but one rule for treating ADD it would be this: Find out what you're good at, and do it. Or, as my brother-in-law who is a teaching golf pro says, "Forget what the books say. Just do what you need to do to put the ball in the hole."

Q: What if you're not good at anything, or what if what you're good at is illegal, dangerous, or simply lacking in any social value, like playing Nintendo?

A: *Everyone* has the seed of a talent. Everyone has some interest that can be turned into a skill that is legal, reasonably safe, and has value both to that person and to society. *Everyone.* The work of treating ADD is to find that talent or interest. It may be hidden or camouflaged. For example, if the activity you're good at is selling drugs, well, that means you have entrepreneurial and sales talents and interests that could be plugged into some legal venture. If the activity you're good at is driving down the highway at 110 mph, then you may have a career in some risk-filled, highly stimulating arena like investing on the commodities exchange or being an investigative reporter. If what you're good at has no social value, like playing Nintendo, you might want to get a job at a computer-game store, or you might want to take a course in designing computer games.

The germ of a great career often lies hidden in the illegal, dangerous, or useless activities we love. Look for that germ cell. If you can't find it, get someone else to help you look.

Q: What do you mean by "structure"?
A: By "structure," I mean any habit or external device that helps make up for what is missing internally, in your mind. For example, the ADD brain is low on filing cabinets. So, you need to set up more filing cabinets outside the brain in order to replace piles with files. An alarm clock is an example of structure. So is a key chain, as well as a basket to put the key chain in every day when you get home. The habits of putting your key chain in the basket and putting your documents into the files also exemplify structure. Useful devices and new habits can help more than any medication.

Q: What are the most important lifestyle changes?
A: The six lifestyle changes I stress the most are:

1. Positive human contact. Due to our disconnected culture, people these days don't get enough smiles, hugs, waves hello, and warm handshakes. Positive human contact is as important as, if not more so than, a good night's sleep or a proper diet.
2. Reduce electronics (e.g., television, video games, the Internet). Studies have shown that too much "electronic time" predisposes to ADD.
3. Sleep. Enough sleep is the amount of sleep that allows you to wake up without an alarm clock. Without enough sleep, you'll act like you have ADD whether or not you have it.
4. Diet. Eat a balanced diet. Eat protein as part of breakfast. Protein is the best long-lasting source of brain fuel. Don't self-medicate with drugs, alcohol, or carbohydrates. Consider taking the various supplements discussed in chapter 25.
5. Exercise. Regular exercise is one of the best tonics you can give

your brain. Even if it's just walking for fifteen minutes, exercise every day. Exercise stimulates the production of epinephrine, dopamine, and serotonin, which is exactly what the medications we treat ADD with do. So exercising is like taking medication for ADD in a holistic, natural way.

6. Prayer or meditation. Both of these help to calm and focus the mind.

Q: What is coaching and tutoring as it applies to ADD?

A: An ADD coach is someone other than a parent or a spouse who can help a person get organized and stay on track. Coaches are available in many shapes and sizes, from the ultraexpensive executive coaches to the ultrainexpensive grandpa who coaches for free. There are national coaching organizations you can contact online for more information.

For many people, the most important intervention is targeted tutoring—tutoring targeted to correct specific problems or symptoms. This is usually reserved for children and young adults, but adults may benefit as well. The tutoring should be targeted to the specific need of the individual, as determined by the history and testing. For example, if you have trouble with written output, the tutoring should address that specifically; if you have trouble with arithmetic, the tutoring should address that; if you have a reading problem, you should get help specifically aimed at that. It is important to address areas of cognitive weakness as early as you can. For global issues of time management, compensatory skills, and self-esteem, a professional educational therapist is best trained in counseling and learning theory. To learn about finding such a professional, go to www.aetonline.org.

Q: What other nonmedication therapies help?

A: The time-tested ones have already been mentioned: identifying and promoting strengths; education; structure; lifestyle changes; coaching, counseling, and tutoring.

Although as yet unproven, physical exercises specifically designed to stimulate the cerebellum may become mainstream interventions. There are various programs that do this, such as the Dore method, the

Brain Gym, the Interactive Metronome, and the groups of exercises prescribed by occupational therapists.

Nutritional remedies can also help. Adding omega-3 fatty acids to the diet is useful for health in general. We suggest fish oil as the best source of the omega-3 fatty acids. Adding antioxidants to the diet can also help. Grape-seed extract is one of nature's most potent sources of antioxidants; so are blueberries.

Q: What about medication?
A: You should never take medication until you know the facts and only if you feel comfortable doing so. Learn what is known before you decide. You'll find that the facts are actually reassuring. When used properly, the medications for ADD are safe and effective. Research shows that medication is the single most effective treatment for ADD. It works for 80 to 90 percent of people who try it. When it works, it increases mental focus, which leads to improved performance in all domains of life. The most commonly used medications are the stimulants, like Ritalin or Adderall, or their long-acting equivalents, like Concerta, Ritalin LA, or Adderall XR. The nonstimulant amantadine has been used to great advantage in treating ADD, as has bupropion (Wellbutrin) and the newest nonstimulant, Strattera. If you are considering taking medication for ADD, be sure to see a doctor who has experience in prescribing them, as subtle adjustments can make a big difference.

Q: What are the dangers of stimulant medications?
A: All can cause a variety of side effects. The most common is appetite suppression. Occurring much less frequently are headache, elevated blood pressure, elevated heart rate, nausea, vomiting, insomnia, the development of tics or twitching, feelings of jitteriness or anxiety, feelings of agitation or even mania, and feelings of depersonalization or paranoia. All these side effects can be reversed by lowering the dose of the medication, changing the medication, or stopping it altogether.

Q: What else should I know about stimulant medications?
A: Here are some quick facts about stimulants, or STs:

- STs take effect in about twenty minutes and last from four to twelve hours, depending upon which one is taken.
- You may stop and start STs at will. For example, you can discontinue them over the summer or on weekends. Unlike antibiotics or antidepressants, you do not need to maintain a steady blood level of STs in order to derive benefit. Obviously, when you stop the STs, you lose the benefit until you start them up again.
- If you start on STs and get some benefit, that does not mean you will need to take STs for the rest of your life. Sometimes you learn new habits while taking STs that carry over to when you aren't taking them, thus allowing you to discontinue the STs.
- There are no *known* dangers associated with long-term use of STs. The side effects that are going to occur usually occur right away. Long-term dangers may appear, but as yet they have not.
- STs are not addicting or habit forming if taken properly. On the other hand, if you grind them up and snort them or inject them, as some people do, then they are dangerous.
- STs do not lead to the abuse of illicit drugs. To the contrary, studies show that taking STs reduces the likelihood that you will self-medicate with other drugs.
- STs or some other nonstimulant medication, like Strattera or Wellbutrin, will work (i.e., improve mental focus without producing side effects that warrant stopping the medication) 80 to 90 percent of the time in people who have ADD. That means that 10 to 20 percent of the time no medication will help.
- You should never compel anyone to take STs or any other medication for ADD. This can create struggles that lead to bad outcomes.

Q: What alternative medications are there to stimulants?
A: Amantadine may be the best of all medications for ADD, but it is not widely used because when it was first tried the doses were too high and patients reported side effects. A doctor on the faculty of Harvard Medical School, William Singer, has pioneered its use at lower doses with excellent results. Not a controlled substance, not a stimulant, and virtually devoid of side effects, amantadine deserves much wider use.

The new medication Strattera, introduced in the winter of 2003, can also be helpful. Classified as a norepinephrine reuptake inhibitor, it is not a controlled substance. It reduces the negative symptoms of ADD for some people, but not for others. It is impossible to predict in advance who will benefit and who will not. You have to try it (under medical supervision, of course) to find out. In addition, the atypical antidepressant Wellbutrin can help treat ADD. Like Strattera, it is not a controlled substance.

CHAPTER 2

THE FEEL OF ADD

Most people who don't have ADD don't understand it. Responding only to the well-advertised negative aspects of ADD, they overly pathologize the condition. So you need to explain to them its complexity: ADD is a mélange of often contradictory tendencies and traits that swirl around within you, stirring up different parts of your life at different times as it makes its inconsistent rounds.

The ingredients of the mélange may include:

- high mental and physical energy (coupled with extreme lassitude at times)
- a fast-moving, easily distracted mind (coupled with an amazingly superfocused mind at times)
- trouble with remembering, planning, and anticipating
- unpredictability and impulsivity
- creativity
- lack of inhibition as compared to others
- disorganization (coupled with remarkable organizational skills in certain domains)
- a tendency toward procrastination (coupled with an I-must-do-it-or-have-it-now attitude at times)

- a high-intensity attitude alternating with a foggy one
- forgetfulness (coupled with an extraordinary recall of certain often irrelevant remote information)
- passionate interests (coupled with an inability to arouse interest at other times)
- an original, often zany way of looking at the world
- irritability (coupled with tenderheartedness)
- a tendency to drink too much alcohol, smoke cigarettes, use other drugs, or get involved with addictive activities such as gambling, shopping, spending, sex, food, and the Internet (coupled with a tendency to abstain altogether at times)
- a tendency to worry unnecessarily (coupled with a tendency not to worry enough when worry is warranted)
- a tendency to be a nonconformist or a maverick
- a tendency to reject help from others (coupled with a tendency to want to give help to others)
- generosity that can go too far
- a tendency to repeat the same mistake many times without learning from it
- a tendency to underestimate the time it takes to complete a task or get to a destination
- various other ingredients, none of which dominates all the time, and any one of which may be absent in a single individual

No two people who have ADD are alike. Variety and inconsistency make it impossible to capture a definitive picture of this fast-moving mind-butterfly.

Nevertheless, even casual observation detects a difference between someone who has ADD and someone who does not. Just because we can't say exactly where non-ADD life leaves off and ADD life begins does not mean that there is no division between the two. As Edmund Burke, the great eighteenth-century statesman, said, "Just because there can be no clear line drawn between night and day, yet no one would deny there is a difference."

So let me describe ADD from my point of view. First of all, I resent the term. Maybe it's just because I have ADD myself, but it seems to me that if anyone has a disorder, it is the people who plod along paying close attention to every little speck and crumb, every little detail and rule, every minor policy and procedure in every minuscule manual. I think these are the people who have a disorder. I call it Attention Surplus Disorder. They did exactly what they were told as children, told on others who did not, and now make a living doing what they're told, telling others what to do, and telling on those who don't.

What kind of a life is that? Wouldn't you rather have attention deficit than attention surplus? If you had to call one a disorder, wouldn't you vote for the surplus? Who wants to pay attention to the myriad details for very long? Is it really a sign of mental health to be able to balance your checkbook, sit still in your chair, and never speak out of turn? As far as I can see, many people who *don't* have ADD are charter members of the Society of the Congenitally Boring. And who do you suppose advanced civilization? Who do you suppose comes up with the new ideas today? People with ADD, of course.

But I can't change the names or the rules. Attention Surplus Disorder will remain the ideal to which people who like to be told what to do aspire. On the other hand, let me recommend the opposite of Attention Surplus Disorder, a syndrome called ADD.

ADD is a way of living that has been with us throughout history. Until recently it went unnamed, even to those who had it. Before the syndrome is named, i.e., diagnosed, life may be filled with pain and misunderstanding. But after the diagnosis is made, one often finds new possibilities and a lever for major improvements in life.

Some people say ADD doesn't even exist, but that's only because they have never had to deal with it in a child or a friend or an employee. Believe me, I can tell you from fifty-five years of personal experience as well as almost twenty-five years of professional experience, ADD is real. It is as real as any other cast of mind, like being optimistic, or being good with words, or being brave. It is real, albeit impossible to measure exactly or to see under a microscope or on an X ray.

Many metaphors come to mind to describe it. Having ADD is like driving in the rain with bad windshield wipers. The windshield gets smudged and blurred as you're speeding along, but you don't slow down. You keep driving, trying your best to see. Why don't you slow down or, better yet, pull over? That is not the way with ADD. You keep going. Faster is better. It is in your blood (and in your brain).

Having ADD is also like listening to a ball game on a radio station that's coming in with a lot of static. The harder you strain to hear what's going on, the more frustrated you get. Once in a while a static-free interval blesses the airwaves, and you can hear the ball game clear as a bell. A cat may meow in the background, but you know it is just a cat, not more static, and the clear signal from the radio allows you to focus on the game. How good this feels! But then, like an unresolved feud, the static returns, and you become more than frustrated. You get mad. You want to break the radio, or kick the cat, or scream at whatever human makes the terrible mistake of inquiring right then as to how you might be feeling.

Having ADD is also like trying to build a house of cards in a windstorm. You must build a structure to protect yourself from the wind before you can even start building with the cards. You put up a lean-to, and feel proud of what you've done, only to see a gust of wind tear it down. So you start again, and once again the wind wins. So you construct the lean-to again. And again. You never get to the cards. But you don't give up. That is another trait of people with ADD. They keep trying. Often, they keep trying the same, doomed way, but they do keep trying.

In other ways having ADD is like being supercharged all the time. I tell kids it's like having a race-car brain. Your brain goes faster than the average brain. Your trouble is putting on the brakes. You get one idea and you have to act on it, and then, what do you know, but you've got another idea before you've finished up with the first one, and so you go for that one, but of course a third idea intercepts the second, and you just have to follow that one, and pretty soon people are calling you disorganized and impulsive and disobedient and defiant and all sorts of impolite words that miss the point completely. Because you're trying so hard to get it right. It's just that you have all these invisible vectors pulling you this way and that, which makes it really hard to stay on task.

Plus, your brain is spilling over all the time. You're drumming your fingers, tapping your feet, humming a song, whistling, looking here, looking there, scratching, stretching, doodling, which leads other people to think you're not paying attention or you're not interested, but you're spilling over so that you *can* pay attention. I can pay a lot better attention to something when I'm taking a walk or listening to music or even when I'm in a crowded, noisy room than when I'm sitting still and surrounded by silence. God save me from the reading rooms in libraries. These are peaceful havens for most people, but for me they are torture chambers.

Someone once said, "Time is the thing that keeps everything from happening all at once." Time parcels out moments into separate bits so that we can do one thing at a time. In ADD, time collapses, making life feel as if everything is happening at once. It's now or never . . . or maybe later. This creates panic. One loses perspective and the ability to select what needs to be done first, what needs to be done second, and what can wait until another day. Instead, you are always on the go, leaping before you look, always trying to keep the world from caving in on top of you.

In the world of ADD, there are only two times: there is *now,* and then there is *not now.* So, if a supervisor says to a person with ADD that a presentation must be ready for a major meeting in three months, the person with ADD thinks to herself, *not now.* She forgets about it until three months from now becomes *now.* Then it is too late. "If only you could get your act together," her exasperated supervisor laments. "You're the most talented person in this company, but until you shape up you're never going to make a difference here or anywhere else."

It is not surprising that depression, toxic worry, and anxiety disorders abound among people with undiagnosed ADD. We never know when we're going to forget something, say the wrong thing, or show up at the wrong place at the wrong time.

Museums. (Have you noticed how I skip around? That's part of the deal with having ADD.) The way I go through a museum is the way some people go through a bargain basement. Some of this, some of that, oh, this one looks nice, but what about that rack over there? I love art, but my way of loving it can make someone think I'm an ignorant Philistine.

On the other hand, sometimes I can sit and look at one painting for a long, long while. I'll get into the world of the painting and buzz around in there until I forget about everything else. In these moments I—like most people with ADD—can superfocus. This ability gives the lie to the notion that we can never pay attention. When we're interested, when our neurotransmitters line up just so, and when structure is in place to help us, we can focus like bloodhounds on a scent.

If there is a separate disorder called Can't Wait in Lines Disorder, I've got it. *Can't* is the wrong word, I guess, because life does require me to wait in lines, and I manage to do it without going berserk and getting arrested. It's just that I hate to wait. When I have to wait I tend to act—often in ways I wish I hadn't.

I'm short on what you might call the intermediate reflective step between impulse and action. Like so many people with ADD, I lack tact. Tact is entirely dependent on the ability to consider your words before uttering them. We ADD types become like the Jim Carrey character in *Liar Liar* when he can't lie. I remember in the fifth grade I noticed my math teacher's hair in a new style and blurted out, "Mr. Cook, is that a toupee you're wearing?" I got kicked out of class.

I've since learned how to stifle most of these gaffes, but I can still get into trouble for saying the wrong thing at the wrong time. That's another tough truth about having ADD. It takes a lot of work just to do the trivial tasks—like staying silent, or resisting telling the cop who stopped us that he looks just like Elmer Fudd.

As you might imagine, intimacy can be a problem if you've got to be constantly changing the subject, pacing, scratching, and blurting out tactless remarks. My wife has learned not to take my tuning out personally, and she does say that when I'm there, I'm really there.

When we first met, she thought I was some kind of a nut, as I would bolt out of restaurants at the end of meals or disappear to another planet during a conversation. She has since grown accustomed to my sudden comings and goings. I am lucky I married her.

Many of us with ADD crave high-stimulus situations. In my case, I love casinos and horse races. I deal with this passion by not going often, and when I do go, I bring a modest sum that I can afford to lose. And lose I usually do! Obviously, a craving for high stimulation can get a person into trouble, which is why ADD is prevalent among criminals and self-destructive risk-takers. ADD is also often found among so-called type A personalities, as well as among manic-depressives, sociopaths, violent people, drug abusers, and alcoholics.

But it is also common among creative and intuitive people in all fields, and among highly energetic, interesting, productive people. You can find high stimulation in being a surgeon, for example, or a trial attorney, or an actor, or a pilot, or a trader on the commodities exchange, or working in a newsroom, or in sales, or in being a race-car driver!

Usually the positive side of ADD doesn't get mentioned when people speak about it. The tendency is to focus on what goes wrong, or at least on what has to be somehow controlled. After all, that's why people seek a diagnosis and why they seek help. Something is wrong. But once the ADD has been diagnosed, and the child or the adult has learned how to take care of whatever was wrong, the brain offers up an untapped realm.

Suddenly, the radio station is tuned in, the windshield is clear, the windstorm has died down and you can start to build that house of cards. You can start to use all the great plans and ideas you've been storing up for years. Now the adult or the child who had been such a problem, such a nudge, such a general pain in the neck to himself and everybody else, starts doing things he'd never been able to do before. He surprises everyone around him. He also surprises himself. I use the male pronoun, but it could just as easily be *she*. Now that we are looking for it and realize that hyperactivity does not have to be part of the picture, we are seeing more and more ADD among females.

People with ADD often have a special "feel" for life, a way of seeing right into the heart of matters, while others have to reason their way along methodically. This is the person who can't tell you how he thought of the solution, or where the idea for the invention came from, or why suddenly he produced such a painting never having painted before, or how he knew the shortcut to the answer for the geometry problem. All she can say is she just saw it, she could feel it.

In places where most people are blind, the person with ADD can, if not see the light, at least feel the light, and she can produce answers, apparently out of the dark. It is important for others to be sensitive to this "sixth sense" many ADD people have, and to nurture it. If the environment insists on rational, linear thinking and "good" behavior all the time, then these people may never develop their intuitive style to the point where they can use it profitably. Indeed, it may atrophy, or, worse, be used in the service of revenge or criminal behavior. But with proper treatment, what at first seemed impaired may soon prove gifted.

What is the treatment all about? Anything that reduces the static and strengthens the true signal. Just making the diagnosis helps muffle the static of guilt and self-recrimination. Building certain kinds of structure into one's life—like lists, timetables, and healthy habits of sleep, diet, and exercise—can sharpen mental focus. Working in small spurts rather than long hauls helps. Breaking down tasks into smaller tasks helps.

The specifics of treatment will vary. Whether it's hiring a secretary who understands ADD, or an accountant who can work with you, or using an automatic bank teller in the right way, or developing a filing system that works for you, or selecting the right home computer, getting the precise aid that you need takes time but can transform unmanageable chaos into, if not order, at least manageable chaos.

Marrying the right person and finding the right job are probably the two most important "treatments" for adults. And for kids it is most important to get rid of ridicule and fear from home and school and promote big dreams.

Many other steps can help, like applying external limits on your dangerous impulses. Wear seat belts when you drive. Observe the speed limit. *Use* a planner, don't just own one! Find support from other people instead of going it alone. Find someone to be in your corner to coach you, to keep you on track.

Medication helps too, but it is far from the whole solution.

A comprehensive treatment plan, one that takes into account many and varied interventions, is the best treatment plan. Over time, it can help a person of any age who has ADD find a new life.

We who have ADD need help and understanding from others. But, then, who doesn't? We probably need more than the average person, as we can be especially exasperating and difficult. We may make messes wherever we go, but with the right help, those messes can be turned into realms of reason and art.

So, if you know someone like me—of any age—who's acting up and daydreaming and forgetting this or that and just not getting with the program, consider ADD before he starts believing all the bad things people are saying about him and it becomes too late.

CHAPTER 3

THE SEVEN HABITS OF

HIGHLY EFFECTIVE ADD-ERS

One way to understand how to get the most out of life with ADD is to consider which qualities lead to happiness and success in people who have ADD. I could fill an entire book with success stories of people who have ADD. Indeed, I am teaming up with Catherine Corman, a former history professor at Harvard and a mother of a child who has ADD, to do just that. We are writing a book about successful, happy adults who have ADD. The book, entitled *ADD—That's Me!*, will be for teens; we want to give them a positive look at ADD and tell them some true stories of how great life can be if you have ADD.

I will tell brief versions of two of those stories here, and then comment on what qualities tend to recur in the lives of adults who are successful and happy in life with ADD.

Bob Lobel is the sports anchor for WBZ-TV, channel 4, the CBS outlet in Boston. He has ADD.

Bob is one of the most popular and experienced figures in the Boston media. He has thrived in a competitive business for more than twenty years. But he is not a shrewd, competitive go-getter. Quite the opposite. He can't focus long enough to be devious. Bob's long suit is creativity. He is a master ad-libber; indeed, he told me that it is much easier for him to ad-lib than to read the copy from the teleprompter.

"Reading copy feels really unnatural to me," he says. "So we have figured out a way for me to half ad-lib, half read." Some of his ad-libs have become part of the regular Boston lexicon, making him somewhat of a local legend.

For example, once, when a player who had been traded from one of the Boston teams had a huge day for the team he had been traded to, Bob ad-libbed on the air that night as he told of the player's great day, "Gee, why can't we get players like that?" That line has become a Boston staple for whenever a player we have let go does well somewhere else—and there are legions of them, starting with Babe Ruth.

Not only is he the master of the ad-lib, quickly making friends with new turns of phrase, Bob is able to make friends with new people so easily that he has lasted a long time in a business where people come and go every week. Instead of stabbing people in the back, Bob pulls knives out of people's backs. He builds bridges others have burned—often not for his own benefit but for the benefit of the hotheaded guy who shouldn't have burned the bridge in the first place and deserves a second chance. Bob will do this and not tell anyone about it. He works behind the scenes to build goodwill—not because he is a saint but because he is basically a guy who loves life and has a heart full of goodwill. He wants to see the good times roll—for everybody. He will make himself look silly, say, by putting on a red nose and antlers on TV to look like Rudolph in the Christmas fund-raiser for Children's Hospital, and do so gladly to make money for a cause he believes in.

All these skills—which don't show up on his school record or his professional résumé—make him one of the most effective and happy men in his business. It also means he often gets the hot story first. People want to call him before they call anyone else.

Bob has two older children from a previous marriage and an eight-year-old with his present wife, who is getting her Ph.D. in psychology. Bob and his wife are unassuming about their star status in Boston. Bob says one of the keys to his work is not taking it too seriously. "Basically, I just try to have fun every day I go to work. I work hard, that's for sure, but I love what I do. I am one of the luckiest guys I know."

Always an underachiever in school, never tagged as one destined for great success, Bob went into broadcasting simply because he liked how he imagined the work to be. He got his start in a small market in New Hampshire. After that, his talent took him to the top of his field.

"Having ADD is one of my greatest assets," he told me. "Looking back, I couldn't have done it without ADD. What makes me unique comes straight from my ADD. I'm like the cutup in sixth grade. I thrive on chaos. I love to ad-lib. I think outside the box. Geez, I can't think inside the box. I can change leads three seconds before airtime and make up the copy as we go on the air. This is just who I am. It comes naturally to me. That's why I think of ADD as a gift, not as a liability."

Bob didn't know he had ADD until midway through his career. When he was in school, no one thought about ADD. When he did get diagnosed, he was already at channel 4 and doing well. He had learned how to deal with his ADD without any formal assistance. He just followed his strengths and didn't get bogged down in negative thinking. He always made sure he had a creative outlet. He didn't try to get good at what he was bad at; instead he tried to get better at what he was good at.

When I asked him how the diagnosis helped him, he said, "Just realizing that there was a name for this really helped. Just knowing that ADD existed helped me a lot. Instead of thinking I was the odd man out, that I was different in a bad way, I realized that I was different, but in a good way. Somehow, knowing that others had this, and that there was a name for it, made it all feel so much better.

"The second thing was that after I got diagnosed I focused even more on just trying to channel all the chaos and energy I always had in my brain in a constructive way. Knowing about the diagnosis helped me do this. And the medication helped me a lot, as well."

Bob takes Ritalin. Once he and his doctor adjusted the medication so he had the right dose of the right medication, it helped tremendously. He became even more effective at "channeling the energy and chaos," to use his terms.

David Neeleman is the CEO of JetBlue Airways, one of the most successful airlines in the world. A couple of years ago I read in a magazine that he had ADD and that he had found out about it by reading *Driven to Distraction,* so I called him up. It took a while to get through the various roadblocks he has to protect him from the world, but when I finally managed to get him on the line he was as open and friendly as if I were an old friend. He invited me to come down to his office in Darien, Connecticut.

I arrived at his office at nine A.M., as scheduled. He arrived at noon. Knowing about ADD, I was not surprised. I made use of my three hours of waiting by talking to many of the people who work for David. Every one of them loved being at JetBlue. Just as being late is a characteristic of ADD, so is inspiring loyalty in others.

Looking younger than his forty-two years, tall, fit, with sandy-blond hair and a smile that spreads across his face as informally and happily as an untucked shirt, David burst into the office and apologized profusely for his lateness. He entertained me with the standard, valid ADD explanations: couldn't find his appointment book, got lost in a conversation on the phone, couldn't remember which office he was supposed to go to, couldn't find his cell phone once he was in the car, and on, and on.

We talked for hours. We talked about his family—he's married and has nine children. We talked a lot about theology and how his faith shapes his everyday life—he's a devout Mormon, but he isn't the least pious or holier-than-thou. In fact, he almost converted me during our interview; but when I told my wife of my enthusiasm she reminded me that I would not like to give up alcohol, nor would she! We talked about his business. And we talked about ADD.

He told me that many of his kids inherited his ADD. Some of them take medication, although David refuses to because he is afraid it might reduce his creativity. (It wouldn't.) His wife keeps hoping he'll try it someday.

He wants his children to have a better time than he had in his education. "Of my nine kids, nine of them struggle in school. They are really smart kids, really creative, but they just struggle. Like Ashley, who is five feet eleven inches tall and drop-dead gorgeous, but if you don't have the confidence and you don't test well, you can grow up thinking you are an idiot. I want to protect her from what I went through. I grew up thinking I was the biggest idiot on the planet. When she had to take a test to get into college she tried medication beforehand, and she came home crying, saying it was the first time she had ever been able to focus and finish the test. She did that a year ago. I have another daughter who is a tenth-grader who does really well even though she is really disorganized. She is the funniest kid to be with! Her room is a disaster, and she is always flying by the seat of her pants, but she has great artistic talent, and she is a great athlete."

When I asked him about his own learning differences, he quickly warmed to the subject. "When I give a speech, I can't write anything down because I can't read it. If I were to stand up in front of a group and start reading, 'This certificate effectively as of July first is given . . .' I just can't do it. I am very self-conscious about reading stuff aloud. I sit in church totally terrified that someone is going to call on me and have me read a Scripture passage aloud, so I rehearse words just in case. But I can hold audiences spellbound when I give talks. They're all extemporaneous. I have never written anything down. I remember one time I was supposed to be testifying before Congress and I had a written statement. I was sweating bullets at the idea of reading it, so finally I said to my government affairs guy, 'I can't read this, there is no way, and if I do I am going to look like a complete idiot.' He said, 'Just paraphrase it, then.' And my testimony went just fine."

That symptom made me believe David had dyslexia. Next I asked about attention. "I never focus for very long. When I was in school I thought I was stupid. My third-grade teacher told my parents that as long as this kid can hire a secretary who can write and read his letters for him, he will do well, but he'll need someone to do all this stuff for him. That kind of stuck with me all the way through high school.

"By the time I got to high school I was getting pretty good grades but I wasn't taking anything hard. I was basically BS-ing my teachers, getting through, but I felt very inferior. But then I went on my mission [Mormon kids have to do a service mission], and that really helped me. It gave me a lot of structure. I was in Brazil, and I learned a foreign language. Soon I was converting people to our faith. I was really, really good at that. One of the best ever. This gave me the confidence I'd never had.

"When I got back I was a changed person. But I still had to go to college. I went to the University of Utah and just hated it."

"Why?" I asked.

"First of all, I was a tremendous procrastinator. I hated to study. I felt like I should be out doing things, moving things along, but here I was stuck studying statistics, which I knew had no application to my life. Finals would come and I was up all night cramming for this stupid stuff. I liked very little of what I was studying, but I knew I had to have an education. But the first opportunity I had to start a business, I just blew out of there. I started a business and it was really successful."

"So you dropped out of college?" I asked, thinking of other hugely successful entrepreneurs, like Michael Dell and Bill Gates, who had done the same.

"Yes, I dropped out."

"And you started a travel business?"

"I found someone who had some time-share condos in Hawaii that he couldn't sell because it was the early eighties and there was a recession. He was paying a one-hundred-fifty-dollar maintenance fee every month for them. I said, 'Look, if I can rent these out for you, I'll pay the hundred fifty dollars. He said, 'Great.' So I started renting them out. It was such a bizarre thing. I was married and had a daughter on the way, and I just found a girl whose mother knew the guy, and I went to talk to him and I got him to rent these condos. So I'd make a couple hundred bucks every time I would rent one. I was doing one or two a day, so I was making two, three, four hundred bucks a day in college.

"I thought, Wow, this is good. And then I thought, Well, let me just combine the rentals with some airfare deals. There were some airlines starting up on the West Coast, so I called them up and said, 'You don't know me, but if I send you some money will you send me tickets?' And they said, 'Sure.' So I started packaging these condos with airfare."

I could see David's mind whirring as he told me this story. He hardly even paused for breath. "In our second year we did about six million in sales, and I had twenty employees. I got other condos, and it was booming, but then the airline went out of business. It took all of my money. I was twenty-two years old. They called me up one day right before Christmas and said, 'We're gone.' 'What do you mean, you're gone?' I was devastated.

"But then June Morris called me. She had a big travel business. My uncle was her attorney, luckily so."

"She heard you had gone out of business?" I asked.

"Well, she knew I was beating the crap out of her because I had all these great packages. When she heard what had happened she was smart enough to hire me. And she got Morris Air out of it. I did the whole thing by myself, but she got a lot of the credit. I thought, Well, she deserves the credit because without her I wouldn't have even been there."

"When you went to work for her she just had a travel agency?"

"Yeah, and then we became Morris Air and nine years later we sold the company for one hundred thirty million dollars."

"What was the key to your success there?" I asked.

"My ability just to know what's important, to cut right through all the crap and get to that nugget, and say, 'Okay, this is the most important thing we've got going, this is the thing we have to focus on, and all this other stuff is just noise.' And that's my greatest talent today. I think it goes with ADD."

After Morris Air, David went to work for Herb Kelleher at Southwest Airlines. The two of them hit it off fabulously well. But then other people got jealous of David because of his tremendous ability to come up with great ideas. For example, when he arrived at Southwest, you couldn't call the airline and buy a ticket by giving a credit-card number. "They had never thought about it," David said. "But I had invented ticketless travel at Morris. So I brought it to Southwest. I invented the electronic ticket. It saved us tens of millions of dollars. But this kind of thing also made people jealous.

"There were six guys in the running for the CEO job and I was seen as being in the mix, but I really, truly didn't want to be the CEO. But they all went to Herb and said, 'Get rid of this guy, he is driving us crazy.' So Herb called me in and he said, 'I have had all these guys coming in and complaining about you, even your best buddy. They all say you need to go.' I was very quiet. It was such an emotional time.

"So he fired me. When I left they tried to give me a big bonus, which I donated to the employee catastrophic fund. They wouldn't publicize that. They wouldn't tell anybody. I was just pissed off because I felt like I was being bought off."

"I thought you quit," I said, remembering some story I had read.

"I got fired. Herb tells everyone I quit, but I got fired. That was probably the most difficult time in my life. It was in May 1994 when I got fired."

"And when did you find out about your having ADD?" I asked.

"It was right after I left Southwest. I read your book. I thought, This is me. I actually wrote to a guy who I was trying to recruit from

Southwest for my new business and I told him, 'Now I know why I failed at Southwest.' The diagnosis explained so much, like why I would sit in meetings and I would just say what came into my mind. And all these guys would be sitting at a table and Herb would be saying something and I would say, 'God, I can't stand sitting here talking about pregnant ramp agents hour after hour! We should get to something important. Why are we dealing with this? Have someone else deal with that!' I would just blurt stuff out. I would try to stop myself, but I couldn't."

"And what do you think are the advantages of having ADD? You mentioned your ability to see what's important, to hyperfocus."

"Yes. Two things, right from your book. A is hyperfocus, and B is creativity. When I see things like ticketless travel, TVs on airplanes, certain route decisions I make, people think I am absolutely out of mind. And they turn out to be great ideas."

"So what advice would you have for the ADD entrepreneur?"

"I would say go with your passion, but know your limits and surround yourself with strong people. Don't surround yourself with yes men, but surround yourself with people who can tell you no and can tell you that this is a stupid idea and these are all the reasons why. If you have people who will give you a push back you're better off."

"And what still gets in your way in terms of your ADD symptoms? What do you still struggle with?"

"Oh, everything. I struggle with a lot of stuff. My car's a wreck. I have two weeks' worth of clothes piled up on my chair right by my bed. My socks are right by my bed in the same place I leave them. My wife is one of these pick-up-after-yourself kind of people. She does it sometimes when people are coming over.

"You know, sometimes I will just go onto a computer at eleven at night, and then I'll go back to ESPN, and then I'll go back over to this, and then I'll go back over to that, and it's one o'clock in the morning and I am doing nothing productive. But I have this nervous thing where I just have to be doing something when I'm not really productive. Lying down in bed and reading my kids a story is like torture to me. I so wish I could do some of that stuff and it wouldn't seem so laborious."

David then went on to tell me about a tree that is leaning against the side of his house. It is dangerous and he needs to call the tree service and have it taken down. He sees the tree every morning from his bathroom window while he shaves, and every morning he resolves to call Foley's Tree Service that day. And each night, when he brushes his teeth, he sees the tree still there, and he realizes another day has passed and Foley has not been called. I offered to call Foley right then and there, but he said no, he needed to do it himself. It's been two years and Foley is still waiting for the call.

"I see the tree every day and say I have to do it. It's the mundane things that are almost impossible for me to do. I can't. I have the worst time paying my bills. I never could pay my bills, not because I didn't have the money, it's just that I would always say I would do it tomorrow, no, I'll do it tonight, no, I'll get it done in the morning. Finally, I just hired someone to do it.

"Then I'll get an e-mail, say, from someone who has spent a day drafting a letter to me about how they want to work for me, and I'll read the first three lines and say, 'I'll get to this later,' and I put it away, and I never respond. I don't get to it, and I don't forward it to Carol [his assistant]. It's maddening that I just can't sit and read some three-page letter. And I have this weather site that I always look at, so I go there and I look at the weather instead of reading the e-mail just because weather disrupts the airplanes. I get these repetition things going. If I would just spend as much time reading the letters as looking at the weather site I would get a lot of this stuff done.

"Another thing that bugs me is that I can't celebrate my successes. The day JetBlue went public I made something like a hundred fifty million dollars. All it made me feel was more responsible."

"More responsible?"

"Yeah. The first thing someone else would do is go buy a new car or something, but I still have my old Yukon that I drive around."

David Neeleman is a humble man. He is also a creative genius in the field of aviation. And he has ADD.

I called him a few months after our conversation and asked him about the tree. Had he called Foley yet?

"No," David replied. "We sold the house."

Both Bob Lobel and David Neeleman show many of the strengths— as well as many of the vulnerabilities—of adults who have ADD. Bob and David prevailed, even though they both still struggle in certain ways.

In getting to know people like Bob and David and hundreds of others like them, I have singled out seven qualities that tend to recur again and again. Here they are:

THE SEVEN HABITS OF HIGHLY EFFECTIVE ADD ADULTS

1. Do what you're good at. Don't spend too much time trying to get good at what you're bad at. (You did enough of that in school.)
2. Delegate what you're bad at to others, as often as possible.
3. Connect your energy to a creative outlet.
4. Get well enough organized to achieve your goals. The key here is "well enough." That doesn't mean you have to be very well organized at all—just well enough organized to achieve your goals.
5. Ask for and heed advice from people you trust—and ignore, as best you can, the dream-breakers and finger-waggers.
6. Make sure you keep up regular contact with a few close friends.
7. Go with your positive side. Even though you have a negative side, make decisions and run your life with your positive side.

CHAPTER 4

ADD SELF-ASSESSMENT

QUIZZES FOR ADULTS:

A SCREENING TEST

The DSM-IV criteria for ADD—which are listed in chapter 11—provide the definitive screening questionnaire for ADD. However, it was not written with adults in mind. There has long been a need for a brief screener for adults. Now that need has been met.

A team of leading experts, in conjunction with the World Health Organization, developed the Adult Self-Report Scale, or ASRS. Led by Ron Kessler of Harvard and Len Adler of NYU, the team refined the questions to the point where 80 percent of the people who score positive on the ASRS will turn out to have ADD when a full evaluation is done.

The ASRS is a screening tool, *not* a definitive diagnostic test. However, it does give a short means of seeing if it is worthwhile to go on to a more detailed diagnostic workup.

If you get a positive result on the test, then you definitely ought to get a full evaluation. However, if you get a negative result, do not assume this means you do not have adult ADD. The test is only 70 percent sensitive. That means it will pick up only 70 percent of the cases of ADD in a random sample of adults.

The test consists of six questions. You should answer each with one of the following responses: "N" for never; "R" for rarely; "S" for sometimes; "O" for often; or "V" for very often.

Here are the questions:

1. How often do you have trouble wrapping up the final details of a project, once the challenging parts have been done? N R S O V
2. How often do you have difficulty getting things in order when you have to do a task that requires organization? N R S O V
3. How often do you have problems remembering appointments or obligations? N R S O V
4. When you have a task that requires a lot of thought, how often do you avoid or delay getting started? N R S O V
5. How often do you fidget or squirm with your hands and feet when you have to sit down for a long time? N R S O V
6. How often do you feel overly active and compelled to do things, as if you were driven by a motor? N R S O V

Here's how you score the test:

If you answered "S," "O," or "V" for questions 1, 2, or 3, give yourself one point for each.

If you answered "O," or "V" for questions 4, 5, or 6, give yourself one point for each.

Now add up your points. A score of 4 or higher is a positive score. That means you ought to consult with your health-care provider and go on to the next step in the diagnostic process.

Remember, this is *not* a diagnostic test. It is just a good, brief screening tool.

A SELF-ASSESSMENT QUIZ

While the ASRS is a statistically valid, short screening tool for adult ADD, the following quiz has no statistical validity whatsoever. I composed it as an additional means of providing a feel for ADD. The more "yes" answers you give on this quiz, the more likely you have ADD. However, there is no cutoff point, as this is purely descriptive, not diagnostic.

This quiz is a good place to start if you are dealing with an adult who doubts that ADD is real. If the person has ADD, she will be surprised at how many questions hit close to home.

A quiz with a similar format appeared in *Driven to Distraction*. However, this quiz is entirely new; it is longer, covering more ground, and the questions highlight aspects of the ADD experience I have learned about since writing *Driven to Distraction*.

General Questions

1. Did you turn to this chapter right away, before you read any of the other chapters in this book?
2. Do you feel that you are underachieving in your life, even though you may have achieved a great deal so far?
3. Are you more generous than most people?
4. Do you have more trouble than the average person with staying on track, especially when what you are doing is less than gripping?
5. Do you feel some regrets about the way you are but also feel unable to find any way to change?
6. Would you have made a good inventor?
7. Do you perceive patterns where other people don't see them?
8. Do you tend to solve problems intuitively rather than logically and methodically?
9. Do words like *logically* and *methodically* bring back bad memories?
10. Do you also relish certain qualities you have, regretting that you can't always present them in such a way that others appreciate them?
11. Are you more tenacious and persistent than the average person?
12. Are you more sentimental than the average person?
13. Do you have an unusually acute sense of smell and sensitivity to touch?
14. When you are sitting, do you frequently drum your fingers on the table or bounce one of your legs up and down using the ball of your foot as a fulcrum?
15. Do you love crossword puzzles, brainteasers, and self-assessment quizzes?

16. Do you love bicycles (even if you don't ride them anymore)?

17. Do you feel that the positives you have accomplished in life you did by accident, by smoke and mirrors, almost as if someone else achieved them, not you?

18. Do you put up a good front, but inwardly wish you could find a better way in life?

19. Do you go off on tangents easily?

20. On the other hand, do you get really annoyed when other people go off on tangents, wishing they'd hurry up and get to the point?

21. Do you drink coffee or consume other caffeine-containing substances (colas, chocolate, Mountain Dew, some teas) in greater quantities than most people do?

22. Did you have many ear infections when you were a child?

23. Do you like situations of danger and risk?

24. Have you missed many opportunities due to procrastination?

25. Although you may be quiet and reserved, does your mind go a mile a minute most of the time?

26. Are you more of a child at heart today than other adults your age?

27. Do you often get something done extraordinarily well and when you're finished have very little idea of how you did it?

28. Do you feel huge letdowns after big events or successes, more than the average person does?

29. Are you totally amazed that so many people can't see through the façades that phony people put up because you can see through them in a second?

30. Do you especially despise hypocrisy?

31. And do you especially admire honesty?

32. Do you wish people were more honest and less politically correct?

33. Did one or both of your parents or their parents drink too much, or suffer from depression or bipolar disorder, or have trouble with gambling, or get into trouble with the law?

34. Do you often drive past the exit you were supposed to take on the highway?

35. Are you chuckling to yourself as you read these questions?

36. Are you a born debater?

37. Were your years of education (school, college, and beyond) marked by underachievement?
38. Are you more prone than the average person to make careless mistakes?
39. Do you feel that if other people knew the real you, they would disapprove of you?
40. Were you the class clown or cutup in school?
41. Did you have trouble completing your education due to problems with organization or getting to class on time?
42. Do you find that marijuana appeals to you because it helps you "chill out"?
43. Do you often make remarks that others consider odd or off the wall?
44. Do you have many different enthusiasms, often wanting to follow more of them than you can possibly keep up with?
45. Do other people comment on how hard it is to get you to stay focused on what they want you to stay focused on, even when you want to focus on that as well?
46. Do you tend to drive fast?
47. Do you often feel an urge to hug the person you are talking to, even if you barely know them, for reasons unrelated to sexual attraction?
48. Did you feel a bit out of it in school, regardless of what grades you got or how socially popular you were?
49. Are you a dreamer?
50. Do you have a sense of humor that is unusual, zany, macabre, or otherwise out of the ordinary?
51. Do you not only think outside the box but have trouble thinking inside the box?
52.
53. Do you find that your thoughts go so fast, your mental organizer can't keep up with them?
54. Were you hyperactive as a child?
55. Do you find driving a car fast to be a soothing experience?
56. Are you much more forgiving than most people?
57. On the other hand, do you rush to take sides against people who take advantage of others?

58. Do you laugh easily?
59. Even though you may not do it, do you enjoy flirting more than the average person does?
60. Are you slightly less coordinated than others your age?
61. Do you love it when life is going fast?
62. Do you simultaneously yearn to fit in but hate to conform?

Questions About Work

63. Do others complain that if you were more motivated or just tried harder you could pay attention better?
64. Do you sometimes focus extraordinarily well, even superfocus?
65. Do you get frustrated because you can't make yourself superfocus on demand?
66. Are you embarrassed by what a mess your pocketbook, desk, or office is?
67. Would you have made a good salesperson?
68. Would you have made a rotten accountant?
69. Even if you don't like doing it, do you do your best work under a deadline?
70. Do you find that you can get more done in twenty minutes while waiting in an airport than in six hours working in your office?
71. Do you wonder why so many people refuse to take chances?
72. Do you love highly stimulating environments, like newsrooms, the floor of the stock exchange (or how you imagine the floor of the stock exchange to be), emergency rooms, courtrooms, or football games?
73. Do you excel in certain areas, but have trouble figuring out how to turn those areas into income generators?
74. Do you have a razor-sharp memory one moment only to be foggy and absentminded the next?
75. Do you have a million new ideas, but have trouble turning them into reality?
76. Do you do your best work when you can be your own boss?
77. Even though you may be at your best when you're your own boss, do you also benefit from having an assistant who can remind you to stay on track?

78. Do you find that you focus better in the midst of a crisis or an emergency than when all is peaceful and calm around you?

79. When you attend a lecture or other presentation, do you feel you could pay better attention if you could get up and pace around at the back of the room?

80. Even though you noticed it at the time and chortled a bit at what you took to be my own oversight, have you forgotten by now that question 52 was left blank?

81. Do you prefer to work in intense bursts, rather than prolonged intervals?

82. Are you an entrepreneur by nature?

83. Do others comment on how creative or original you are?

84. Do you find that sitting in a meeting is almost always a total waste of your time and agonizing to boot?

Questions About Home Life

85. Are you much more of a night person than a morning person?

86. Do you often offend people without meaning to?

87. Is your own humor sometimes mistaken for an insult?

88. Have you ever gotten divorced?

89. Do you usually know the point a person is getting to before they get there?

90. Do members of your family complain that you often interrupt?

91. Are you much more energetic than other people your age?

92. Are you now, or have you ever been, concerned that you drink too much alcohol?

93. Do you now or did you ever smoke cigarettes?

94. Are you a maverick?

95. Even though you may be a maverick, have you found yourself working for someone or married to someone who wants you to conform?

96. In romance, have you often made the mistake of dating, or even marrying, someone who belittles you, reprimands you, and tries to control you?

97. Do others see more that is good and valuable in you than you do?

98. Do you find that your spouse has to do most of the organizing and planning?

99. Does your spouse/partner resent how much he or she has to do for you to make a go of it with you?

100. Does your partner often tell you how much she or he cares about you but at the same time tells you that she or he is going to leave you unless you can get your act together?

101. Has the quality of your sex life declined due to emotional conflicts with your spouse?

102. Do you find that you have trouble sustaining attention when you are making love, even though you are aroused and interested?

103. Do you think you have a higher level of sexual interest, drive, and curiosity than others your age?

104. Are you thinking about many other things in the back of your mind as you read through this quiz?

105. Is what you are looking forward to doing after you put this quiz down something other than what you are supposed to do next?

106. Do you carry an anger and frustration within you that comes out too easily or at the wrong times?

107. Do you find that you feel much more mentally focused after you exercise?

108. Do you find that you have trouble putting your thoughts into words?

109. Does your spouse tell you that you are a difficult person with whom to communicate?

110. Are you dyslexic or a very slow reader?

111. Do you waste vast quantities of time roaming around on the Internet, sending and receiving e-mails, playing electronic games, and otherwise diverting yourself from what you originally sat down at your computer to do?

112. Do you love children but also find that you get bored trying to read to them or play a board game with them?

113. Do you feel that your life could be much, much better if only you

could make one major change or breakthrough . . . but you don't know what it is?

114. Is your idea of a perfect dinner party to arrive, have a drink, eat the food, and go home with as little chitchat and dillydallying as possible?

115. Do you sometimes smile in a conversation in hopes that it will be a sufficient contribution, because you have totally lost track of what is being talked about?

116. Do you find it difficult to explain the rules of a game, not because you don't know them but because you just can't stand the laborious process of imparting them, step by step?

117. Do you have recurring dreams in which you are mortified to discover you are walking around naked in public?

118. No matter how hard you try to be on time, do you usually arrive late?

119. Do you pray that your children never have to go through what you went through as a child and what you go through now?

120. Do you have trouble lingering when you make love?

121. Do you have trouble lingering in general? For example, if you see something beautiful, like a sunset or a painting, do you have trouble savoring it for more than a few seconds before you feel the need to move on, even though you liked the sunset or the painting?

122. Do you sometimes get exceedingly annoyed (even if you don't show it) when someone interrupts you when you're reading the newspaper or working on your computer, even though the interruption was intended to be pleasant?

123. If you have made it this far into this quiz, are you surprised that you have paid attention this long?

124. Do you love basements and attics, even if yours are messy?

125. Even if you don't talk about them much, do you think about the big questions in life more than you imagine the average person does?

126. Do you feel a great deal of secret shame about how disorganized you are?

127. Even though the questions in this quiz are diverse, can you intuit

the theme that ties them all together, even if you can't explain it logically in words?

128. If you read all the questions in this quiz, and you made it all the way to this question, question 128, let me ask you, was there a point at which you said to yourself, "Wow. How does he know this? This is *me*!"?

CHAPTER 5

WON'T PAY ATTENTION, OR CAN'T?

THE CRUX OF THE MATTER

Pay attention!

But what if you can't? What if, no matter how hard you try, your attention goes where *it* wants to, not where you want it to?

"If you just tried hard enough, you *could* pay attention!" For centuries, that's been the exasperated refrain of teachers, parents, spouses, partners, mates, friends, coaches, employers, and all others who can't get someone else to focus. It makes people angry because they assume that to pay attention, all a person has to do is want to.

How wrong that is! Effort alone can't focus your mind any more than effort alone can focus your vision or cause you to fall asleep or fall in love. Many forces must combine to create visual focus, sleep, love, or attention; and many forces can detract from all four as well.

We are concerned here about attention. Certainly effort—"wanting to"—is one of the many factors that bolster attention, but it is just one of them. For example, if you are preoccupied with some pressing problem, you will have to struggle to pay attention to anything else no matter how much you might want to. Or, if you are hungry, you will not zero in mentally nearly as well as if you are well fed. If you have a cold or some other illness, you will not be able to focus your mind on much of anything except how lousy you feel. If there is a jackhammer blasting outside your window, that noise will detract from your ability to pay attention inside. If you have just broken up with a girlfriend or boyfriend, your mind will likely be on the breakup instead of where it's "supposed" to be. If you're depressed or anxious, your mind wanders. If you are in physical pain, the pain diverts your attention. If you are sleepy, you have trouble focusing your mind. Those are just a few of the critical factors we know about. There are many more.

Having ADD is one of the many conditions that influence attention. Even though it happens to be one of the most powerful, it is commonly overlooked.

For thousands of years, teachers, parents, spouses, employers, and just about everyone else missed the crucial point that paying attention is not always under voluntary control. *Sometimes* it is; if you ask people to pay attention, they can force themselves to do so for a few seconds. But after a few seconds, the mind's guard goes off duty, and the mind— impish sprite that it is—wanders off to wherever curiosity leads it.

No one can stand guard over his or her mind for very long. As an experiment, try it yourself. Try to force yourself to pay attention to something boring, like a technical journal or a conversation you have no interest in. You can force yourself to do it, but only for about as long as you can hold your breath. Pretty soon, you exhale. You forget you're trying to pay attention and your mind goes where *it* wants to go. To bring it back, you must first of all realize that it has disappeared, which you won't realize because you and your mind are now engrossed in your new thoughts, wherever they have gone. If a fly buzzes by, you might catch yourself and come back to the boring journal, only to drift away once again seconds later.

For reasons we don't quite understand, soon after you command yourself to pay attention, you forget that you have commanded yourself to pay attention. No matter how much you *want* to force yourself to pay attention, boredom allows curiosity to find the key and open the dungeon door, allowing attention to escape and find some interesting place to visit.

Attention behaves this way for people who do not have ADD. For people who have ADD it is the same, only more so. They pay attention even more inconsistently than non-ADD people do. It is not that they won't pay attention more consistently. They can't.

Let me tell a story to illustrate the point. One of the first adults I treated for ADD was a poet who lived in the Boston area. He wrote beautiful poetry that gained lavish critical acclaim. However, there is not much of a market for poetry, even good poetry. So this man, let's call him Hank, had to find other jobs to earn a living. One of his favorites was driving a school bus, as he really liked children.

One day he came to see me and told me that he was worried he might lose his job driving the bus. This was terribly upsetting: he needed the job, and he liked it, to boot. When I asked him why he might lose his job, he told me what had happened the day before.

"I drove my bus into the school parking lot, just as I do every day," he said. "All the kids piled onto the bus, just as they do every day. Once they had all taken their seats, I started to drive. I drove the route, just as I do every day. Then I drove the bus back to the bus yard to drop it off and pick up my car, just as I do every day. But when I turned off the ignition and looked around, I saw that the bus was still full of children. I hadn't made one stop. None of the kids had said anything. I guess they thought they were on some kind of field trip or something. None of them seemed to mind, though."

"Why didn't you make any stops?" I asked.

"Because I had started to work on a poem in my imagination. I got really focused on the poem. Driving the route I could do on automatic pilot. But making the stops? Well, that required attention in the present moment, but my attention was completely wrapped up in the poem."

As it turned out, the man was so well liked that he did not lose his job, but he and I decided together that driving the bus was probably not a good idea, given the possible risks.

In ADD, you can get so wrapped up in one project that you all but forget who and where you are. You do not suffer from a deficit of attention but a wandering of attention. Your mind does not go empty, it goes elsewhere. The term attention *deficit* disorder completely misses this point. It is not a deficit of attention that we ADD-ers have, it is that our attention likes to go where it wants to and we can't always control it.

This is not without benefits. The poem Hank was working on in his mind while he drove his bus past the appointed stops might have won him a Pulitzer Prize. But his not making the stops almost cost him his job.

The goal in treating ADD is not to prevent these mental excursions but to bring them more under voluntary control. We wouldn't want to eliminate them; it is during these mental excursions that some of our best ideas appear. Creativity, after all, does not happen on schedule or on demand. It happens unpredictably. Since impulsivity is one of the core symptoms of ADD, it stands to reason that people who have ADD tend to be more creative than their non-ADD counterparts.

To preserve the best of ADD while controlling what gets in the way is the goal of what is called (somewhat blithely) treatment. Effort helps treatment, but effort alone can't come close to creating the dramatic change in a person's world that a comprehensive plan of treatment can. To tell a person who has ADD to try harder is about as helpful as telling someone who is nearsighted to squint harder.

CHAPTER 6

AN EVIL, AN ILLNESS, OR A KIND OF MIND?

FROM STIGMA TO SCIENCE

For most of human history the mind has been a locked vault. We have used our minds, but we haven't known how we did so. The exploration of the psyche has been a dark science, if a science at all—more black magic than anything else. We have used crude terms generated out of stark ignorance to explain how we think, feel, and behave. We relied on three simple pairs of opposite adjectives to make our "diagnoses."

To describe mental acuity—or lack thereof—we had *smart* and *stupid*. To describe types of behavior, we had *good* and *bad*. To describe how a person dealt with emotion, we had *strong* and *weak*.

But for severe cases we reserved special adjectives.

For severe cases of stupidity, we invented pseudoscientific terms, like *idiot, moron,* or *imbecile*. These were all once considered meaningful diagnostic terms, as clinically accurate as, say, *hyperthyroidism* or *hypopituitarism*.

For severe cases of disruptive behavior we hatched fervid terms, like *crazy, possessed,* or *evil*. Indeed, madness and evil have always intertwined in the popular imagination.

For severe cases of emotional distress we applied scornful terms, like *coward, weakling,* or *misfit*. At our most sophisticated we could invent a nonsense term, like *nervous breakdown,* a term that has absolutely no scientific or neurological meaning whatsoever. We invented this term in our attempt to sound as if we knew what was going on when a person suddenly couldn't cope with life, when, in fact, we had no idea.

Historically, the treatments for the mild cases, the cases of stupidity, badness, or weakness, were all the same: *try harder; shape up; get a grip.* If that didn't work, you might be punished to see if pain or humiliation would motivate you to try harder. If that failed, you were simply dismissed as inferior.

The treatments for the severe cases were, well, severe. If you were an idiot; or if you were crazy, possessed, or evil; or if you were a coward or a misfit, you risked being tortured, even put to death. Society did not tolerate severe problems of the mind. Not knowing what else to do, we blamed the sufferer.

It is little wonder that for thousands of years rational understanding of problems of the mind foundered on the rocks of stigma when presented to the general public. People did not want to be "diagnosed" with stupidity, badness, or weakness, not only because the terms reeked but also because the "treatments" were horrific. And they certainly did not want their children to get stuck with one of those diagnoses or, God forbid, one of those "treatments," either.

Now, even though our knowledge should have rendered those old moral diagnoses obsolete, stigma persists. That's why nowhere in all of medicine is the gap wider between current knowledge and the application of that knowledge than in the field of mental health.

If you look at the basic symptoms of ADD—distractibility, impulsivity, and restlessness—you will realize that there have always been people who were especially high in all three of those core symptoms. But until the twentieth century, the lens through which those people were viewed was the lens of morality. The moral diagnosis a person received spelled trouble for the sufferer.

In the twentieth century doctors gradually ground a new lens through which to view these symptoms. With the help of the lens of science, a medical diagnosis could take the place of the moral diagnosis, but only if people were willing to use the new lens. Many were not. Thankfully, some brave doctors were.

One such doctor was Charles Bradley. In 1937 he made a startling discovery. He had set up a hospital ward for boys whose behavior was out of control. Saving these boys from the euphemistically named "reform schools" of the day, where they received daily beatings, Bradley tried looking through the lens of science at behavior that was out of control.

One day he had an idea that was to prove how helpful that lens could be. He decided to give the boys a medication, a stimulant medication to be exact. He had read in a journal that some adults who had used this medication to lose weight reported behavioral and mood changes that Bradley thought might benefit his boys. So he gave it a try. I imagine his head nurse must have thought he had gone round the bend when he announced, "Let's give them all a stimulant!"

He gave them an amphetamine. This stimulant didn't rev up the boys. Instead it stimulated focus. It was like putting on the brakes in their brains. Stimulating the brakes slows down the car; stimulant medication stimulated the inhibitory circuits in the brains of these boys. At last, they could control their behavior. It was a stunning discovery.

Here was a medical treatment—stimulant medication—that worked where thousands of years of "moral" interventions—various applications of shame and pain—had failed.

But, like most great discoveries, this one disturbed many people. The idea of a medication being able to help the brain where willpower couldn't threatened some people's world view as deeply as Copernicus stating that the earth was not the center of the solar system. We like to be in control, we humans!

However, the benefits were so dramatic that others picked up on what Bradley was doing, and the medical treatment of what we now call ADD began, as did more intensive medical research.

The research led to the discovery that this condition not only could cause hyperactive behavior but also could cause attention to drift away involuntarily. The discovery of this invisible symptom—the wandering of attention—led to a new name for the condition, attention deficit disorder, or ADD.

In the 1970s researchers realized that this condition did not necessarily go away during childhood. It had been assumed that ADD went away during puberty, but pioneers in the field, like Leopold

Bellak, Hans Hussey, and Paul Wender, observed that while this sometimes happened, it was not always the case—some children continued to have ADD into adulthood. Thanks to their observations, the whole field of ADD opened up. We now estimate that at least 60 percent of children who have ADD continue to have it into adulthood.

Furthermore, as researchers looked at groups of people more closely, they realized that girls and women could have ADD, not just boys and men. The females were less disruptive and so they called less attention to themselves, which led to their being diagnosed less often. While not as common in females, ADD does affect girls and women. The ratio is estimated to be about 3:1, males to females.

Often the females show less impulsivity and hyperactivity, but more inattention and a quiet daydreaminess. Authors like Sari Solden, Kathleen Nadeau, and Patricia Quinn have written excellent books about women and girls who have ADD.

As the understanding of ADD grew, so did the numbers of people receiving treatment. The shroud of stigma began to lift, but many people still contended that ADD was more a moral failing than a real, biologically based condition.

But the research in the 1990s shattered the "moral" diagnosis and made it clear that something was going on in ADD at a biological level.

Alan Zametkin's famous PET (positron emission tomography) scan study published in the *The New England Journal of Medicine* showed differences in glucose metabolism in the brains of adults who had ADD as compared to adults who did not. These results were not consistent enough to become a diagnostic test, but they encouraged others to keep looking.

Then they looked using the MRI (magnetic resonance imaging), and they found more differences. The brain volume was slightly decreased in subjects who had ADD. More specifically, it was decreased in the frontal lobes, the corpus callosum, the caudate nucleus, and the vermis of the cerebellum. All of these regions are associated with symptoms of ADD.

Furthermore, new genetic studies showed that ADD runs in families. Heritability is a statistic based on weighing genetic influences against environmental influences. It is calculated through twin studies and adoption studies. The heritability of ADD was figured to be about 75 percent, which is very high for a condition in the behavioral sciences.

Furthermore, as the human genome project reached its fruition, researchers began to identify a host of genes that influence the production of neurotransmitters, enzymes, and carrier molecules associated with ADD. Each one of these genes could become part of a genetic profile associated with ADD. Due to the great variability among people who have ADD, and due to the many genes involved, and due to the environmental influences over the expression of these genes, we do not have a genetic test for ADD yet. But we have definitely established that there is a genetic influence over this condition.

We've come a long way since Dr. Bradley's innovative work in 1937. It no longer makes any sense to think of ADD as a moral failing; it clearly has a biological basis to it. *It* is probably many *its*; and as we sort ADD out, we will probably name a host of conditions now covered by this one umbrella. But none of those conditions is going to be called *laziness* or *stupidity*.

If ADD is a kind of mind, rooted in anatomy, genetics, and biochemistry, where does that leave discipline and hard work? Discipline and hard work will always matter, of course. They simply are not enough—nowhere nearly—to treat what can go awry in the brain, and certainly not what goes awry in what we call ADD.

"Oh, c'mon," the skeptic says with a snort. "*If a kid really wants to buckle down and pay attention, he can. If he had a gun to his head I bet he would.*" Actually, no. Even if he had a gun to his head ready to blow his brains out the minute he drifted off, sooner or later he'd forget the gun was there, and he would drift off. The only way to make sure he stayed on task would be for the person holding the gun to remind him it was there every ten seconds or so. But if the person were willing to do that, the gun would be unnecessary. Reminders alone would do the trick. Fear alone wouldn't keep him focused, but reminders would. Structure is a far more effective tool than fear is in dealing with ADD.

Since I can't post an X ray on this page and say, "See? There's the broken bone, right there!" I have to resort to words. Words, however, can do the job. Like the simple words said to me by a little boy who had ADD: "My thoughts are like butterflies. They are beautiful, but they fly away." After treatment he said, "Now I can put a net around the butterflies."

CHAPTER 7

THE ITCH AT THE CORE OF ADD

"For some reason, I always do something to mess up my successes. I get the jitters, I can't stop myself, and I do something stupid like get drunk and mouth off or not show up for the crucial meeting, or something. Why on earth do I do this?"

This man, whom I started treating many years ago, had a certain kind of ADD, the kind that creates an itch deep inside, an itch that often gets scratched in dangerous ways and at the worst times.

"Right in the middle of talking to someone I don't even know or care about I'll sometimes get this urge out of nowhere to toss my drink in his face. Just for the fun of it. Just to see how he'd react. I don't do it, thank God, but I get the urge to. Does that mean I'm crazy?"

No, he's not crazy. But he does have this prickly kind of ADD, a kind that generates an all-but-unscratchable lifelong itch, an itch that can lead to enormous success and productivity or acute embarrassment, even utter disaster.

Says another patient, "No matter how well my life is going, I always feel a vague dissatisfaction, as if I'm not doing something right, or I'm missing some important ingredient that other people have that makes them feel happy. I certainly have no right to complain. I have a good life. But I am not happy. I really never have been. My husband doesn't know what to say to me. What makes it even worse is that he blames himself sometimes for how I feel. But it is not his fault. It's just me. Something is wrong inside. Is this simply the way it's always going to be for me?"

No, it doesn't always have to be that way. She has ADD, a certain type of ADD that makes her always feel slightly out of kilter, slightly dissatisfied, slightly unhappy. And sometimes *very* unhappy—but for reasons she can't comprehend. There is no comprehensible, external reason. Her sadness derives from her internal wiring. What she suffers from is not depression. Depression comes on for an extended period, then clears up for an extended period. This woman can get attacked by sadness for a day or a week or an hour—and it can clear up in as short a time as well. That is not depression. It's this prickly kind of ADD.

"Everyday life is just too bloody boring for me. I always feel a need to do something to stir things up. I'll make a wisecrack or say something totally off the wall or politically incorrect. I know I'm not supposed to do that, and I try to hold back, but I just can't. What's wrong with me?"

He has this certain type of ADD. Whether it is what's wrong with him or what's right with him depends on how he manages what goes on inside of him.

"I can't resist romance. I just love men! I love my family and my work and I don't want to do anything to jeopardize that, but, on the other hand, I love getting close to people, and when it is a man, I just can't keep the erotic element out. I can't imagine my life without serious flirting. I saw a therapist and he told me I have a histrionic personality disorder. But when I read about that, it wasn't me. I'm not a silly, superficial woman. I'm just oversexed, I guess. But it doesn't feel like I should feel bad about it. It feels healthy and good. But I know it's dangerous. What's wrong? Am I a bad person?"

No, she is not bad or histrionic. She does have this certain type of ADD in which high stimulation becomes a biological necessity to feel fully engaged and alive. That's why she says it feels healthy. When she satisfies her need for high stimulation—in her case, through sexual stimulation—she feels alert and good. When she doesn't, she doesn't feel good.

People who have ADD often don't like how they feel inside. It is difficult to describe exactly what they don't like about how they feel, except to say that they feel bored, or off, or logy, or at sea.

What can begin as a mildly unpleasant feeling can escalate in seconds into a veritable crisis. They feel they *must* do something to change how they feel. Within moments, they are operating on a level beyond their rational control.

It is in these moments that they can make impulsive, self-destructive decisions. They start an argument or a fight. They blow up in anger. They create a crisis out of nothing. They down half a bottle of vodka, or make a wild investment on the stock exchange, or jump into bed with someone they would have done better to avoid.

What they don't understand—and the wide world certainly does not understand—is that these reckless acts do stem from a biological need to alter their inner state. In pain, they feel compelled to seek relief immediately. It helps if they can develop a repertoire of adaptive, healthy ways to change their inner state.

To explain better what's going on, let me ask you to consider if you think the following people have anything in common:

- The type A, hard-driving workaholic who can't relax
- The so-called type T, or thrill-seeking individual
- The extreme-sports athlete
- The compulsive consumer of erotic literature
- The sex addict
- The compulsive gambler
- The alcoholic or the person who can't quit smoking
- The person who abuses other drugs
- The compulsive overeater
- The rage-a-holic
- People who describe themselves as having "an addictive personality"
- The adult with ADD

I suggest that they all have something in common. They all have an itch they can't ever quite scratch. Their attempts to scratch may lead them to become workaholics, or to take extreme risks, or to scratch the itch with drugs, alcohol, food, sex, or gambling. There are good ways to scratch and bad.

Traditionally, people look at this problem through the lens of morality, a lens that was discussed previously. People who do the various things named above usually receive a judgment, not a diagnosis. At best, people say they don't have their priorities straight. At worst, they are condemned.

But I want to invite you now to look at what's going on through the lens of brain science, not the lens of morality.

Could it be that all of these people share a problem of peculiar brain chemistry? Specifically, could it be, based on an inherited pattern of neurotransmitters, receptors, and carrier molecules, that they are not as able as other people to find pleasure in the ordinary ways most people can? Could it be, based on this genetic variant, that they must resort to extraordinary means to feel fully alive?

About a decade ago Kenneth Blum and other researchers suggested the existence of a condition they named the reward deficiency syndrome, or RDS. People who have RDS are not able to feel pleasure as easily as others. The gene involved in their model (and there are many other genes proposed now) is the A1 allele of the dopamine D2 receptor. People who have this variant are not as able as those who don't have it to reap the pleasurable benefits of dopamine.

Dopamine is one of the chief chemical mediators of pleasure. Anything that gives you a squirt of dopamine tends to make you feel good. Exercise can do this. So can making love. So can any kind of creative activity in which your imagination gets deeply involved. So can drinking, gambling, taking extreme risks, eating ice cream and other carbohydrates, taking various drugs, and smoking cigarettes. In other words, as I said before, there are good ways and bad ways to get your squirt of dopamine.

People who have RDS are more apt to turn to both the good and the bad ways excessively, because moderate ways don't produce as much pleasure as they do for other people. A good-morning kiss and a hug on their way out the door don't do as much for them as they do for others. They have to do more to get the squirt of dopamine than other people do. So they do more. They may exercise more than others, or make love more, or engage in more creative activity. And they may drink more than is good for them, or gamble more or eat more ice cream or take more extreme risks, all because they need to do more in order to feel as good as others do with less.

This model does oversimplify the pleasure circuitry in the brain. Much more goes into creating the physical sensations of joy or well-being or satisfaction or ecstasy than merely a squirt of dopamine. What's important here is not the exact anatomy or biochemical pathways involved—we'll be figuring those out for decades to come—but the fact that they differ from person to person based upon genetic variations.

In other words, people vary in their ability to feel pleasure given a certain stimulus. Some people feel pleasure more easily than others. And how you find pleasure in life is one of the key determinants of health and success.

If you have a certain kind of genetic makeup you may be predisposed to developing an addiction, or a near-addiction, not because you are a bad person but because your wiring doesn't afford you the more ordinary ways of getting pleasure that other people's wiring does.

This genetic variant often shows up in people who have ADD. That's one reason why addictions are so common in people who have ADD. But it also shows up frequently in highly creative people in all fields. There is an interesting link between near-addictions and creativity.

I have been drawn to literary people my entire life. My heroes during my adolescence were Dostoyevsky and Shakespeare. I was an English major in college. I have always liked to write, and many of my closest friends are writers, editors, publishers, agents, columnists, or other kinds of workers in the word business. I have always been intrigued by a commonality I have noted in literary people. They tend to be highly creative, witty, ironic, a tad cynical, and a tad depressed. They tend to drink a lot of alcohol, or be in recovery from having done so. They tend to harbor great dreams, but over the years lose faith in their ability to fulfill those dreams. And yet they also tend to be tenacious, working hard even as they lose hope that their work will pay off.

They share other traits. They have an extraordinary eye and ear for what is genuine. They pick up on the telling detail—a man's pulling up his socks as he talks, or a woman's licking her lips just before offering criticism—others overlook. They like to know exactly what happened. They love gossip. They abhor hypocrisy and spot it in an instant. They love honesty, and yearn for one honest conversation in a day.

As a psychiatrist, I have come to think of the literary type in genetic terms. I believe they inherit the genes that predispose toward RDS, as well as the genes that predispose toward verbal dexterity, keen powers of observation, a highly developed sense of irony, and a touch of depression. Due to the RDS, they can't find sufficient pleasure in ordinary life. So they resort to extraordinary means. For example, they write. They submit to that unforgiving discipline to try to improve upon life by creating order, even beauty, out of chaos. That is an extraordinary effort to find ordinary pleasure. When it works, they get a squirt of dopamine, and some endorphins and other pleasure mediators as well. They can get a milder shot of pleasure in other "word" ways, such as through a witty conversation or by reading a piece of writing that they love.

But they also often turn to alcohol or other drugs in their effort to improve upon ordinary life. As Ogden Nash, one of the great exemplars of this type, wrote, "Candy is dandy, but liquor is quicker." Ogden Nash didn't know that both candy and liquor stimulate dopamine.

I extrapolate from what I have learned from my literary friends to include all creative people. I call them dreamers. Whatever genes predispose creativity and being a dreamer, those same genes often appear in people who have trouble finding pleasure in ordinary life—a trait we're calling RDS.

Now add ADD to the picture. ADD abounds among people who have both the dreamer genes and the RDS genes. It is so common that one title I considered for this book was *Beautiful Dreamers: The Story of ADD.* "RDS dreamers" does not include everyone who has ADD, but the category does constitute one interesting kind of ADD.

Let me explain how the itch that's at the core of this kind of ADD derives from both the dreamer genes and the RDS genes.

First of all, when you can't find pleasure as easily as others do, that causes an "itch" inside you. You want to find satisfaction, but you can't. So you resort to extraordinary means. Some are adaptive and helpful; others are maladaptive and hurtful.

Second, if you are creative by nature, you live with another kind of itch. You are always inventing new expressions of that creativity: new plots for books if you are a writer, new melodies if you are a musician, new recipes if you are a chef, new routines if you are a stand-up comic, new images if you are a poet, and on and on, depending upon what you do. When the first nubbin of the new idea breaks into your consciousness it causes excitement, but also a strange kind of pain. It demands attention as it vies with your other ideas to be developed to the fullest and expressed.

Those two forces combine to create a feeling that craves resolution. When you then add to this volatile combination the genes for ADD, which reduce impulse control as well as the ability to screen out incoming stimuli, you can see why the man at the beginning of the chapter feels the desire, out of nowhere, to throw his drink into the face of the person he is talking to; or the woman needs serious flirting to feel alive. It's all about trying—somehow—to scratch a remote but potent and unignorable itch.

With this kind of ADD, each day brings crucial moments. They are the moments when you first sense the itch. When you first feel the itch—and it can happen a hundred times a day—beware!

At that moment, you can go in one of two dangerous directions. You may lapse into a state of depressive brooding. This is usually a prelude to compulsive or addictive activity, be it sex, drugs, or risky behavior.

Or you may lurch into action. You may actually throw the drink. Or you may make the deal you know you shouldn't. Or you may get into bed with someone you really don't want to.

Neither of those two directions leads to a good place.

The best way to scratch the itch is to engage in some kind of creative activity. Play. Draw the person you're talking to into an unusual conversation. Maybe tell him you just had the idea of throwing a drink in his face. Tell him in a way that is not offensive, of course, but don't suppress your own need to be real. That only makes the itch worse.

Connect with the discomfort you're feeling—the itch—and try to let it guide you to a place where you can transform it—i.e., scratch it—through creative activity. Creativity is your gift. Use it.

Let the discomfort guide you by feeling it rather than trying to replace it with something else. Most creative work begins with pain. Let the pain guide you to discover the sculpture hidden in the rock, or the recipe hidden among the ingredients, or the conversation hidden between the two people standing together at the cocktail party.

This principle makes sense for everyone, but it is especially important for people who have ADD because in them the itch is so powerful, and their ability to control how they scratch it can be so limited.

They—we—must make a plan, set up structures, and develop habits. At the top of the list for us adults who have ADD is to marry the right person and find the right job. Put ourselves in situations where our creativity can be valued and expressed. Avoid situations in which we will be tempted to swerve toward near-addictions or full addictions. Stay away from people who instill fear through ridicule.

And, above all, cultivate connections in which our best selves can emerge. Cultivate creative outlets—with people, with activities, with pieces of music or periods of meditation—that are always available to us, so that when we feel the itch, we have adaptive alternatives to the maladaptive patterns that can ruin our lives.

When I use the word *connection* or the term *creative outlet* I am referring to a method by which you can transform the pain of the itch into the satisfaction of an itch scratched. I don't mean that you must go write a poem or create a work of art each time you feel the itch—although most poems and works of art have indeed been composed in reaction to such an itch.

I mean, simply, that when you feel the itch you should try to bear with the pain, instead of suppressing it, and allow it to lead you through a labyrinth. The labyrinth may be a conversation that began with your feeling bored (a sure harbinger of the itch!). Instead of gulping down your drink to alleviate the boredom, you speak to the person attentively. You allow the creative process to lead you into the unknown territory called spontaneous conversation. Being who you are, if you stay at it, the chances are good that what began as a boring conversation will turn into an interesting one. The itch will be transformed into pleasure. Your creativity will have done the scratching.

There are other readily available adaptive methods of scratching. Exercise is one of the best. Of course, you can't start doing jumping jacks at the cocktail party (then again, you might!), but if you are alone in your office you can. Meditation and prayer are also both very good.

With forethought, you can arm yourself with strategies that work for you. For most people who have this kind of ADD, some creative outlet or stable connection makes for the best means of scratching. Not only do these strategies steer you clear of the perils of ADD, they lead you into realms where great achievement and personal happiness are most likely to be found.

PART TWO

◆

Three Stories That Tell *the* Story

CHAPTER 8

THE BENEVIANS:

HOW THIS DIAGNOSIS CAN CHANGE YOUR

LIFE FOR THE BETTER—AT ANY AGE

The best way to give you a true feel for ADD and teach effective ways of dealing with it is by taking you into the actual lives of people who have it. They are the best teachers. These next three chapters tell three true stories, profiling people of various backgrounds, ages, and genders. I chose the kinds of people in whom the diagnosis is often missed, or for whom the struggle was great. For the more straightforward, uncomplicated examples, I would refer you to the early pages of *Driven to Distraction.*

The first story is about a family. (The names in chapters 8 through 10 have been changed, but all the other information included is true.) Various members of the Benevian family have been coming to my center in Sudbury since 2001, so I know them well. Both parents are well educated. Paul, the dad, works as an environmental planner and also served on the school committee for their town, and Nan, the mom, is active in the PTA and has a career working as a consultant in research and design. I don't really know what "research and design" means, but I do know that this mom is smart and happy. Paul and Nan have a good marriage. They live in an affluent suburb of Boston, and the kids attend the public schools, good schools.

When I asked Nan whether she'd be willing to tell her family's story for this book, she enthusiastically agreed, being particularly keen that other parents become aware of the hidden traps she fell into before she got the help that was needed.

The two Benevian kids, Sophie and Lucas, were fifteen and eleven. Both were strong students. No behavioral issues, no hyperactivity issues. In fact, Lucas was maybe the reverse; he was a kid who would play alone for hours at a time at a train table when he was young. So, never any signs of hyperactivity in their childhood. When they started school, they did very well. In fact, they started reading early and they were both reading at third-grade level when they entered first grade. Paul and Nan actually thought about skipping first grade for Lucas and moving him right to second grade, except his kindergarten teachers felt that he was a bit socially immature, so they decided against it.

Said Nan proudly of her daughter, "Sophie was extroverted. A very outgoing kid, social, popular. Got along with adults, got along with kids. Very active. Dancing. Lots of activities. Really, you know, just a great all-around kid. Her homeroom teacher and English teacher in sixth grade pulled me aside at the first teacher conference and said, 'I'm driving that child to Harvard.' "

However, the following year, things took a turn for the worse. Sophie began complaining that she wasn't good in math and science. Toward the end of seventh grade, her grades started to drop off. Said Nan of her daughter, "She was starting to hang around with some kids we weren't crazy about, kids who were much less academically talented. Sophie didn't seem to be as interested in things as she had been, like sports or activities or much of anything. She would occasionally get into bits of trouble. She actually got into a pushing fight with another girl in front of the school and got detention for that. So I asked for the team meeting.

"The team was surprised to see us, because Sophie was a smart kid. What was the problem? I said, 'Our perception is she might be slacking off a little.' They all looked at their record books and were surprised by what they found. 'Oh, my God, yes, she is,' they said. So, they put a little heat on her, and she rose to the occasion."

Soon after, however, they came to another jarring transition. Eighth grade in this town is at the high school. That meant Sophie was leaving the middle school and going up to the high school with the group of friends that her parents weren't crazy about.

Nan and Paul reassured themselves that their daughter was a level-headed, smart kid. Sophie was put in advanced math and advanced English. She came home at the end of the first semester with honor-roll grades, but grades that were lower than they were used to seeing. When they asked what was going on, Sophie replied, "Get out of my life! These are perfectly good grades. If my friends came home with these grades, their parents would be ecstatic!"

Nan made an appointment with the school guidance counselor. "That's when we found out that Sophie wasn't doing her homework. I said, 'Excuse me, my child isn't doing her homework?' Turned out she had missed scads of homework. To a person, every teacher said, 'She's a nice kid, she's a respectful kid, she's a smart kid, but she's under-performing. She's not working up to her potential.' And they reported huge variability in her scores."

Such variability is one of the tip-offs for ADD, but at this point the Benevians didn't know about ADD. "The teachers said the problem was due to the adjustment to the new school and to the excitement of being in high school and social life and all that. But, they said, she still needs to do her homework. And if she would do her homework, then she would be okay. We went home to her and we said, 'Homework is not optional.' " Nan laughed at this in retrospect. " 'You must do your homework!' I commanded. But she didn't do her homework. Instead, all sorts of acting up started that we'd never seen before. She was ar-gumentative, defiant, and really very difficult."

Now thirteen, Sophie was having lots of arguments with her par-ents. "We were carefully checking up on schoolwork, which Sophie resented tremendously. We were leaning on her about her overuse of the computer. She spent a lot of time on the phone and on the computer, IM-ing (using Instant Messenger). It was obvious that she wasn't putting in the time she should have been putting in for homework. So we tried to set aside certain hours for work. Everything became a battle. When the midterm reports came home, she hadn't improved.

"One of her teachers proposed that we call Sophie in and have a meeting with Sophie present. At first, she just sat back and folded her arms as her teacher said to her, 'Sophie, you are a social leader. We see you out in the hall. You're the last one in the classroom because you're out in the hall talking to your friends. You could be an academic leader. You're a bright kid. What's going on? You need to do your homework. This is serious. You may not think this is an important year, but it *is* an important year.' I was thinking, Hallelujah! Somebody else is saying this besides me. And then the teacher put it to her: 'Sophie, why don't you do your homework?' "

"By now she didn't have that thirteen-year-old smirk on her face. With real clarity in her eyes she replied, 'I don't know why I don't do it. I honestly don't know. I can't tell you why I don't do my homework.' "

That is the honest answer in the world of ADD. These kids and adults have no idea why their best efforts produce lousy results one day and superb results the next. They don't understand it any better than the people around them do.

At this point, unfortunately, Nan and Paul thought Sophie's problems were due to her peer group. At a loss as to what to do, they threatened to move her to a private school, which Sophie resisted because of her friends. Sophie told her parents, "My friends are the most important thing in my life. They understand me; you don't. You can't take me out of this school. I won't go. I'll sabotage the admission test. And if you make me go, I'll get myself kicked out of the next school."

Paul and Nan consulted a psychotherapist, Ann. To their great surprise, Ann asked whether they had considered whether Sophie might have ADD. "She was the first person ever to suggest that to us. I said, 'What?!' in disbelief. 'There's nothing in her childhood that would indicate ADD.' 'I know that,' Ann replied. 'But when I was at Columbia Health Services, I used to see students who were in medical school and law school getting their advanced degrees who never before had come up against this level of challenge when all of a sudden they started to have enormous difficulty and they couldn't understand why.' I told Ann I'd file her idea in my mind."

Up to now, Nan had thought of ADD as something only young boys could get. "ADD never would have occurred to me. But Ann explained how it can present differently, especially in girls. Girls have a lower activity level than boys. So it's more difficult to diagnose ADD in girls than in boys. And it's particularly difficult to diagnose it at an adolescent age or beyond. People just don't expect to see it appear for the first time at that point. It's more unusual. Even though I respected Ann and took what she said quite seriously, I didn't know what to do about it at the time."

Then came an upsetting incident: a screaming argument about nothing in particular that lasted several hours. Sophie threatened to run away, even packed her bags. Somehow Nan and Paul talked her out of it, but problems continued.

Explained Nan: "Within three or four weeks she adopted a behavior of stalking me around the house. If I gave her an answer that she didn't like, she would just stay on my heels and keep yelling at me, 'You don't understand me. You don't know what's going on in my life.' She would be verbally abusive to me and would tell me everything that was wrong with me: I had yelled at the children too much; I was always too busy."

Sophie pushed all Nan's maternal buttons. "If she got an answer from me that she didn't like, such as, 'You're grounded for this weekend because you have homework that you haven't turned in,' she would explode with a litany of complaints against me to the point where she actually once cornered me in my room, and wouldn't let me out. She was screaming at me. Finally, I walked over to pick up the phone to call Paul to say he needed to get home. When she then ripped the phone out of my hand, I said, 'Okay, I have to go get my cell phone so I can call Daddy, because I need some help because I can't handle you right now.' I had to physically move her out of my way. I didn't want to touch her, but I had to in order to get out of the room. Amazingly enough, she let me do it. But as I walked out, she continued to scream at me. I got my phone, and I called Paul and I told him to come home. He came home right away and he took her out of the house."

Nan then phoned their therapist, Ann, who advised her to take Sophie to a psychiatric hospital. For any parent, this has got to be one of the most traumatic experiences of their lives. It must feel as if the bottom is just falling out. However, this emergency—more common than you might think—often leads to major improvement.

"It was really tough," Nan said. "Ann and I talked about options." Nan called their health plan and found out what they'd cover and at which hospital. "It felt good to have a plan. I called Paul on his cell and said, 'I don't know where you are, but come home and pick me up.

We're taking her to Children's Hospital.' So he came and he picked me up. I got in the backseat and we started on the way. Soon Sophie asked, 'Where are we going?' And I said, 'Sophie, we're taking you to Children's Hospital for a psychiatric evaluation.' I was prepared for her to leap out of the car or something, but she just went silent."

At the hospital, they waited two hours only to find out that there was no one on call in psychiatry. They arrived back home at midnight. "I was hysterical. Sophie was sullen. We all stayed home the next day."

What surprises many parents is how much of what is involved in getting care comes down to details like insurance and availability of doctors. Nan finally identified the right hospital for a psychiatric evaluation. "We couldn't get an appointment for a couple of days. When we did go in, we spent the day there. A whole team of people talked to Sophie: a psychiatrist, a social worker, and a resident. When they got back to us, I said to them, 'I'd really like you to evaluate whether you think this child has ADD.' After a while they brought us all back together and they said, 'No, we don't think this child has ADD. We think that this is a transition to adolescence. You're making the transition, she's making the transition, and you're all just having a difficult time making the transition. We recommend family counseling.' "

In the late 1970s and early 1980s, this was the standard drill for psychiatric professionals. It is a good drill. For the previous decades, the ruling theory had been psychoanalytic, which focused on the individual, not a system: there is one patient and one doctor. The idea of a family system was a radical idea evolving at this time. But, like any good idea, family systems theory can be overdone. As helpful as it might be, family therapy was not at the top of the list of what Sophie needed then. Diagnosis, education, and medical treatment were.

The Benevians took the advice and found a family therapist. Nan again filed the idea that Sophie might have ADD. "We did the family counseling, and we worked on a few things, but Sophie quit going after two or three appointments."

Summer came and went, surprisingly free of conflict. The family looked forward to Sophie's new school year, thinking ninth grade was going to be much better. "Then her midterm grades came home," said Nan. "She had C's and some D's. We went to parent conferences and found out that in addition to the C's and D's, she had an F in math.

She had forged her father's signature on the progress report. I left that meeting crying and totally devastated.

"But before that, a couple of weeks into the term, Sophie had come home one Wednesday—I work at home on Wednesdays, so I can be there for any spontaneous conversations—and plopped herself down in my office told me, 'Mom, I think I have ADD.' "

It continues to amaze me how often adolescents make the diagnosis for themselves before the adults do. I think this is because they don't talk to as many experts as their parents do, and so they are not dissuaded from the diagnosis, as Nan and Paul had been.

Nan asked her daughter what made her think she had ADD.

Sophie told her, "Well, when I sit in the classroom, I can't wait to get out. I just stare at the clock. I stare out the window. Or I stare out the window of the door. I can't sit still. You know, give me a new pen or something and that makes it more fun for me to take notes, and that helps, but I just can't sit there."

Nan didn't know what to think, but decided to have Sophie re-evaluated. "I wasn't thinking that she had ADD, but I thought another evaluation might help us get to the bottom of what was going on once and for all. Above all, I was pleased that Sophie herself was reaching out for help."

The best advice I can give parents is this: Don't give up until you have an explanation that makes sense to *you*. Don't take what the doctor says as if it were necessarily true if it doesn't ring true to you. Get a second opinion. Get a third opinion. Knowledge in medical science has become so vast that no doctor on this earth, even the most brilliant and conscientious, can keep up with everything, even in his or her own specialty. The best doctors will tell you this, and they will welcome a second opinion.

Nan did seek another opinion, which she ended up getting at my center in Sudbury. Before the appointment, she stayed up all night reading *Driven to Distraction*. "I cried, because I saw Paul, I saw Sophie, and I saw Lucas. I said, 'Oh, my God!' I left the book on Paul's bedside table and I said, 'You need to read this.' I wasn't going to say anything else to him. I simply said, 'You need to read this for yourself.' "

The diagnosis came back with little question about Sophie having ADD. Still, the Benevians were reluctant to take the next step and put

Sophie on medication. Of course, all parents feel that way. Who would want their child to take medication unless they were sure it was necessary?

Both the neuropsychologist and the psychiatrist, Dr. Cerulli, who met with Sophie used the same analogy. "It's like giving someone with poor vision eyeglasses. It's really about a chemical adjustment in the brain so your kid is able, *able,* to function better. This is something that can really have a positive impact on your kid."

While all physicians or medical professionals worry about the side effects of taking medication, if the medication is properly prescribed the side effects should be minimal. What people don't consider is what the side effects of *not* taking medication might be. Most people who oppose the use of medication fear that medication will have negative effects on the brain, even though such negative effects have never been demonstrated. We now know from solid research that repeated episodes of failure and frustration can have serious negative effects on the brain. And we know that chronic failure acts like a huge load of toxic stress and that this most definitely causes damage to the brain. It can lead to cognitive decline—in other words, you can lose intelligence—and it can cause depression. Those are pretty serious side effects, if you ask me.

Said Nan: "At a basic level, the idea of having my kid on an amphetamine was really difficult for me. Nobody around our house is on any kind of medication. And we don't do drugs. Actually, my husband is an alcoholic, so we don't even have alcohol around. The idea of having my kid taking a controlled substance just did not appeal to me at all. And not understanding very much about what it was chemically, and what it was doing, made me even more apprehensive."

The family thought about the issue and then went back to see Dr. Cerulli. "What really convinced me was that after Dr. Cerulli looked at her record she said, 'From looking at this record, there's no question in my mind that she has ADD. This is not a borderline case.' " After seeing Dr. Cerulli and hearing her evaluation, I thought, Well, if Sophie's willing to do this . . . And she was. For a kid who doesn't want anybody messing in her life, to then be willing to take medication, well, that brought me to where I was willing to do it. That was a big step. And I thought, Well, let's see what happens. And, son of a gun! She noticed a positive effect the first day."

When medication works, it works quickly. It can be pretty amazing. Sophie came home and said, "Mom, you're not going to believe this. I walked into English and we had a substitute teacher. And we were supposed to read a chapter and write a response. Instead of my doing one chapter, I did three. And I finished before everybody!"

Nan and Paul realized that Sophie had not been paying attention in class because she *couldn't*. Sophie couldn't do her homework because she wasn't able to pay attention in class. All of a sudden they had an explanation for their daughter's behavior. It didn't have anything to do with motivation; it had everything to do with her brain. They decided to lay off her for a while and let her begin to get back into better study habits and better self-esteem. "I could see now how much her self-confidence had suffered in eighth grade. There was an incredible amount of stress in the house. Nobody wanted to come home. It was horrible. At different times Paul and I said to each other, 'We can't go on like this. This is crazy.' "

The youngest Benevian had also been suffering. "Lucas was really a victim. He witnessed all of the arguments and suffered from all of the stress. He would occasionally even hide under the dining room table, not that that was an effective place to hide!" Nan laughed. "But it was just kind of a symbolic thing like, 'Oh, my God, let me run for cover!' "

Sophie was cruel to her brother. "We came down hard on her because you don't get to be mean to people in our house. You just don't. But every opportunity she got, she was. You can see, it was very, very tough at home. But then in ninth grade, her fourteenth year, things got so much better when we got the right diagnosis and she went on medication. She's still rebuilding her self-confidence and figuring out what she wants to do academically and athletically." Nan went on to describe Sophie's academic progress, which was immense. She did have trouble with foreign languages, as people with ADD often do. But, in general, she went from a frustrated student to one who could soar, getting the most out of her creative mind as well as finding ways to impose structure on her work. She moved up to honors in history and English and began to regain a lot of the confidence she'd lost. "Her teachers think she's fantastic now," Nan said. "Her history teacher nominated one of her essays for an award and it actually won!

"It's been a year of rebuilding. We did continue to investigate private schools with her, and she liked several private schools that we were looking at. But she didn't want to change. She is very close to her friends. At one point she said, 'It seems like you want to send me away,' which broke my heart. It seemed reasonable to let her stay in her current school because she was improving. If we could just straighten out a few things, like maybe get her some better study habits, then we thought this could work. We're continuing to work on that. She still resists our involvement and we continue to struggle, but it's so much better than it was. It's really so much better than it was."

This is usually the way with the treatment for ADD. Medication gives you a strong, positive boost in the right direction at the outset. The benefits last, but you soon discover that that is not enough to get you to where you want to go. Learning about ADD, which I call the education part of treatment, is also crucial and highly therapeutic, as it allows everyone involved to reframe the problem in a medical, as opposed to a moral, condemning, context. But then the hard work of learning strategies and structures must begin. This is a lifelong effort; it never ends. I am still working on it in my own life. This is the tiring part of having ADD.

In addition, you often discover, as the Benevians did, that there is more to the problem than ADD alone. Indeed, ADD usually occurs with some other syndrome, such as depression; an anxiety disorder, like obsessive-compulsive disorder or generalized anxiety; substance abuse; a learning disability, like dyslexia; a behavioral problem, like conduct disorder; or another mood disorder, like bipolar disorder.

Indeed, you can see signs of depression as well as bipolar disorder in Sophie's history. Her loss of interest in activities that used to interest her, her drop in grades, her changing friends from a positive to a negative group—all these suggest depression.

In addition, her extreme symptoms of irritability—stalking her mother, arguing constantly, getting into prolonged shouting matches, becoming so unmanageable as to have to be brought to a hospital— point toward the manic pole of bipolar disorder, as does her sleeping problem (she has difficulty getting to sleep at night as well as getting up in the morning). When irritability is the chief symptom, you need four additional symptoms from the following list in order to make the diagnosis of mania (more on this in chapter 15):

- distractibility (notice that this symptom occurs in many conditions, not just ADD)
- increased activity or agitation
- grandiosity (exaggerated ideas of self-importance)
- flight of ideas (ideas that seem to fly from one topic to the next, often without any logical connection)
- involvement in activities that have bad outcomes, like drug use, sexual escapades, dangerous risk-taking, and the like
- a decreased need for sleep
- excessive talkativeness

Sophie did not have enough of these to make the diagnosis, which is why she was diagnosed with ADD alone at the beginning. But her mood continued to fluctuate more than was normal for a fourteen-year-old girl. Later, Sophie was also prescribed Celexa. The combination of the Adderall and Celexa has helped tremendously in Sophie's being able to get on top of her schoolwork. Said Nan, "Knowing what's going on makes such a huge difference. Life is much, much better for us all."

As is often the case, the diagnosis of ADD in one member of a family leads to the diagnosis in another member. In the Benevian family, Lucas was next. A smart kid, Lucas was a bit introverted. When he was a child, he spent hours and hours with Legos and trains.

Nan was distressed to hear from Lucas's first-grade teacher that her son did the minimum. "She said, 'He's not completing his work. He's just not with the program.' I was shocked. For a kid who can spend hours building Legos, why is he not finishing his work at school?"

Lucas managed to hang in there for second and third grades. Academically, he was doing great. He figured out how to stay on task and get his stuff done, but he never fit in. He didn't have a lot of friends, but that wasn't much of an issue until he started getting teased on the bus. "When he was in third grade he said to me, 'Mom, is there a different bus I can take to school?' And I said, 'Yes, there is, Lucas, but it would take you to Pinewood,' which is a different school than he was in. And he said, 'Really? I can go to Pinewood?' "

Lucas changed schools and had a good year in fourth grade, although his teacher said there were self-control issues: tapping his pencil and lots of fidgeting, coupled with stream-of-consciousness talking. The kids were wonderful and accepting of him, but his teacher felt that he was turning kids off a little bit. He sometimes bragged about how smart he was. He couldn't connect conversationally with other kids.

In fifth grade, Lucas had a terrific teacher who noted that he needed more physical space than other kids. She gave him a chair at the end of the room, allowing him more room to spread out. At the teacher conference, Lucas's teacher told Nan, "He's doing great. I realize he needs a little bit of physical accommodation. And he fidgets a little, but I just walk over to my desk and I have some squishy things for kids to play with and I hand one of them to him. Or sometimes if I feel like he's distracted from the conversation, I just go tap on his shoulder and he comes right back."

It is vital that a teacher doesn't see ADD as an excuse and is flexible enough to do what Lucas's teacher did. It is extremely important in a child's ADD treatment to get his teacher on your side. If you don't have such a teacher, move heaven and earth to get one. Just as the keys to happiness and success in adult ADD are to marry the right person and find the right job, the keys to happiness and success in childhood are to have the right parents and find the right teachers.

Nan was thrilled that Lucas was thriving in school as she and Paul were trying to resolve Sophie's issues. And then they went to a teacher conference several months later. "I'll never forget the look on that teacher's face; it was so incredibly concerned, it was alarming. She said, 'Lucas is unraveling before my eyes. He can't stay focused. He doesn't pay attention to what his assignments are.' And she actually had a full-time aide in the classroom, because she had ten or eleven kids on ed plans out of a total of twenty kids in the class. She said, 'There's a lot of support in this classroom, and even with that Lucas is not staying with us.' "

Nan knew what was coming. She had already started to think about Lucas in terms of a possible diagnosis of ADD. Just being educated allowed her to deal with Lucas's situation more efficiently.

"After learning about ADD," Nan explained, "I had decided that Lucas's time spent with train tables and building was the hyperfocusing that can go with ADD. And I thought his social immaturity and some other things we had seen were probably ADD-related. I wanted to have him evaluated so he didn't end up in the same situation as So-phie was now in, having crashed and burned in eighth grade. I wanted to get going with Lucas and understand what, if any, issues he had. But then we found out that he was already starting to crash and burn!"

At that moment, they were having Sophie evaluated. Lucas was next on the list, and after he was seen, it was clear—not ambiguous at all—that Lucas had ADHD. He too went to see Dr. Cerulli. And when he went on medication, his teacher noticed amazing things right away.

Lucas noticed it right away as well. Dr. Cerulli put him on a lower dosage than Sophie because Lucas was saying he was having a difficult time getting to sleep at night. (Insomnia can be a side effect of stimu-lant medication; lowering the dose often takes care of it.) The problem was that Lucas's teacher noticed he wasn't making it through the day. Between one and two o'clock he would dramatically start to lose his focus. His dosage was raised to 15 mg extended release. He came home the first day and said to Nan, "Mom, it's not enough. I know it's not enough." He was immediately increased to 20 mg, where he has stayed.

Finding the right dose of the right medication can take time. It is a process of trial and error, as we do not yet have any tests that can tell us in advance which medication will work best in a given individual, or what dose will be the right one. Just make sure you work with a doctor who understands that adjustments need to be made and knows how to make them. The goal is to get improvement in the negative symptoms, like loss of focus or disorganization, without side effects. It can take some time to get there, but 80 percent of the time one medication or another will help people who have ADD. Of course, that means that 20 percent of the time medication will not help. I'm in that 20 percent. Medication does not help me, so I don't take it. But 80 percent of peo-ple will be helped if they give it a try and stay with it long enough to find the right medication and the right dosage.

Lucas's teacher reported incredible results. He was able to stay on task. He didn't fidget anymore. Throughout the entire day, he was re-ally with the class, connecting well with the kids.

"Before we had him diagnosed and started treatment, it had actu-ally reached the point where if he had a question, he would be right on his teacher's heels," said Nan. "He would be right up against her, kind of crazy about getting the answer that he wanted. He got very impatient. She noticed he had spatial issues in the hallway, not realizing that he was too close to people, that he was bumping people. And he was running in the halls when he wasn't supposed to be running in the halls. So there was a variety of problem behaviors. After we started treatment, she noticed an improvement in nearly all of them.

"Let me back up again to say that the first time I suspected there might be a problem, although I didn't know at the time what it was, was when we went to the open house in fifth grade for Lucas. The children had all done self-portraits. They had all been asked to write a poem about themselves. Lucas's was in stark contrast to the others. I'll read it to you:

> *My hair is like short threads of energy.*
> *My hands are like small machines of power and speed.*
> *My heart holds much anger*
> *that is black as the farthest reaches of space.*
> *I live in video games*
> *and eat game cubes.*

"I was just overcome with sadness for this child who had all this anger. I didn't understand. So I thought, Oh, my God, this poor kid is a victim of all the difficulty we had in the family when we were dealing with Sophie before. I thought I should get him to a counselor and really work out these issues. And then, when I learned about ADD, I thought, Oh, my God, this kid's brain is flying at ninety-five thousand miles an hour. That's what's going on. Everybody's telling him to sit still and control himself. And he's angry because he can't. That's not what his brain is wanting him to do. I began to understand the poem only after I considered ADHD as a problem for him."

As upsetting as Lucas's poem was, it also showed how original and creative he was, and is. Now he is making good use of that creativity, but doesn't feel full of anger.

There's yet another Benevian to discuss in this chapter. Nan's husband, Paul, is the oldest of three boys from what Nan describes as "a fractured family." His parents were divorced when he was twelve, and each has remarried and divorced several times.

Paul realized a few years ago that he was an alcoholic. There were also issues in his marriage with Nan that needed to be addressed, and that's when they began seeing Ann, their trusted therapist. When Ann asked, "What's going on with you guys?" Paul replied, "Well, we're having problems and there's a lot of issues. Nan wanted this new house. I didn't really want to buy it. But Nan really wanted to. So that's going on. And I might be drinking too much." Ann quickly steered Paul to AA, and he's been going ever since.

That's only part of Paul's story. After reading *Driven to Distraction*, Nan realized how much her husband fidgeted, tapped a pencil, and engaged in other nervous behavior. "When he was serving on the school committee, I would see his impatience, as he would tap a pencil or shift in his seat. I could see it in bold relief." Nan never considered it as part of a larger pattern of symptoms until she read *Driven to Distraction*. Then, late at night, reading the book, she thought, "Yup, the alcoholism, his hyperactivity—it all makes sense."

It is not uncommon for entire families to be diagnosed with ADD. It is also common for all but one member to be diagnosed. ADD does seem to be genetic, and it certainly runs in families.

It was Paul's turn to see Dr. Cerulli. She thought he had mild ADD, with mild depression. Paul went on Adderall with the goal of being a more balanced person at work and at home. Reported Nan, "It had the general effect of making him think about his behaviors and understand his behaviors better. It has made a positive difference for him."

Nan looks back at her family's tumultuous journey with some anger. "To have been through a psychiatric evaluation with Sophie and have it come out that she didn't have it, that cost us almost a year's worth of continued agony. It sent us down a whole other path that would have been reasonable to go down in terms of family dynamics and family counseling. But we needed a correct diagnosis first for that to be fully effective. There needs to be better education with practitioners and the community of therapists about this issue."

She's also continually evolving as a parent. "In retrospect, I learned how to do things differently because I understand now. Now that I understand what my kids have been dealing with, I can be such a better mother. I have a fair amount of guilt looking back over all those years, but there's no point in that. Moving forward, Paul and I are trying to be better parents. And in terms of medication, obviously, any responsible person is going to question what kinds of medication their kid is taking. In fact, my parents were horrified when we started Sophie on medication. I had to explain to them why."

Now Nan is struggling to understand what all this means for the long term. Lucas's pediatrician recently lectured her about how the goal was to get her son off his medication. All the while, Nan was thinking to herself, "Well, yes, but I can't imagine this child being in any educational institution without having medication to help him focus. It's not his fault if he can't. And it's not a negative if he can't. It's just who he is. And then maybe he'll get a job someday that perfectly suits him and his circuitry. But in the meantime, this is what he needs to function well in the environment that he's in—in the school environment."

This has been a long journey for the Benevians, and it's not over yet. Paul has just given my book to his mother for her to think about. Joked Nan, "And then I start looking around and think: who else?"

CHAPTER 9

JOEY:

WHEN THERE'S MORE THAN ADD

Telling Joey's story is unlike telling any other in this book because I was never Joey's doctor or one of his consultants; Joey, his sister, and his parents are close friends of mine.

Joey's story illustrates what a confusing and tiring maze a parent can navigate while trying to get all the services needed for one child with many different kinds of problems. One diagnosis doesn't begin to tell you what's going on. For these children (or adults), getting the right kind of help means visiting different specialists, each of whom may not understand what the other specialist is doing. The parent—or, in the case of adults, the adult patient—becomes the person who somehow has to find the appropriate resources. No one guide exists to tell you all the different treatments and specialists who could help.

Joey's mom, Hannah, has a Ph.D. in psychology, but, as she said to me, "What I have learned raising Joey ought to earn me a second Ph.D. I knew something about the brain from my training in neuro-psychology, but almost all that I really needed I had to learn along the way." Joey's dad, Peter, also has a Ph.D. in psychology. Both Hannah and Peter (mostly Hannah) had to spend thousands of hours, over many years, searching through all that is known in the field of children's learning and emotional problems, then somehow evaluating the treatments, and, finally, implementing the treatments they decided to pursue.

To ease this agonizingly labor-intensive, expensive, and rather hit-or-miss process, Dr. Peter Jensen, professor of child psychiatry at Columbia University, founded a national organization called the Center for the Advancement of Children's Mental Health (CACMH). When the CACMH gets up to full speed, parents will not have to learn and do everything on their own, inventing the wheel over and over again, as Joey's parents, and millions of other parents, have had to do. The CACMH is a nonprofit organization, and it relies on private donations. If you would like to learn more about the CACMH, or contribute to it, you can visit its website, which is Kidsmentalhealth.org.

Dr. Jensen has also written the best book on how to secure services and get the best help for children with attention deficit disorder. It is called *Making the System Work for Your Child with ADHD* (Guilford Press, 2004).

If two people with Ph.D.'s in psychology found the process of getting help for Joey frustrating, exhausting, and confusing, imagine what it is like for parents who have no such training and limited resources. If you are such a parent, I would refer you to the CACMH or the various organizations listed at the back of this book. *Finding the right help is the key to obtaining the best results.* You can also start by calling the medical school closest to you and asking for the department of child psychiatry. Teaching hospitals—those associated with a medical school—tend to be up on the latest developments, but even they don't know everything. That's why, as you will see, Hannah had to search to find what Joey needed.

Joey was adopted at birth. The second child and first boy in the family, Joey found love and warmth as soon as he arrived. An adorable baby, Joey did well in many ways, but he also had some problems early on. He bit other children when he was two and a half years old. Hannah's pediatrician wasn't sure what to advise, so Hannah turned to the preschool team in her town and she followed their advice: she took Joey to an occupational therapist.

Joey was diagnosed with sensory integration disorder, which I discuss later in this book. It commonly accompanies ADD. The best book about it is *The Out-of-Sync Child,* by Carol Stock Kranowitz. Kids with SI, as it is called, can be skittish, jumpy, overreactive, and hypersensitive to various sensory modalities, while at the same time they seek extra sensation through excessive behaviors, like hyperactivity, rocking, kicking, or, as in Joey's case, biting.

The occupational therapist prescribed brushing, a treatment developed by the person who pioneered the study of SI, Dr. A. Jean Ayres. For fifteen to twenty minutes twice a day Hannah would brush Joey's skin with a soft-bristled brush. The brushing—which does not hurt—stimulates the brain in ways that help integrate sensory experiences. Gradually, the child does not feel the need to gain extraordinary sensory stimulation and at the same time can enjoy normal levels of stimulation without overreacting. The treatment worked. Joey stopped biting.

From brushing, the treatment moved on to more advanced interventions. These included various exercises that helped Joey coordinate his movements, balance himself, and become more aware of others in a social setting. He participated in a program called the Brain Gym, which prescribes an array of exercises based on a theory called educational kinesiology. It may sound far-fetched, but it has worked for lots of kids. (For more information, go to www.Braingym.com.)

Joey had major speech problems. On the advice of the preschool team, Hannah brought Joey to a speech-language pathologist, from whom he received speech therapy. Joey continues to get speech therapy today and it continues to help.

Hannah took Joey to an audiologist when he was five and again when he was six, just to make sure that his hearing was all right and that he didn't have auditory processing disorder, or APD. (Do you get the feeling that Hannah was constantly in motion, either in her mind or in her car, trying to get Joey all the help he needed and make sure she left no stone unturned? She was.) In APD, a child can hear and understand words, but he can't *process* them, he can't make use of them. For example, he can understand the directions but he doesn't follow them—not because he is being defiant, but because he is unable to take what he understands and turn it into the appropriate actions. The best book about APD is *Like Sound Through Water,* by Karen Foli.

The audiologist found Joey's hearing to be normal, and did not find signs of APD. Another stone turned. Time spent, but not wasted.

By the time Joey was in the second grade, he had made progress, but he was still clearly behind the other kids in major areas. His biggest problem was reading. He couldn't do it. Other kids were learning to read, but Joey couldn't even memorize the alphabet. He reversed all his letters and felt totally confused by words.

Enter Orton Gillingham. The Orton Gillingham method of tutoring is one of the best treatments for dyslexia. After Joey was evaluated by a specialist, the tutoring began: one hour a day, five days a week. It is intensive tutoring in which the child uses all sight, sound, and touch to get into the world of phonemes, letters, and words.

Joey learned to read. He still had trouble with numbers, though, and so the tutor turned her attention to that. Such tutoring is still part of Joey's education.

By now, not only was Hannah getting her second Ph.D., she needed a second mortgage. While the public school system offered all the help Joey was getting, Hannah and Peter could see that it was just not going to happen in a timely fashion. So, they drew upon savings and reduced their retirement contributions to pay tuition for a Montessori school for Joey, as well as the tutoring, which was extra. The bill was about twenty-five thousand dollars per year. Peter worked longer hours and traveled more. The burden for following through on treatment fell to Hannah alone.

As time went by, Joey needed less and less tutoring. However, starting in second grade he needed more and more help getting organized and paying attention. More worrying on Hannah's part led to more searching, which led to a new expert. A new evaluation led to the diagnosis of attention deficit disorder. Hannah's latest specialist, a child psychiatrist, started Joey on stimulant medication. First he was put on Ritalin. It didn't help, and it caused side effects. The doctor then suggested Adderall, which did help a little bit and didn't cause side effects. It is worth noting here that if one stimulant medication doesn't work, another one might.

Being a highly creative and sensitive child, Joey began to imagine all kinds of dangers in the world as he got older. By third grade he was often extremely anxious, and given to periods of depression—a new set of concerns for Hannah to wrestle with and somehow try to solve. At this point the psychiatrist suggested that Luvox, a selective serotonin reuptake inhibitor (SSRI) with a good track record in kids, be added to Joey's regimen. The Luvox worked; it considerably reduced Joey's anxiety and depression.

However, in fourth grade Joey's anxiety and sensory sensitivity combined to create a new, practically unbearable problem. Joey couldn't stand noise. He would burst into tears or totally withdraw if he were in a noisy place or in a loud group. This is not good if you are a fourth-grade boy!

Once again, Hannah had to look around for help. "Can't stand noise" is not one of the standard symptoms a pediatrician has ready-made treatments for, nor do most child psychiatrists. Even the occupational therapists and the SI experts didn't know precisely what to say because their treatments had already been tried.

Step back and just imagine for a moment how this symptom might have been dealt with by another parent in another place at another time. A sensitive, anxious, highly creative boy like Joey who started to cause problems over something "stupid" like disliking noise would not have received much sympathy. As he became more and more of a nudge, putting his hands over his ears and crying, teachers and parents might well have responded with harsh discipline. "What? You don't like that noise? Well, get over it before I give you something to really make noise about!" The child would have been taunted, beaten, and repeatedly misunderstood until something terrible happened.

Joey was lucky. He had Hannah. Once again, she went to work, asking around, searching. Again, she found a treatment that helped. It is called the Tomatis method, named after its founder, Dr. Alfred A. Tomatis.

Hannah described how it worked: "Joey began the program to help his attention and to help him with his noise problem, what they call auditory overload. In a mildly noisy classroom, or in an auditorium for school activities, arts, or music, he would become overwhelmed and shut down. He looked uncomfortable and unhappy. He would burst into tears or stand rigid, hoping to get through the event.

"The program consists of an initial quantitative test of hearing, a two-phase program using a device known as the Electronic Ear, which is a recorded tape played on a specific tape recorder with particular headphones. There is an auditory pretest, interviews, clinical tests, and auditory posttests as well.

"In the first phase of treatment, Joey listened to classical music with two audio channels which were set specifically for him at the right frequencies, with pulsating beats which exercise the auditory system. In the second phase of treatment, Joey used a microphone attached to the headset. He would begin by humming into the microphone and end by reading and composing ideas over the specific music being played into the headphones. He could hear his own humming or his own words and the music as well. Each phase of this was programmed according to his pretesting auditory results.

"Joey seemed to be soothed by the music. When I listened to the music, it sounded quite distorted at different points to my ear. But for him, it was not uncomfortable. The program required patience because he was expected to listen daily for one and a half to two hours over a period of several months in each phase of the program. While listening he was allowed to read or do nothing—but he could not watch TV or do anything else. Although the program was intense, we were in constant phone or e-mail contact with clinicians both in Boston and in Bainbridge, Washington, where this particular Tomatis program originated. It is known as the Open Ear Center Tomatis and Lift Program.

"It became obvious that Joey's tolerance for noisy stimulation had increased. He was able to stay, even participate, and definitely focus better in a high-stimulus situation. Along with this, Joey got better at describing what he was feeling rather than becoming rigid with discomfort. His teacher noticed that he could speak better, paid more attention for longer periods, and could tolerate lively academic discussions, even participate in them. The improvement was dramatic.

"At home, I noticed that we could go out in crowded situations without him shutting down. His speech became clearer. He could keep on task with homework more easily despite distractions that in the past would have completely captivated him. He felt the change himself. He felt more comfortable in his classroom and didn't mind being asked to participate in dramatic productions, music, classroom, or school-wide activities. His mood was more even, his ability to refocus when he became distracted increased, and he just became a different child in the classroom. He felt more resilient and capable of handling day-to-day life. Altogether, his natural creative juices, capable mind, agile sense of humor, and empathic wise spirit emerged more as his trademark."

Hannah put it beautifully. *That's* what I mean when I stress in this book that treatment is not just about reducing negative symptoms; it is even more about identifying and promoting strengths.

Labor-intensive as it was, the Tomatis method helped Joey in ways that the other treatments had not been able to.

A new crisis soon loomed. (Hannah expected crises by now.) Joey's Montessori school ended in the sixth grade. He was not ready for a mainstream, public-school setting, but neither was he well suited for most of the special-education schools in the Boston area.

Once again, Hannah had to go on a search. There was no standard, obvious solution to the problem. Driven by her enormous love for this unusual boy whose gifts were now starting to emerge for all to see, Hannah, in her dogged way, found exactly what Joey needed.

The Corwin Russell School looks like a bomb shelter. It is a brick and cinder-block building out in the middle of nowhere, next to a cellphone tower. It is also the perfect school for Joey. The woman who runs it, Jane Jakuc, has an uncanny talent not only for finding the hidden gifts in all her students but also for selecting faculty who can do the same.

This is how the school succinctly describes itself: "The Corwin-Russell School @ Broccoli Hall is an independent school for high-potential students eleven to nineteen years old with varied learning styles, average to superior intelligence, exceptional creativity, attentional issues, untapped interests, talents, and strengths, and disparity between innate ability and past production." That is the school Joey needed.

Joey is now thriving at Corwin-Russell @ Broccoli Hall. The "@ Broccoli Hall" is a whimsical addition to the name of the school that Jane and her staff dreamed up during a sleepy part of some summer day. Many people now call the school Broccoli Hall, which amuses me when I think of the more formally named schools ending with the word *Hall*. Jane doesn't exactly thumb her nose at those schools. But there is a playful, iconoclastic message in "Broccoli," one that Joey and the other students there need and benefit from. They need to know that they are not less than the students at, say, Rosemary Hall, just different. As different as broccoli is from, say, rosemary.

The day he arrived at Broccoli Hall, Joey felt at home. He has played Caliban in their production of Shakespeare's *The Tempest*, and will act in another play later in the year. He still continues to have trouble with coordination and attention, even though he takes medication and gets tutoring. When I told Hannah about the cerebellar stimulation that helped my son Jack so much, she looked into it and signed up Joey. A group of students at Broccoli Hall now do the cerebellar exercises (I discuss this innovative but unproven treatment in more detail in chapter 29).

Joey's medications have also been readjusted. The child psychiatrist who prescribes his medications is trying him on the new medication Strattera, in the hope that it will be more effective than stimulants. Strattera is a norepinephrine reuptake inhibitor, and it has been found to be effective in treating ADD in children as well as in adults.

In addition, this doctor is changing Joey's SSRI from Luvox to Lexapro in the hope of getting as good results but with no side effects. This process of trial and error reflects the state of the science/art of psychopharmacology. We don't know in advance how a given medication will affect a given child. So we must try one and then try another until we get the best results.

Hannah has overseen all this. When you review all that Hannah has found for Joey since he first needed help at age two and a half, you see a daunting list. The standard treatments were tutoring and medication, along with finding the right school. All helped, but they didn't do the full job. What Hannah sought out and added to the standard regimen made a huge difference, but her devotion made the biggest difference.

Hannah had already learned some of the secrets of different brains from Joey's older sister, Rachel. Rachel had ADD and various other learning differences. Hannah had already worked for years on her behalf, trying to get services from her town, but at the same time trying not to alienate the people she was depending on to provide those services.

Ultimately, Hannah and Peter had to pay for most of the services out of their own pockets. Luckily, by working extra hours, they were able to earn the additional income they needed to do this.

The gloomy reality is that most people just can't do this. We need to spend more money to help our children become the people they can be. When you look at what Hannah did for Joey—and also for Rachel—you can see that good treatments exist, treatments we did not have a generation ago, and that excellent diagnostic processes also exist. It's because we know much more about the brain now.

However, bringing the benefits of that knowledge to individual children costs money. We ought to spend it. We ought to make what we know usable for all who need it. No one matters more than our children. If "no child left behind" is ever to become anything more significant than a catchy political slogan, it will require, first, that we understand that words like *slow* and *stupid* are meaningless; second, that we acknowledge that *every* brain contains within it the seeds of valuable talents; and third, it will take a commitment on the part of voters and policy-makers, not just heroic parents like Hannah and Peter, to provide the funding and leadership required to offer the astonishing benefits of our recently gained knowledge to children everywhere.

Only then will no child be left behind. Only then can our society gain strength, when each child finds and develops his gifts, whatever they might be. Then they can be like Joey, who, in spite of obstacles many would have deemed impossible, did find "his natural creative juices, capable mind, agile sense of humor, and empathic wise spirit."

CHAPTER 10

THE O'BRIEN FAMILY:

A HOUSEFUL OF ADD

What if everyone in your family had ADD, including you, your spouse, and your *seven* children? "Just shoot me now!" you might reply. I would have thought it impossible for any parent or set of parents to manage such an endless typhoon had I not spent the last ten years watching Nancy O'Brien guide herself and her family through that very storm.

Her story proves that one person and one family can prevail against ridiculous odds with little help. Her story also shows some of the history of the feisty syndrome we now call ADD, from its being all but unknown to its being marginally known but misunderstood to where it is today, better known and not quite as misunderstood. Nancy's remarkable story drives home the point that mastering the power inherent in ADD takes a rugged spirit and daily effort, requiring enormously more work than simply taking a pill every day—but it can be done, even under the most difficult circumstances. As you will see, a pill eventually *did* help Nancy a great deal, and it helped other members of her family, but it took much more than medication for her to find the life she and her family today enjoy.

I promised "difficult cases" in this book, and Nancy's is one of the most difficult. She had to learn about ADD herself; she had to wrestle with the dismissive skepticism of many people, including doctors; above all, she had to raise seven children who had ADD, even as she discovered and coped with her own ADD and that of her husband. That she prevailed proves it can be done, and done without expensive help; it can be done by parents, both of whom have jobs outside the home; and it can be done without going crazy along the way.

My patient since 1994, Nancy is one of the sanest women I know—a good thing, since life has dealt her some of the craziest problems fate can contrive. "Just my good Irish luck," she says with an ironic smile.

But it took a lot more than sanity and luck for her to see her seven children into adulthood intact. Exactly how this woman did it makes for a story that not only inspires but instructs.

Born in 1944, as a girl and young adult, Nancy didn't know anything about ADD. But by attending the school of hard knocks for most of her life, she eventually became one of the world's experts on the topic.

She was the seventh child in a family of seven. Her parents ran a small junior college in Boston, and her whole family was crowded into one small apartment.

Being teachers, Nancy's parents stressed the importance of doing well in school. All of Nancy's siblings managed to do that. But not Nancy. "School was pure hell," she said. "I hated it with a passion. I *still* hate school. My only memories of it are really bad memories.

"I was in the second grade and I was told to stand out in the hallway because I had been talking in class. This was very painful because I was really a very well-behaved student. Somehow or other I must have been caught talking, so there I was, put out in the hallway. That symbolizes me in school. Alone in the hallway, feeling ashamed and totally misunderstood.

"I remember another time, in first grade, when my mother had given me a doughnut for a snack. I put it in the drawer of my desk, where it gradually got all moldy and crushed; I couldn't figure out how to get it out without being noticed and made fun of, yet I didn't dare tell anybody it was there. Soon that doughnut became a monster, a horrible, dreaded thing. Day in and day out I lived in fear that somebody was going to find this disgusting, moldy doughnut and blame me for not getting rid of it."

Many kids could have gotten into this predicament, but it is particularly typical of a child (or even an adult) with ADD not to know what to do about a doughnut left in her desk—or a million other situations that to other people have an obvious, logical solution.

While other people would simply take the doughnut out of the desk and throw it away, the ADD person can't see the obvious solution. So she puts off doing what—obviously—needs to be done. Once this happens, she panics whenever she thinks of the problem—be it a doughnut in a desk, or an undone assignment, or an unpaid bill, or an apology that needs to be made, or a mess that needs to be cleared, or any of a million other items. The panic leads to more procrastination, which in turn leads to more panic, which leads to still more procrastination, as the doughnut, or whatever else it is, grows thicker and thicker with mold.

Even when she moved to another school, her misery continued. "It was terrible from day one. They were doing cursive writing. The only thing on the blackboard was Palmer method, another nightmare for me. It's that slanted, perfect writing. Most of the Catholic schools around here, if not all of them, made you learn that method. You were tested on it once a year, and you had to pass the test. But all I had learned in my other school was printing. I couldn't read anything they put on the blackboard, because it was all Palmer cursive! I didn't dare tell anyone because I was really, really shy. I still am, actually. So, I just had to figure it out on my own."

Figuring it out on your own: the life story for millions of people throughout history who had ADD before anyone knew about ADD. Most people think of ADD as some newfangled diagnosis. The only thing new is the name. Its symptoms are as old as the hills. There have always been children and adults who were particularly distractible, impulsive, and restless. Until the diagnosis of ADD came along, however, these children and adults were given not a medical but a moral diagnosis. They were dismissed as being bad, lazy, willful, or incorrigible. Their "treatment" often was to be punished and shamed: put in the hallway, ridiculed by the teacher, or beaten. Their "treatment" as adults was to fail and underachieve, as others regarded them with pity or scorn—except for the ones who beat the odds and became hugely successful by dint of intuition, creative talent, and dogged determination.

Those of us who had ADD before the medical diagnosis came into being had to figure it out on our own. We were like street kids, surviving on our wits and wiles, doing all we could to avoid the moral diagnosis and the severe punishments that came with it.

Before anyone knew about ADD or dyslexia or any of the learning problems we are lucky enough to know a little bit about today, Nancy's solution was the only solution: suck it up. Try harder. Back when she was in elementary school, in the 1950s, you were lucky if you didn't get a spanking in school if you had trouble. The idea of different kinds of minds and different styles of learning was simply gibberish.

"I figured it out. But school was extremely, extremely difficult for me because I couldn't concentrate." In the 1950s, that would have been dismissed as a weak excuse. Back then, the teacher might have said, "Try harder. If you try hard enough, you can do anything." Good old "hard work conquers all." One of our most treasured values, and rightly so. But the truth is, while hard work always helps, and may be the key to any great achievement, hard work alone does not conquer all. You can work hard banging your head against a brick wall all day and the brick wall will not fall.

Nancy *was* trying hard. "It wasn't that I didn't want to learn, and it wasn't that I didn't show up virtually every day, although I was late an awful lot. It's that nothing penetrated. Somehow I managed, though. But it was very, very hard.

"At one point they made me take an IQ test to see how smart I was. They never told me what my IQ turned out to be, but one day a teacher announced that there was somebody in the class who had the third highest IQ but the seventh to the lowest marks. I knew that person was me. How mortifying. I ultimately concluded I must be lazy or unmotivated in some ways because everybody else was able to do better. I knew I had the intelligence, but I just couldn't figure out why I couldn't use it in school. It bothered me terribly. You know, my parents *ran a school.* And every one of my siblings was either in college, through college, getting their master's, or achieving at some other high academic level. But not me. I was a mess, in a home where education was everything. I just couldn't figure it out."

The ordeal went on. "I did my homework, all the while not understanding what the heck I was doing. But I did it all the same. Just the doing of it turned out to be enough to get me through. Oddly enough, the one thing I *could* do really well was memorize, and that helped. For example, in religion class we had to memorize catechism. And in English we did a lot of poetry. So I did pretty well in religion and English, because I was able to memorize catechism and long poems. I did an association thing to help me remember, and then I'd forget what the association was."

All people have their own special skills. Instead of just identifying deficiencies, schools should try to identify and promote those special skills as early on as possible. For example, in my own case, growing up on Cape Cod, I was lucky enough to go to schools where my love of words was appreciated and valued, even though my handwriting was poor and my spelling was worse. While I got help with handwriting and spelling, the teachers put their greatest emphasis on helping me take pride in and develop what I could do with words, however I wrote or spelled them. Too often, teachers and parents focus all their attention on weaknesses, but it is the talents and strengths that get you through. They are what you build a career upon. In Nancy's case, it was her ability to memorize that saved her educational career.

Nancy's education was interrupted. "I got pregnant at the very end of my junior year so I had to leave school. I missed some, but I did graduate right on time." She gave birth to Warren, her oldest, between eleventh and twelfth grade. "I married Warren's father about a year after Warren was born. I was really depressed. Really, really depressed. I've worked in a psych unit as a nurse for years, and I have yet to meet anybody as depressed as I was then." At that, Nancy laughed her rueful laugh.

This is the kind of predicament untreated ADD can get you into. Here is an intelligent woman impulsively getting pregnant when she didn't want to, marrying a man who turned out not to be good for her, all the while underachieving in school and having no idea why. Nancy was barely surviving.

But life just went on, day after day. "Warren was unbelievably hyperactive. There's no doubt in my mind that his hyperactivity contributed to my depression. He just never slept. Never. He was awake all the time. And he was moving constantly. You couldn't keep him in a crib.

"Before I married Warren's father, I was living at home with my parents, which was hell. I had this hyperactive kid and they weren't helpful in any way. That's not to say they didn't want to be or didn't try to be, but they weren't. They were no help—and they never had been any help to me growing up. Not because they didn't want to be; they just didn't know how."

Back then, parents didn't know what was going on if their child had ADD; they didn't know what to do. So they did nothing, or, worse, did harm. Many kids like Nancy received daily beatings during their years in school, and then their parents turned their backs on them as they entered adulthood. These parents simply did not know what else to do.

"Somewhere along the line I had a church wedding with Warren's father, a small, private church wedding. And then I had another kid, Robert, and then I became more depressed. There was no help. Nobody noticed. Nobody cared that I was just totally depressed."

Nancy's ordeal in the early 1960s points out how little we knew back then. Not only was ADD poorly understood, so was depression. To make matters worse, all problems related to the mind were considered shameful: marks of weakness, flaws in character. And even if you did summon up the courage to admit to being depressed, you might not get any help. Even if you did get "help," it might be the kind of help that made your problems worse, like barbiturates—"mother's little helper"—or prolonged hospitalization.

Nancy's parents eventually helped them buy a two-family house in Brighton. "We were living there, and my husband was working. And I had the two kids. But I was so depressed, I had trouble even getting out of bed. That went on for a long time. I got to the point where I could not stand to be this depressed anymore so I got out the phone book, came across St. Elizabeth's Hospital, and started seeing a psychiatrist there in 1966. He turned out to be a wonderful guy. I saw him for maybe two years.

"He was knowledgeable, and he was understanding. The fact that he was Irish was helpful, because I had a lot of that Irish stuff going on. He was an alcoholic and I had a lot of that stuff going on too." Again, Nancy laughed her wry and rueful laugh. "On his suggestion I started going to AA. That opened up a new life. I went from my tiny, narrow, miserable, sick existence to a whole new world with a whole new bunch of people, all the people I met in AA."

Nancy continued therapy from the mid-1960s to the mid-1970s.

She and her husband had two more children, Kathryn and Nancy. "After a while I realized that my choice in marriage was very destructive. I decided I had to turn my life around. I got a divorce."

Nancy's eyes sparkled as she went on. "I was like a lunatic at this point. I wasn't depressed anymore. Instead I was completely enraged all the time. Angry, angry, angry. I didn't know why, and I couldn't figure it out. I just knew that nothing was working and my life really sucked. I was working as hard as I could to make it not suck. But it was still terrible. I kept going to my AA meetings, and they would say, 'One day at a time, first things first,' and all those sayings that they have.

"Anyway, I got a part-time job, and I moved to Maine with my four kids. My parents gave me enough money to keep me going, which in retrospect was probably a bad idea. I needed to crash long before I did. But maybe there was no place to crash to then. I don't know.

"But I do remember standing at the back window washing the dishes and thinking to myself, I can't wash one more dish. I cannot spend my life washing dishes. I was literally going to go insane if I had to keep washing dishes. My life couldn't be those dishes. I had to do something. I thought about it for a couple of minutes and I thought, Hmm. Nursing. Nurses are the most organized people I have ever seen. I am the most disorganized person I can imagine. But it worked for me. I got a college degree and a nursing degree."

Here's another example of an ADD-er with sheer grit. "I sat myself down and I said, 'No matter what, I'm going to sit and I'm going to study this book. And I'm going to sit and study it until I get it. If I don't get it, I'm not going to bed.' I just made a commitment to myself. I knew that I was smart and I concluded it didn't really matter why I couldn't do it, I was going to do it anyway. I started getting A's in every class I took. I came up with lots of gimmicks to force myself to concentrate. When I found myself drifting off and daydreaming, I would stop and take a deliberate break. Gimmicks like that."

Nancy remarried. Her new husband, Paul, helped with the housework while she pursued her degree. "I would sit down and start at seven o'clock every night in the same spot. I'd take the breaks as I needed them, but I would always stay until it was midnight. Seven to midnight was a huge amount of time because I had these kids. But that's what I did. In school, I taped every lecture and I would listen to the tapes when I got home. I would transcribe each lecture virtually word for word. Then I'd memorize it because I could memorize. That's really how I got through the science courses, like inorganic chemistry, with lots of formulas and details to memorize. Even if I understood them, I couldn't remember them. So I just memorized the lectures, word for word."

She got her RN and BSN. "I did really well. I earned a 3.65 average. So that was good. But I still had a lot of the ADD symptoms, you know? Even now, my memory is still terrible."

Nancy had her fifth child before nursing school, her sixth and seventh afterward. She hated to see how each one of them struggled in the same ways she had. She didn't want them to have to resort to the extreme measures she had had to use to finally do well in an educational setting. "I had no answers for my kids, but we kept looking. My sister found out that there was a place at the Franciscan Hospital in Brighton that gave an evaluation to kids who were really having trouble—any kind of problem, physical, emotional, whatever. So, we brought Warren there. He stayed for five days. They did every psychological and physical exam possible. Finally the doctor said to us, 'He has two problems. He's slightly farsighted, and he has minimal brain dysfunction.' Translation—ADD."

At last, Nancy had a diagnosis, an explanation for why this child, now nine, had been so terribly difficult from the moment he was born. Here was an answer: the greatest relief of all. It is often the case both for parents and for adults who get diagnosed with ADD; just knowing the reason for the problems is perhaps the greatest therapy of all.

But then the story took a turn for the worse. Nancy was ready to charge into school and tell Warren's fourth-grade teacher what was really going on, why the boy whose IQ tested at 150 was such a poor student. When she asked her doctor if he would write letters to Warren's teachers or if they should call him, the doctor shook his head. "Neither. Nobody's going to believe you, or believe me, for that matter. Everything I've told you is true, but nobody will believe either of us. It will take decades before this diagnosis gains any credence with teachers and the public. I'm also sorry to tell you this, but in a few years, when Warren is twelve or thirteen, he's probably going to get into all kinds of trouble."

It amazes me, some thirty-five years later, how prophetic that doctor was. It makes me wonder how many medical conditions—

especially those relating to the mind—we now are dismissing as trivial or nonexistent will prove to be serious, valid, and treatable decades hence.

Nancy was a prisoner of the times in 1969, but she didn't give up. Following the doctor's suggestion, she started Warren on a stimulant medication. It helped tremendously. When she explained the reason for his sudden improvement to his teachers, not only did they dismiss the diagnosis, as the doctor had told her they would, they went on to insist that the medication was not the cause of his doing better, but discipline and hard work were.

Nancy was so impressed with Warren's progress on medication that she decided to try one pill herself. "I thought, My God, this is what I have been looking for all of my life. It was incredible. It just completely changed my whole outlook on everything. It made me focus. I remember thinking, Geez, I could do anything now. I could do all the projects and stuff I don't want to do, that I've been putting off, that I hate. All I wanted to do was accomplish stuff. Just one pill did that. But after I took the one pill I decided—this is so sad—I decided that I liked it so much and it worked so well that I better never ever take it again because I could become addicted to it. I had been going to AA, and I was afraid that I was going to become a drug addict. You know, they tell you in AA that you might mainline heroin after you take Ritalin. So, I never took it again. In fact, I stopped giving it to Warren as well. I was worried about what it might do to him too. That turned out to be a big mistake because, as the doctor predicted, he went on to have a whole lot of trouble at school. He's very smart, but he had a terrible time. He barely graduated high school."

While Warren later returned to medication and went on to much success, Nancy struggled for years with and for her kids, watching while they wrestled with many of the same problems she'd had in school, as well as some new ones, like misconduct. Still afraid of medication, and unable to get anyone to take the diagnosis of ADD seriously, she made do, with her husband's help and her own ingenuity and tenacity.

The family moved to Arizona for a while, then back to Massachusetts. Nancy became a psychiatric nurse and worked in the drug and alcohol unit at the VA hospital in Boston, where she was amazed to find that many vets had undiagnosed ADD. When she would suggest to the doctors on the unit that these men who were in for treatment for substance abuse might have underlying ADD as the cause of their addictions, the doctors dismissed her opinion out of hand. They insisted that ADD was a diagnosis found only in children, that you grew out of it during puberty, and that it was unrelated to substance abuse.

Nancy was right, and the doctors were wrong. ADD does not necessarily go away during puberty. And ADD is strongly associated with addictions in adults. If the ADD gets treated it becomes much easier for these adults to give up the substance they are basically using as a form of medication. Only, it's the wrong medication. In other words, if you provide them with the correct medication, perhaps Ritalin or another stimulant, they can then give up the incorrect medication, like alcohol or cocaine.

Once again, Nancy was ahead of her time. And she still was afraid to allow herself to take the medication she knew could dramatically help her. However, she was learning some strategies with schools. By the time her seventh child, Nicholas, started his education, Nancy was no longer cowed by school authorities. "When Nicholas started kindergarten, on the first day of school I met with the teacher and said to her, 'I think that you're going to find that he is hyperactive. I want you to watch him. If there are any signs of this, I want to know.'

"At first, everything was fine. And then I started getting little notes tipping me off that there was a problem. So, I went and I spoke with his teacher again. She just said, 'Oh, no, no. He's fine.' So, that was it for kindergarten. First grade, same process. It was like a carbon copy of kindergarten. 'Really nice kid,' the teacher would say. 'He's just a little of this and a little of that.' "

When he started third grade, she finally felt something had to be done. Just as she had with Warren almost twenty years before, Nancy found an expert who could do an evaluation. Now the times were more favorable. In addition to a diagnosis, Nancy was referred to Paul Wender's excellent book on ADD.

As she sat in her backyard and read the book, she was stunned. Now she knew for sure what she had sort of known all along. *Everyone* in the family had ADD: the kids had it, her husband, Paul, had it, and she herself had it.

Of course, the struggle was still not over. Truly, the struggle is never over in life with ADD. But now it became even clearer that everyone in the family needed help. Nancy set about trying to make sure they all got it. Not just medication, but guidance, structure, support, career counseling, help with substance abuse, relationship building, cheerleading—all the interventions people with ADD need.

One of her first stops was Nicholas's school. "They didn't get it at all. They didn't know anything about ADD or its impact on kids in school. I spent a lot of time with guidance counselors at the school and with a psychologist, who actually had a Ph.D. She was very critical of me early on, mainly because she didn't know anything about ADD. Ultimately, she admitted as much. No one at the school knew anything about it. It was an unknown. And remember, this was the early nineties, not that long ago."

Even today, millions of parents find themselves in Nancy's situation. It is up to them to somehow negotiate the various rules and regulations of the public-school system, or, if the child is in a private school, to persuade the school to take the issue seriously. You can do this alone. You will find a list of resources around the country at the end of this book. Contact someone near you.

In dealing with schools, my best advice is to make friends with the teacher. Make friends before you make requests. Many parents are understandably so desperate and wound up that they all but attack the teacher with their requests, almost before they say hello.

Before you do anything else, I urge you to make friends with the teacher. It takes only a few minutes to shake hands; maybe bring in some cookies or offer to help at pickup time. When you do that, your chances of getting the help you need, without having to go through the bureaucracy, go way up.

This didn't work for Nancy. She had to work the system. "What I figured out was that the person who has the most people on their side in any given meeting wins. Luckily for me, I had a pool of people I could pull from and it didn't really matter who they were as long as they were warm bodies and they were on my side." If you don't have a team already, go to the back of this book, find someone near you, and begin to build your team.

Said Nancy, "My brother was running an educational foundation, so I got him and one of his teachers, who was a specialist in learning disabilities, to come with me. When they brought in more, I brought in more. At the end of every meeting, I got what I wanted because I had more people there.

"This was crucial, because Nicholas's fourth-grade teacher had started off the year by telling me that he didn't believe in ADD, that there was no such thing. He said the problems Nicholas had were all a matter of discipline. Same old stuff as I got back in the sixties. He told Nicholas if he really, really tried to do his work, he could. I looked him straight in the eye and said, 'That's a mean and abusive thing to say to my child because he really does want to do his work, but he can't.' By then I'd just had it with the whole process. I decided I had to go above this teacher because there was no changing him or his way of thinking. Like so many others, he was absolutely not open to facts, research, or any kind of scientific evidence I brought in. It was like dealing with a bigot or a racist.

"But guess what? You won't believe this. At the end of the school year, that teacher told me that he'd been diagnosed with depression, but he was starting to think what he really had was ADD! Can you believe it? He was very grateful that I had spent so much time with him and with Nicholas. All I wanted to do was kill the guy. He was such an idiot."

In high school, it became difficult for Nicholas because the teachers wanted to mainstream him. Nancy didn't let them, which she now feels was a mistake. "He went into one of these 'special' programs in the school that basically isolates the kids with learning differences. That's really all that's special about them. He didn't do well there. So he left. But he's going to go back and finish, and he'll be in the mainstream this time. He's very bright. I know he'll do well."

And Nancy's other children? "Let's see. Robert's living in Arizona and works for the telephone company. He's married, he's got a couple of kids, and loves it. He's happy as a clam. He was diagnosed with ADD out there and was on medication for a while, but he said his wife asked him to stop taking it because it made him really irritable. So he doesn't take it. He can be his usual, jovial, ADD self at home and at work and people love him."

Of course, finding the right job and marrying the right person are keys to happiness for us all. The reason I emphasize this for adults who have ADD is that they so often make the same mistake in both areas.

They marry and work for people who are caricatures of a mean fifth-grade schoolteacher. Of course, they need precisely the opposite: a boss and a spouse who recognize and value their talents and can deal with their shortcomings without demeaning them in the process.

Nancy has a daughter who shares both her name and her profession. "She has a degree in nursing. She had a terrible time in school with ADD, but she managed to get a GED. Then she went to college and got a degree in nursing. She started a master's program to become a nurse practitioner, but she's never finished it. I'm not sure why. I think she makes it more difficult on herself by not taking the meds. Maybe that's why she hasn't finished her master's. I don't know."

Life is also a struggle for her daughter Kathryn. "She's very bright, and when you talk to her, she'll tell you she doesn't have the typical problems concentrating. She can sit down and read and her mind doesn't wander; at least that's what she says. But her behavior would make you think that she has ADD because she's job-hopping like crazy and moving from one state to another and goal-hopping. Everything is always in flux with her. She can't seem to get much accomplished or find a real direction and stick with something.

"She's thirty-four, she's single, and right now she lives with my two sisters, but she hates it, so she's moving again. Life is a struggle for her. But she has two degrees. She put herself through Emerson College and graduated on the dean's list. She then went back to school and got another undergraduate degree, in English. She says she wants to get a teaching degree and teach English, but she keeps moving. She moves away and becomes horribly homesick, and then moves back. Still, she's very responsible and works hard. She always has a job. She paid for all her education herself. She's just totally disorganized in terms of making a plan for her life and then acting on it and sticking with it.

"As soon as I say anything to her about medication, she jumps up and walks away. But I'll tell you an odd story. Kathryn has two cats, and she loves her cats. They're her children. One day the cats started to fight, and one of them was starting to injure the other one seriously. It got to the point she was going to have to give one of them away. I suggested she put one of them on Prozac. She didn't want to do it, but I said, 'What do you have to lose? You're going to have to get rid of the cat otherwise.' So she called Tufts Veterinary School. It turned out there was a guy doing research on cats and Prozac. He started the cat on Prozac. It's taken the cat several weeks, but the cats are back to being best friends now. So there's a little crack in her armor against medication. I'm hoping that this will be an inroad, and maybe she'll get some help."

Nancy went on about how talented her daughter was in other ways. "She can sell a house. She can buy any piece of property, sell it, and turn a profit in a month, with no realtor. So she can handle that stress and organization, no problem. But her life is just drifting."

There are thousands of women and men just like Nancy's daughter Kathryn: adults who have untreated ADD. They are tremendously talented, but drifting. To call them underachievers is an understatement. When people offer help, these folks usually reject the offer, not out of anger but out of an abiding preference to go it alone. They are not loners so much as they are stubbornly committed to doing life according to their own plan, even if they don't have a plan!

They certainly don't all need medication, but they all certainly could benefit from some kind of a treatment plan other than just bumping along to the beat of their own drums. Usually, they can't even hear their own drums. They just know they don't want to march to anyone else's.

If you know such a person, my best advice to you is to persist. You might try giving him this book to read, or, if reading is out of the question, summarize the book. If that fails, try having someone he trusts speak to him after you have first educated that person about ADD. Or let him know of benefits of treatment he might not have thought of: like lowering his golf score or improving the experience of lovemaking. Treating ADD improves anything you do that requires mental focus, and that includes just about everything you do while you're awake.

Don't get into a fight with these people. Adults who have ADD are just like kids who have ADD: they love to argue and fight. That's more stimulating than listening to suggestions about how to improve their lives.

Don't argue or fight or struggle, but also don't give up. Persist. Try this, try that. It is never too late to treat ADD. The oldest patient I have treated was eighty-six. She said the treatment changed her life, allowing her to focus and not get bored while being with her great-grandchildren.

It was certainly not too late for Nancy to learn about ADD as an adult, and to help her husband and her children. When she gave a book about ADD to her nineteen-year-old son, Kevin, she wasn't sure if he'd read it, but he did. I asked Kevin about it, and this is what he said to me: "It was amazing. It was like finding religion. I thought I was just going to go through life kind of half-assed. I had been doing sub-par, just getting by. And all of a sudden there's a promise for a solution or cure."

Kevin saw a doctor, was diagnosed with ADD, and started on Cylert, a stimulant medication that is not used widely any longer due to damage it can possibly cause to the liver. It didn't damage Kevin's liver and it did help him focus. "The relief of knowing I wasn't stupid, the insight, the diagnosis, plus the medication, turned things around for me."

There was another step Kevin needed to take. Like many adults with ADD, he was self-medicating with alcohol and marijuana. Chronic pot smoking can make ADD worse. Getting ADD diagnosed and treated helped enough that he applied to law school and got in, but before he started he was smart enough to give up his marijuana. "I stopped smoking pot about a month before law school started," he said, "and that was dramatic. Before I quit I said to myself, You're in a cloud, man. When I quit pot, the cloud went away."

We are still learning about why it is so common that people who have undiagnosed and untreated ADD self-medicate with various drugs, as well as indulge in activities like gambling, shopping, eating or fasting, spending, viewing pornography, or having compulsively driven sexual escapades. Whatever the reason, it is well known now that a disproportionate percentage of people who have ADD struggle with addictions or unhealthy pleasure-seeking habits that are not quite addictions but nonetheless over time impair the person's mood, performance, and health. It may be that such people have an as yet undefined variant of ADD that has been called by Kenneth Blum the reward deficiency syndrome. Indeed, the underlying neurochemistry may be identical, and define both this subtype of addiction-prone ADD and the reward deficiency syndrome itself. For more about this, see chapters 7 and 19.

Whatever their underlying brain biology may be, people who have ADD need to change their inner state often and regularly. They can't stand the feel of regular, unchanged life for long.

Children may try to change their inner state by getting into fights or arguments. That is not their conscious motivation, but they may be drawn to conflict, as moths to a flame, out of a biological drive. Conflict changes their inner state. It is riveting. Let's face it: an argument is far more engrossing than peace and harmony. In seeking conflict, the child is unwittingly self-medicating with a powerful drug: adrenaline. Adrenaline is nature's own stimulant medication. When a person (of any age) feels excited, fearful, combative, or stressed, he or she naturally pumps out adrenaline and cortisol.

Children—and adults—who have ADD learn early on that with the aid of adrenaline they can tune in and enjoy life more easily. Therefore, when they feel bored or logy or vaguely out of sorts they learn that they can feel better by seeking excitement, danger, conflict, or even a fight. It is not that they are "bad," but that they are bored, and so they instinctively seek to change their inner state. For someone who has ADD, being bored is like being asphyxiated. It cannot be endured for more than a minute or so. When bored, the person with ADD feels compelled to do something immediately to bring the world back up to speed. Adrenaline can do this in a heartbeat.

Another easy way to change their inner state is with potions and drugs. Some are legal, like alcohol, caffeine, and nicotine; some are illegal, like marijuana, cocaine, or Ecstasy. People with ADD are far more likely to misuse all of these drugs than the average person. Or they may turn to certain highly stimulating activities to change how they feel, like gambling, sexual adventures, and the other activities already mentioned.

It is an important part of treatment, first of all, to acknowledge what is going on—not to deny it—and then to find other, more adaptive ways of changing your inner state. For example, the legal drug caffeine can help, but you must be careful not to use it in high doses, as the side effects can be unpleasant and even dangerous. Prescription drugs like Ritalin and the other stimulants can help, when they are used carefully and conservatively.

However, drugs are only one way to change your inner state, and, in the long run, not the best way. Finding adaptive ways to regulate the unpleasant inner feelings that so often besiege people of all ages who have ADD is one of the most important keys to a happy and healthy life. Learning how to find pleasure in ordinary activities that can be done by oneself can save the life of someone who has ADD. Each person can find her own favorites. For me, watching professional sports, especially football, is one; watching mindless TV, especially *Law & Order* and *The Practice,* is another; reading the sports section of the newspaper is a third; and reading Robert B. Parker's Spencer novels is a fourth. Nothing very constructive on that list—but nothing dangerous, either. We all need time to recharge our batteries.

Of course, there are many constructive ways of changing your inner state. Physical exercise is a superb way. Finding a form of exercise that you love can work wonders. Music is another way. And so is what Kevin did: finding an activity that was engrossing, adaptive, and compelling—namely, going to law school. In later chapters, on the nonmedication treatment of ADD, we offer many more tips on how to change your inner state in an adaptive way.

Kevin is now a lawyer. He took Ritalin in law school and sat in the front row in the auditorium, right next to the teacher. Sitting in the front row in classes is another good idea for people who have ADD. Kevin was able to concentrate well enough to excel in law school.

He's been married for five years. Not only has he found the right job, one of the two keys to a happy life with ADD, he hooked up with the right partner, the other key. His wife helped him stay on track. "She's been helpful in the same way my mom was helpful to my dad, and a lot of women are helpful to guys with ADD. She does everything I can't do, like bills, and she also manages a clothing store. She's amazing. I'm very lucky to have found her."

They're thinking about having children. His reasoning is not the standard reasoning, but, then, in the land of ADD nothing is standard. "We're starting to feel like we better have kids or we'll be bored out of our minds. I mean, I hate kids. I don't want kids—I really don't like them. But, you know, you do need them."

I would bet money that Kevin will be one of the best dads around. He says he hates kids, but I am certain that his kids will change his mind. People with ADD usually do wonderfully with children because the ADD brain is so playful and disinhibited—like kids.

Kevin's life is not perfect, but it is far better than he ever thought it could be when he was nineteen. He wrestles with organization, time management, and the other "executive functions" folks with ADD always wrestle with. But he has found the right job and married the right person. He is happy and fulfilled.

Nancy filled me in on James. He had terrible trouble through most of school. He was always tall and stood out—which made his lapses in concentration all the more noticeable. He took various medications, and none helped. The one time he took Ritalin he got wildly agitated and had a terrible time, so, of course, he never took it again.

Nancy said, "The doctors tried him on Tegretol and Depakote, which are good for bipolar, but they were awful for James. So then they tried antidepressants, and they were lousy as well. He left school, went to a special school, left that, went to a therapeutic school, left there, and then screwed around for a couple of years." Nancy chuckled the weary chuckle of a mother who has seen it all. "But then, last year, he somehow or other walked into a carpenter's shop and they took him on. He's been there for a year, and now he's a carpenter's apprentice. Two more years and then he'll be eligible to join the union. He's twenty-five, and I think he's finally found his niche. He drinks too much, so he might still get into trouble, but I think he'll be okay." Nancy took a deep breath and let it out.

I have heard that deep breath, the long inhale and the long exhale, hundreds of times from moms and dads who have hung in there with their kids. Nancy is the only parent I know who's hung in there with seven!

It should be easier for all parents than it was for Nancy since we know so much more now. Easier, but never easy. Usually, kids who have ADD also have other problems. Maybe they abuse drugs or alcohol. Maybe they are depressed. Maybe they also have a reading problem or some other learning disability. Maybe they were abused as toddlers. Maybe they are chronically angry, or chronically unmotivated, or just chronically difficult.

Such young adults constitute a growing epidemic. If you are the parent of such an individual, I have two major bits of advice. First, don't give up. I have treated some young people for years, basically trying to keep them from totally self-destructing, before they finally got it together and started to live good lives. Second, never worry alone. You need a whole team of supports—from a spouse, to friends, to teachers or coaches, to relatives, to anyone who will listen who is wise and cares.

You need a good doctor on that team. We put that list of resources at the end of the book to help you find one. Find a doctor who will hang in there with you, no matter what, as the going usually gets tough. Find a doctor who can laugh. Find a doctor who does not parrot simple answers. Find a doctor you like and your child (or young adult) likes. Find a doctor who knows what he is talking about, but doesn't claim to have all the answers. Find a doctor who gives you hope. Not all doctors will have all these qualities, but don't stop looking until you find one about whom you can at least say, "I like her, I believe she knows what she's doing, and if I'm in a crisis I wouldn't hesitate to call her."

As Nancy well knows, treating ADD is a continual process. "It's not over in a week or a month or a year. It's never over." When she was referred to me as a patient, we revisited the issue of medication. I told Nancy that it was extremely unlikely that stimulant medication would precipitate a relapse from her sobriety, but that I wouldn't prescribe it until she felt comfortable. When that day came, and Nancy started to take stimulant medication again, the results were as positive as they had been the first time she tried it. "I would say that it made an immediate difference and continues to lead improvement for me," she said. "From the first pill until today, I'd have to say that my life continues to be more full. I think that is probably the best term: 'more full.' I don't have enough hours in the day for all the things that interest me. And that's a problem, because there are so many interesting things out there. I set my alarm clock in the morning even on the days I don't work. Life is still getting better."

PART THREE

◆

Making the Diagnosis of ADD

CHAPTER 11

THE STEPS TO DIAGNOSIS

Once you get a feel for ADD, you might start to think almost everybody has it. Because its symptoms abound in modern life, ADD is a seductive diagnosis; it is easy to imagine you have ADD when you do not. Therefore, it is essential that you not diagnose yourself.

The word *diagnosis* literally means "to know through and through." To get a diagnosis you should consult with a professional who knows how to get to know you through and through. Don't worry; there are effective shortcuts to doing this. You don't have to spend a year with the person who is making the diagnosis. But you ought to consult with someone who can spend more than a few minutes with you. Beyond telling you if you have ADD, the person who diagnoses you should be able to suggest to you where your strengths and talents lie. It is upon your strengths and talents that you build a happy life.

Various professionals are qualified to diagnose ADD. Child psychiatrists and developmental pediatricians have the most training in this area. Child psychiatrists diagnose and treat both children and adults. Developmental pediatricians deal only with children. Unfortunately, both child psychiatrists and developmental pediatricians are in short supply.

If you can't find a child psychiatrist or a developmental pediatrician and you want an evaluation for a child, then a pediatric neurologist, a general pediatrician, a child psychologist, or a family physician may be able to help you. You should ask if she has experience diagnosing and treating ADD. If not, then ask for a referral to a specialist who does. If you can't find one, then call the department of child psychiatry at your nearest medical school. All states have at least one medical school and many states have more than one. These academic centers are reliable sources either for an evaluation or for a referral to a good practitioner. We also provide a listing of resources at the end of this book.

If you want an evaluation for an adult, and you can't find a child psychiatrist in your area, then you might get help from an adult psychiatrist, although adult psychiatrists are notoriously weak in this area, as ADD is usually not part of their training. You might consult with an adult psychologist; most psychologists do have some training in ADD. You might also get help from your primary-care physician. In all cases, make sure to ask if he has experience in diagnosing and treating ADD *in adults*. There are reasons why 85 percent of the ADD in adults remains undiagnosed and untreated; one of them is that it is hard to find doctors who know how to diagnose and treat adult ADD. If you can't find such a person, my advice is the same as it is for children: consult the department of child psychiatry (remember, most child psychiatrists also treat adults) at the nearest medical school, or look in the listing at the back of this book.

Once you find someone good to do the evaluation, the hard part is over. Just be sure you have found someone good. The best way to make sure the person is good is to ask other people who have been to that doctor or that center. Also, trust your gut. If you don't feel right, go see someone else, no matter how qualified the doctor might be or how stellar her reputation.

The evaluation itself will vary, depending upon who does it. There is no one right way to do it, nor is there a set amount of time the process should take. Sometimes an evaluation can be completed in an hour. In other cases, it can take weeks to complete an evaluation, because various medical tests and neuropsychological tests have to be scheduled and reviewed. What is done and how long it takes all depends upon how complex the case is. However, the basic steps should include:

1. Taking a history from the identified patient (child or adult). The history should identify potential strengths and talents as well as pinpoint problems and conflicts, with special emphasis on school history.
2. Taking a history about the identified patient from someone else (parents or spouse or significant other). This is because people who have ADD tend to be poor self-observers. Their view of themselves is often at odds with everyone else's.
3. In the case of children, reviewing comments from the current teachers and past teachers. This is crucial.
4. Reviewing medical or pediatric history.
5. Getting neuropsychological testing, if indicated.
6. Getting additional medical tests if the history leads the doctor to think they are necessary, such as a test looking for a sleep disorder; a test of thyroid function; a test for lead in the blood; a test of adrenal function; a standard electroencephalogram, or EEG (if a seizure disorder is suspected); getting tests for food allergies, chemical sensitivities, or other environmental allergies. These last three items may prove over time to be far more significant than we think they are now (more on this later in this chapter).
7. Other tests. In our center, we now offer the quantitative electroencephalogram, or qEEG, as part of the diagnostic workup. Next to the history, we believe this is the best available test for ADD both in children and in adults. In addition, a brain scan called a SPECT scan can be useful for selected, complex cases (more on the qEEG and the SPECT in the next chapter).

Steps 1 and 2—taking a history both from the identified patient (child or adult) and from someone else (parents, spouse, or significant other)—constitute the crux of the evaluation. Although not usually considered a test, the history is the best method of assessment that we have. Sometimes it is the only "test" that will be needed. If, based on the history, the diagnosis is obvious, the process can end right there.

The most common misconception about how to diagnose ADD, a

misconception subscribed to by most schools and many professionals, is that there is a "test" for ADD, a psychological test or brain scan, that absolutely pins down the diagnosis. But there is no such test. The closest we have to it is the history. The history is more valuable than any paper-pencil test or neuropsychological test or brain scan.

It is the individual's own story—what we doctors call the history—that makes or breaks the diagnosis of ADD,

Whoever does the evaluation will be trying to understand the entire person, both strengths and weaknesses, talents, and areas of trouble. Identifying the strengths and talents is important; successful treatment builds on those strengths and talents.

The evaluator will ask about the various symptoms associated with ADD. Everyone has many of these symptoms. In order for the condition to be considered a disorder, your life must be impaired in some way by these symptoms. Unless there is impairment, ADD is just a trait, not a disorder.

The disorder is defined by the presence or absence of symptoms as set forth in the DSM-IV. This is a good screening tool for children, but not as good for adults (in the next chapter we describe a good screening test for adult ADD). There are two clusters of symptoms, one describing symptoms of inattention, the other describing symptoms of hyperactivity and impulsivity. To qualify for the diagnosis, you need to meet the criteria set forth in cluster 1 or in cluster 2, as follows:

1. Six (or more) of the following symptoms of inattention have persisted for at least six months to a degree that is maladaptive and inconsistent with developmental level:

   Inattention:
   a. often fails to give close attention to details or makes careless mistakes in schoolwork, work, or other activities
   b. often has difficulty sustaining attention in tasks or play activities
   c. often does not seem to listen when spoken to directly
   d. often does not follow through on instructions and fails to finish schoolwork, chores, or duties in the workplace (not due to oppositional behavior or failure to understand instructions)

    e. often has difficulty organizing tasks and activities

    f. often avoids, dislikes, or is reluctant to engage in tasks that re-
quire sustained mental effort

    g. often loses things necessary for tasks or activities

    h. is often easily distracted by extraneous stimuli

    i. is often forgetful in daily activities

2. Six (or more) of the following symptoms of hyperactivity and impulsivity have persisted for at least six months to a degree that is
maladaptive and inconsistent with developmental level:

Hyperactivity

    a. often fidgets with hands or feet or squirms in seat

    b. often leaves seat in classroom or in other situations in which re-
maining seated is expected

    c. often runs about or climbs excessively when it is inappropriate
(in adolescents or adults, may be limited to subjective feelings
of restlessness)

    d. often has difficulty playing or engaging in leisure activities
quietly

    e. is often "on the go" or acts as if "driven by a motor"

    f. often talks excessively

Impulsivity

    g. often blurts out answers before questions have been completed

    h. often has difficulty awaiting turn

    i. often interrupts or intrudes on others

To receive a diagnosis of ADD you must have six out the nine symptoms on one or both of the clusters: inattention or impulsivity and
hyperactivity. Your symptoms must date back to childhood. There is
no such thing as adult-onset ADD; we call that modern life!

Furthermore, the symptoms must impair your life in some way for
ADD to be diagnosed. And symptoms must occur in two or more
areas of your life. Typically for children the areas include home,
school, and social settings; and for adults they include home, work,
and social settings.

The evaluator will be looking for a full picture of what is going on, not just trying to enumerate the symptoms of ADD. I want to reemphasize here how helpful it can be if an assessment of strengths and talents enters into the process, not just the description of problems.

Step 3—getting comments from teachers—mainly refers to evaluations of children, but if adults have saved these comments they can be very useful. Comments from teachers can help identify strengths as well as problems. These comments are telling. I like to ask for narrative comments from teachers, rather than checklists of symptoms, as I think checklists "lead the witness," so to speak. I want to know what the teacher says in response to a prompt like "Tell me about this child." If the child has ADD, the symptoms will usually appear in the narrative teacher comments, unless the class is small and so well structured and the teacher so talented that the classroom environment essentially "cures" the ADD while the child is there.

Adults can bring in old teacher comments, if they happen to have saved them or their mothers did. In addition, the adult's spouse or partner or friend can add useful comments on the adult's current situation.

Step 4—a review of medical history, with comments from the pediatrician or primary-care doctor if relevant—is important because various medical conditions can look like ADD or complicate the treatment of ADD.

Step 5—neuropsychological testing—can also be helpful, but it's not always necessary. This kind of testing assesses many components of a person's cognitive style. Sometimes people think that this testing is "the test" for ADD. It is not. However, it is useful and at times is indispensable, especially when you are trying to elucidate an associated learning disability.

Furthermore, if you are trying to get accommodations, such as untimed testing, many schools and boards require neuropsychological testing. The person who does the evaluation can recommend how detailed the testing should be in your individual case.

At our center, we do an abbreviated battery of neuropsychological tests as part of all our evaluations; we do the full battery of tests only when we need a better definition of a learning problem, or because a school or a board requires the complete battery of tests. The full battery is expensive (around two thousand dollars) and time-consuming, so it should not be part of every evaluation.

Step 6—other medical tests—raises two specific issues I want to address. The first regards sleep. As many as 60 percent of children and adults diagnosed with ADD suffer from sleep impairments of one kind or another. Even if you don't think you have a sleep disorder, you very well might, as people are not able to assess their sleep while asleep. Hence, it is worthwhile to consider getting a test in a sleep laboratory. It is a simple procedure. You go to the sleep lab and spend the night. While you sleep, the sleep technician performs the tests and makes the observations that lead to a diagnosis of your sleep pattern. If there is an abnormality, corrective steps can be prescribed.

The second issue is the role that environmental toxins and chemical sensitivities *might* play in producing the symptoms of ADD. We live in a world filled with chemicals. They're in the air, in our food, in the insulation we put in buildings, in the carpets we put on floors, in the synthetic fabrics we wear, in the soaps and lotions we bathe and wash with, even in the very medicines we use to treat our illnesses.

Who can say what all these chemicals are doing to us? I don't know nearly enough to make that assessment. In my years of practice, I have treated one woman whose ADD was clearly due to chemical sensitivities. Her case was so severe that she became disabled and is still unable to work. Only one case in more than twenty years doesn't sound alarming. However, I'll bet there are hundreds of cases I have missed because I didn't know what symptoms to look for in the history or what tests to order.

As we learn more about the causes and treatments for the Gulf War syndrome or the damage done by Agent Orange, as we piece together what's causing the various examples of the ominously named "sick building syndrome," as we learn more about spores, fungi, prions, slow viruses, mycoplasmas, and all manner of allergens, we will collect new evidence that should guide us more effectively.

It is difficult to know what to advise when so much is unknown and untested. For now, I think we all should at least think about chemical exposure. Think about what you eat. Think about what you breathe. Think about what's in your rugs and carpets, what's in your clothes, what's in your insulation and your paint. If you or anyone in your family develops unexplained symptoms, including rashes, chronic respiratory distress, diminished energy, nonspecific aches and pains, mild impairment of memory, reduced capacity to solve problems or think clearly, or reduced attention span, I would suggest you visit an allergist or a specialist in environmental medicine.

To locate such a specialist and to learn more, you can consult the website of the American Academy of Allergy, Asthma, and Immunology at www.aaaai.org. You can also consult the website of the American College of Occupational and Environmental Medicine at www.acoem.org.

As for taking these factors into account when making the diagnosis of ADD, I ask only for medical records and pertinent environmental and dietary history. I do not routinely suggest a consultation with a specialist in allergy or environmental medicine unless some unexplained symptoms urge me to do so.

Other tests are needed only when specifically indicated. For example, if your history leads the doctor to suspect you might have thyroid dysfunction, a blood test will be ordered to assess that. If you have a history of exposure to lead, a blood test for that would be in order. Without going through a complete list of all the possible reasons to get a blood test or other medical test, suffice it to say that the person doing the evaluation should be able to determine if such testing is necessary. Most of the time it is not.

Step 7—additional tests—may or may not be part of your evaluation. New tests are being developed all the time. As of now, no additional test is considered as a standard part of a workup. However, there are two that I think can be quite useful: the qEEG and in selected cases the SPECT scan. I discuss them both in the following chapter.

CHAPTER 12

THE QEEG AND THE SPECT SCAN:

TWO USEFUL NEW TESTS

NOT WIDELY USED

The qEEG and the SPECT scan are both tests of brain function that have been around for more than a decade. Neither has entered the mainstream of psychiatry, but both should provide useful information that can shape decisions on diagnosis and treatment.

The qEEG, or quantitative electroencephalogram, is a kind of brain-wave test that has been refined to the point that it can help in diagnosing ADD in children and adults.

Studies done prior to 1997 did not show any brain-wave pattern that was specific enough even to suggest a diagnosis of ADD. Therefore, the technique was abandoned as a diagnostic tool. However, with changes in the qEEG machine and alterations in the design of the research, a brain-wave pattern was identified that was characteristic of ADD.

People with ADD tend to show a pattern of underarousal in areas in the cortex, or outer layer, of the brain. This so-called cortical hypoarousal is identified by the presence of more slow waves, or so-called theta waves, over fast waves, or so-called beta waves. By measuring the ratio of the fast waves to the slow waves, the test can help diagnose ADD.

Using this new finding, studies done since 1997 have shown that the qEEG is accurate up to 90 percent of the time in making the diagnosis. It is good enough now that the American Academy of Pediatrics, in their 2004 monograph on ADD, stated, "new brain wave analysis techniques like quantitative electroencephalograms will help experts more clearly document the neurologic and behavioral nature [of ADD]."

It is certainly not 100 percent accurate, and it most definitely cannot replace the history as the core of the evaluation, but we think it is good enough that we now recommend it as a standard part of the evaluation and we use it at our center in Sudbury, Massachusetts. It can be done in the doctor's office, or a referral can be made to a center that has a qEEG machine. It is not essential that it be done, but it is helpful.

Not only can it help make the diagnosis, it can help in selecting treatment. New studies have shown that people who show the characteristic pattern of cortical hypoarousal are likely to respond well to stimulant medication. This provides an elegant physiological link between diagnosis and treatment.

Now that this test has a solid, evidence-based foundation, it could find its most practical application in the offices of busy primary-care physicians, or PCPs. About two-thirds of the cases of ADD that are diagnosed in this country are diagnosed not by specialists like John Ratey and me but by PCPs, including pediatricians, family physicians, internists, and other nonspecialists. Most of these doctors simply can't follow the diagnostic process I recommend because they are too busy. As much as they would like to, it is hopelessly unrealistic. These doctors have to see too many patients every day to allow an hour or more for just one. To do so would be to deny essential care to many others. Furthermore, even if they could find other doctors to bring into their practice (which they usually can't, as PCPs are in short supply) and opened up an hour or two to spend doing an evaluation for ADD, insurance companies would not pay for that amount of time. So, it is not going to happen. These primary-care doctors are doing the very best they can under extremely difficult conditions.

The qEEG could improve the diagnostic reliability of their necessarily hurried evaluations. While not foolproof, a qEEG could drastically reduce the chance for misdiagnosis, especially in the primary-care doctor's whirlwind office. It will take some time for the qEEG machine to find its way into clinics and hospitals around the country, but when it does, diagnostic reliability will rise.

The SPECT scan—or single proton emission computerized tomography scan—is a tool cardiologists often use to assess blood flow in the heart. This test also deserves to be used more than it is in psychiatry. We psychiatrists have been slow to pick up on its usefulness in our field. However, one psychiatrist, Daniel Amen in Irvine, California, has been using SPECT in his practice for years. The use of SPECT in psychiatry is controversial, as many experts say it is not helpful. However, Amen has developed it so well that I went out to his clinic and reviewed how he uses SPECT.

I came away excited and eager to learn more. I even had my own brain scanned, and I learned that I had some of the early changes that can be associated with the development of Alzheimer's later on. Dr. Amen advised me on what steps to take to reduce the likelihood of my developing Alzheimer's, like making sure I use my brain actively and creatively as much as possible, making sure my cholesterol is maintained in the normal range, making sure my blood pressure is also maintained at a proper level, and getting regular physical exercise.

He also showed me various scans from his data bank of the thousands of scans he has done. Being a novice, I didn't quite know what to make of what I saw, but I wanted to learn more.

I came away convinced that there is a place for SPECT in clinical psychiatry. Just the educational value alone—being able to show a patient a picture of what's going on in his brain—is enormous.

However, SPECT is far from being a diagnostic test for ADD. It has specific indications, and should only be used in those instances when it is called for.

As of now, SPECT scanning as a tool in clinical psychiatry is at an impasse. One doctor—Daniel Amen—does the majority of it, while the authorities in academia await studies that will either validate or refute it. We need those studies. Amen is gearing up to do some himself, but others will need to do them as well before the SPECT will become widely used. John Ratey and I have been thinking of joining in that effort ourselves.

It is obviously helpful to be able to look at the brain before you try to treat it. Perhaps SPECT will prove to be the most practical way for psychiatrists to do that. Both John Ratey and I believe that Amen makes a good case for the clinical use of SPECT. However, we are also cautious, and we hope to help those who have the resources to do more studies independent of Amen to do so.

As doctors, we rely on our best clinical judgment. We want as much scientific validation as we can find, but we can't always have all that we want. In presenting to you the debate around SPECT, I am implicitly presenting to you the debate around other kinds of new approaches to diagnosis and treatment. The qEEG has good research behind it, but we would, of course, like more. The techniques of cerebellar stimulation that will be discussed in chapter 29 need more studies to confirm or refute their usefulness. The use of nutritional supplements to treat ADD, like omega-3 fatty acids or spirulina (super blue-green algae), needs to be studied further, even though a great deal of evidence supports their usefulness in bolstering health in general.

I resolve this dilemma with Hippocrates's advice, "First do no harm." In the case of SPECT, the only potential harm is a small dose of radiation and the money you pay to have it done. With your doctor's help, you can do a cost/benefit analysis to see if you should get a SPECT. I would suggest applying the same kind of analysis to the other new and as yet unproved techniques and remedies we discuss in this book or you encounter in your travels through the amazing, confusing, information-infused world we have created.

If you now feel thoroughly confused about how to make a diagnosis, go back to steps 1 and 2 in chapter 11: the history. A careful history taken from two people, the person you think might have ADD and someone else, like a parent or a spouse. Hang your diagnostic hat on that. If your doctor needs more help, look to the other tests I mentioned. However, most of the time the correct diagnosis resides in the history, waiting to be found. All your doctor has to do is look carefully. The other tests I mentioned can offer additional useful information, but the history tells the most, by far.

CHAPTER 13

HOW DO YOU TELL A CHILD

ABOUT THE DIAGNOSIS OF ADD?

Once the diagnosis of ADD is made, the question quickly comes up for parents: What should I tell my child?

Parents understandably worry that their child might feel labeled or set apart from other kids if told that she has ADD. They're right. If the information is not conveyed properly, hearing about this diagnosis can upset a child and sometimes do damage.

However, if you and your doctor are careful about how you bring it up, hearing about this diagnosis can really help a child.

Let me take you through a typical scenario in which I present the diagnosis of ADD to an eight-year-old boy. Let's name this boy Jed.

Mom and Dad are sitting in my office along with Jed. Jed has gone through the evaluation process at my center, which includes an interview with a clinician and some testing. His parents have also been interviewed by a clinician, and they have brought in comments from teachers. I am now meeting with them to go over the results of the evaluation. Prior to this meeting I have spoken with the psychologist who did the intake interviews and with the neuropsychologist who did the testing. A neuropsychologist is psychologist who has additional training in the neurological aspects of psychology.

Jed is sitting in the big, green basket-type chair I have in my office.

Kids love it. They can put their feet up on the ottoman that goes with the chair, which makes them feel quite relaxed, and rather royal. I have various little toys and knickknacks around the office that usually make kids feel that what I'm up to is more about fun than anything else— a clock shaped like a chicken; a table lamp that has feet and toes; a baseball I bought at "21" in New York that is dyed pink and green; a photograph of Ted Williams at the end of a swing and a photograph of Babe Ruth standing in the dugout with Lou Gehrig; a painting of a funny-looking mermaid that has a caption underneath, "Sometimes different is better"; a wall clock in which all the numbers have fallen to the bottom of the well of the clock, and the words "WHO CARES?" are written in the center; to name but a few.

The parents usually sit next to each other in a love seat near the child. And I sit in my chair opposite them.

As we settle in, I pick up Jed's chart, write the date, and say, "Did you have fun meeting with Dr. Coakley-Welch?" Jed smiles a little, but doesn't reply. He has just met me, after all.

I look at the parents, whom I have spoken to prior to this meeting. I have told them I think Jed has ADD, and we have discussed how they'd like him to be told about it, if at all. They have accepted my invitation for me to do the talking and see what develops.

"Well, Jed," I say, "you've come here a couple of times and we have asked you lots of questions and you have played some games with Dr. Coakley-Welch, and now I am going to tell you what we've found out."

Jed is looking at my rug, which has clowns, trapeze artists, angels, and other fanciful figures stitched into its design.

"Would you like to know?" I want to make sure I have at least a little bit of Jed's attention. He nods yes. "Well, I have great news for you. You have an awesome mind. You are one cool dude. Your brain is just spectacular."

Jed looks up at me for the first time. He has never been told this before. In fact, he usually hears just the opposite. He is really listening now. "You have something called ADD," I tell him. "Guess what? I have it too. And two of my kids have it as well. It's a cool thing to have." Now I point to a color photograph of my three kids that I have hanging above my desk. They are on the beach in their pajamas, playing in shallow water. Kids like this photograph.

I go on. "You know what ADD is? ADD means you have a race-car brain. You know what a turbocharged engine is?"

Jed nods yes. I don't know if he really knows what it means—I don't—but, like me, he's heard the term and he can guess.

"Well, your brain is turbocharged. That means it can go really, really fast. The only problem is that sometimes it can't put on the brakes. And sometimes it needs special motor oil so it won't overheat and break down. But with the right motor oil and the right brakes, it wins lots of races."

Jed looks at me, wanting to hear more.

"You know how sometimes you have trouble paying attention in school?" He nods. "That's because your mind is zipping around all over the place. You have new ideas all the time." He nods. "And that's great! That's why you're going to have fun all your life and do amazing things. But I want to become like the man who takes care of your race car, only it's your brain that I take care of. I'm going to help your brain learn how to put on the brakes."

Jed nods like he thinks this is a good idea. His parents smile.

That's how I tell kids about ADD. It's no big deal. You don't need to make more of it than it needs to be. On the other hand, it is a bad idea to keep it secret because this implies there is something shameful or bad about ADD.

Parents need to learn more, and so do teachers, but children really don't. It is important that they do not feel defined by ADD. Having ADD is like being left-handed; it is *part* of who you are, not who you are.

If a child has more questions, of course you should answer them. Here are some common questions—with my answers—that kids ask:

Q: My friend Jimmy has ADD and he is weird. Just because I have ADD, am I like him?

A: You know you're not like him. If you have blond hair, that doesn't mean you are like all the kids who have blond hair, does it? Well, having ADD is like having blond hair.

Q: Does having ADD mean I'm stupid?

A: No, not at all. It means you have a quick mind. It means you can do things that lots of people can't do because you are so quick. It means you have a gift.

Q: I don't want to have ADD. Can I get rid of it?

A: If you tell me why you don't want to have it, I can help you get rid of most of the parts of it you don't want to have. Then I bet I can help you turn it into something you want to have!

Q: Should I tell my friends about the medication I take?

A: Not unless you really want to. It is nobody else's business. Some kids don't understand ADD and they don't understand what the medication really does. So, it is better to keep it between you and your parents unless you know and trust the friend.

Q: Will I always have ADD?

A: Only if you're lucky! ADD does go away for some people when they're teenagers, but for most people it stays. By then, you will have learned how to deal with it so well, you'll enjoy having it.

Q: Why is it called ADD? I don't think I have a disorder.

A: Good for you! It is a dumb term. Why don't we make up a name for it we both like? [I love doing this with kids. With grown-ups too.]

Q: My brother teases me because I have ADD. What should I do?

A: Hmm. Why don't you tell your mom or dad that we need to have a meeting with them and you and your brother to explain what ADD is. Your brother is probably a little jealous that you are getting this extra attention because of your ADD. So let's have a meeting and deal with all that.

Q: Can I still be a [fill in the blank here] when I grow up if I have ADD?

A: You can be absolutely anything you want to be when you grow up. ADD does not have to hold you back as long as we take care of it now. In fact, it can become a real advantage for you! How about that? One of my grown-up patients calls ADD his ADD-vantage.

Q: You have ADD. How did you get through medical school and write books now?

A: I did many of the things I am teaching you how to do. Most of all, I tried to do what I loved and I asked for help when I needed it.

Try to answer any question a child has about ADD, but keep the answer simple and brief. As they get older, they might want to read a book about ADD, but I wouldn't push that; they don't need to become experts on ADD, just experts on living their lives as fully and well as they can.

CHAPTER 14

CONDITIONS THAT

COEXIST WITH ADD

If you have read any other books or articles about ADD, you have probably encountered a nasty bit of medical jargon, the term co-morbidity. It refers to other conditions that often develop along with ADD. For example, you might suffer from depression in addition to having ADD. Depression would then be called comorbid.

I hate the term. I don't think ADD is morbid; therefore, whatever comes with it can't be comorbid. We doctors emphasize pathology, so in our articles and books we use words like *morbidity, comorbidity,* and *mortality.* So far, I haven't heard anyone mention comortality. That term might be used when a person dies from two diseases at once: his cancer and heart disease proved to be comortal. Or maybe when two people die in each other's company of the same disease?

In any case, I think we do much better to emphasize health, which is why I reject the term comorbid. However, it is important to know about other conditions that often infiltrate a life with ADD.

Of course, much that is wonderful coexists with ADD. I have mentioned this before, but it bears repeating: at the heart of ADD lies a bonanza of potentially wonderful qualities. Treatment should always aim to identify and develop these.

But coexisting problems can get in the way of developing all that is wonderful. So, it is important to know about them.

Among the most common of these are mood disorders, which occur in about 25 percent of people who have ADD. Mood disorders include depression; mild depression, or what is now called dysthymia; and manic-depressive illness, or what is now called bipolar disorder. Like ADD, these tend to run in families and be quite heritable. Sometimes it can be hard to tell the difference between ADD and bipolar disorder. About 20 percent of people who have ADD may also have bipolar disorder. I will discuss this in more detail in the next chapter.

Substance abuse and addictions of various kinds also are common in people who have ADD. I devote a chapter to this topic elsewhere in this book. About 40 percent of adults who have ADD drink too much alcohol; about 20 percent abuse cocaine, marijuana, or other illicit drugs. Furthermore, Joseph Biederman and his group at Massachusetts General Hospital estimate that about 50 percent of adults with ADD can't quit smoking cigarettes or using other tobacco products.

Antisocial personality disorder, which is a fancy term for adults who have a porous conscience and frequently break rules and laws, develops about 15 percent of the time in people who have ADD. This is often preceded in childhood by milder versions of the same condition, called oppositional defiant disorder (ODD) or conduct disorder (CD).

Learning problems, most notably dyslexia, arise in around 20 percent of people who have ADD. I devote a separate chapter to dyslexia later in this book. Basically, dyslexia refers to an unexplained (i.e., not due to some obvious cause, like not going to school or being blind) difficulty in reading and spelling your native language. People who have dyslexia may learn to read, but as they get older they continue to read slowly, stumble when they read aloud, and never develop what is called fluency—which means reading as automatically and effortlessly as you ride a bike.

Anxiety disorders also frequently accompany ADD. In fact, most adults who have ADD suffer from a mild version of one specific anxiety disorder, post-traumatic stress disorder (PTSD). This is because growing up with undiagnosed, untreated ADD usually leads to many episodes of mild trauma, episodes of humiliation, rejection, and failure, as well as the more severe kinds of trauma, like physical, sexual, and verbal abuse. Having ADD may itself predispose to developing PTSD because people with ADD frequently get themselves into situations in which trauma is likely to occur, and they are accomplished at blocking out the painful event, which prevents their assimilating it or learning how to avoid it in the future.

That's a long list of problems that can crop up with ADD. However, each one of them is treatable. As long as your doctor and you know about and look for these conditions, they are not difficult to find, nor need they cripple you.

Furthermore, when you treat the ADD, these other conditions usually get somewhat better, and sometimes they get totally better. That's because the ADD may have been causing the coexisting condition. For example, depression may develop in people who have ADD because they have felt so frustrated year after year, from not succeeding in reaching whatever goals they have set for themselves. Once the ADD gets treated and they become better focused, they start to achieve their goals, and their depression subsides. Or, when you treat the ADD in someone who has an addiction, he becomes able to give up his addiction because he was using the addiction to self-medicate his undiagnosed ADD.

On the other hand, when you treat the ADD, the other conditions may actually get worse. For example, depression may intensify when ADD is treated. This is because when a person gains greater focus, she may focus on what an abominable life she's created. In this case, the depression must be treated along with the ADD.

Take heart. This can be done. All of the coexisting conditions improve with proper treatment. It takes time; none of them will disappear overnight. But, within a matter of months, you should expect to see improvement not only in the symptoms related to the ADD but in the symptoms related to the coexisting conditions as well. It is important that your doctor and you look for these conditions. About 75 percent of people with ADD also have one or another of them. So, be on the lookout for coexisting conditions, and once you identify them, make sure you get proper treatment for them as well.

CHAPTER 15

BIPOLAR DISORDER OR ADD?

HOW TO TELL THE DIFFERENCE

Until the mid-1990s, no one ever considered bipolar disorder as a possibility in children or adolescents. The prevailing belief was that bipolar disorder didn't exist in young people, that it afflicted only adults. Then, in 1995, Dr. Janet Wozniak, a brilliant young child psychiatrist at Harvard and Massachusetts General Hospital, published a seminal paper in the *Journal of the American Academy of Child and Adolescent Psychiatry* called "Mania-Like Symptoms Suggestive of Childhood-Onset Bipolar Disorder in a Clinically Referred Sample." That paper changed everything.

Wozniak saw what every other clinician was seeing. However, every other clinician except Wozniak failed to appreciate what they were seeing because, according to prevailing beliefs, they weren't supposed to be seeing it. Once Wozniak pointed out what was to be seen, we all realized that there were children who fit the description of bipolar disorder, and that there had been such children all along. We had simply been diagnosing them with some other condition, like borderline personality disorder, conduct disorder, oppositional defiant disorder, ADD, post-traumatic stress disorder, or, more bluntly, bad character or an evil core.

Wozniak and the rest of her team, headed by Dr. Joseph Biederman at Massachusetts General Hospital, deserve a lot of credit. It is a truism that we see what we are looking for and thereby often miss what we don't expect to see. As the great American philosopher Yogi Berra said, "If I didn't believe it, I wouldn't have seen it." For years, clinicians had been seeing children who fit the description of mania as laid out in the various diagnostic manuals, but because they had not expected to see a child exhibit that pattern of symptoms, they didn't put the bipolar name to what they were seeing.

Not long after Wozniak's paper was published, clinicians all around the country began to diagnose bipolar disorder in children. Then, in 1999, Demitri and Janice Papolos published a book for the general public called *The Bipolar Child.* Juvenile bipolar disorder, as it came to be called, had arrived. At last, a group of children who had been largely misunderstood began to find the diagnosis that fit them best. This in turn led to the treatment that they desperately needed.

As with all new diagnoses, this one complicated an already complicated array of psychiatric diagnoses. What was bipolar and what was ADD and what was oppositional defiant disorder and what was just a naughty child? Who could tell for sure?

The symptoms of bipolar disorder overlap with those of many other diagnoses. They overlap considerably with the symptoms of ADD, especially ADD with pronounced hyperactivity and impulsivity. Clinicians and parents everywhere scratched their heads as we struggled to tell the difference.

When the diagnosis of childhood bipolar disorder became widely known, some doctors applied it too often. It is not because the doctors were conspiring to overdiagnose bipolar disorder; they—we—were simply trying to learn how to make use of this new diagnosis and apply it correctly. This happened—and still does happen—with ADD. Once ADD became widely known, it was overdiagnosed in some areas of the country, but underdiagnosed in others. That is what I believe has happened to childhood bipolar disorder. It can be overapplied, but it can also be missed altogether.

My colleague Peter Metz, who is a child psychiatrist and former head of the division of child psychiatry at the University of Massachusetts Medical School, is one of the most astute diagnosticians I know. As the saying goes, he has seen it all, and then some.

When I told him I was going to write about childhood bipolar disorder for this book, he put his hand to his forehead and said, "Save me!" When I asked him what he meant he said, "All day in my clinic I see kids who are on all kinds of medications for bipolar disorder when what they really need is some stability at home. They have social problems, not medical ones. Bipolar is becoming like ADD used to be. It's a catchall for kids who get into fights, can't be controlled, have bad moods, use drugs, do whatever they want, and don't listen to their parents or their teachers. Desperate parents bring them to overbooked doctors who don't know what to do with them. These doctors don't have the time or the resources to offer them the in-depth evaluation that they ought to get, or the total life makeover that they need. So they call them bipolar and put them on serious medications."

"Peter," I asked, "don't you believe bipolar exists in kids?"

"Oh, sure it does," he replied, "and Wozniak's paper was a huge breakthrough. I'm just talking about when the diagnosis gets overdone. There are tons more kids with social problems than kids who have bipolar disorder. That's my point. And I don't like the fact that making the diagnosis of bipolar disorder often dodges the more difficult question of trying to deal with the complicated social issues."

As with ADD, there is no surefire test for bipolar disorder. Therefore, it is possible to fudge the diagnosis of bipolar disorder in the way that Peter Metz worries about.

To complicate the situation even more, social problems usually accompany both ADD and bipolar disorder, so it is not an either-or situation. Usually, you must contend with social problems in addition to the symptoms of ADD and bipolar disorder.

But to bring some clarity to this complex picture, let me turn to bipolar disorder in adults and compare that to ADD in adults.

The hallmark of bipolar disorder is mood swings. These are not ordinary mood swings, though. They are huge, tumultuous mood swings that include periods of what's called mania. If you have ever met an adult who is manic, you won't have forgotten it. You might not have known the name for what was going on, but you knew for sure that *something* strange and mighty was driving that person.

The manic adult feels unusually elated or high. He typically imagines he possesses extraordinary powers. In the extreme, he might believe he is God or Jesus Christ. In milder versions, he believes he can do anything, pull off huge business deals overnight, bring peace to the

Middle East, or find a cure for cancer. Such "grandiosity," as it is called, may not even be that extreme, but it is markedly more pronounced than any nonbipolar individual, even a very confident individual, ever exhibits.

Along with the person's mood rising, his speech goes faster, while ideas come in tangled bunches. Here is a typical sentence from a manic adult: "Good morning, Dr. Hallowell, I can see the tie you are wearing has the colors of the rainbow, which is a refraction of light through mist often accompanied by feelings of hope, which is of course a delusionary process associated with the wish for a pot of gold at the end of a rainbow, which may be related to a bow tie or a tie into a new way of thinking, which, I might add, I have been working on all night long while the rest of the world, including no doubt you, Dr. Hallowell, slept the sleep of the weary, which is simply the sorry state so many people find themselves in, but no longer will, once they have the will to understand what I have been working on all night long, a long theory of edges, each one of which interdigitates into a matrix of overlapping planes, not one of which edges beyond the overarching construct of ineffable mystery, which I don't expect you to understand at this early hour of the day, but which I do intend to explain to you when we have our appointment later on, if later on does indeed become now, which now that I refer to is, I believe, three o'clock this afternoon, am I right?"

If you reread that sentence, you will find sense amid nonsense, which is usually the state of a manic mind.

Sometimes, however, the mood shifts not upward toward the grandiose but toward the irritable. A manic person may become extraordinarily angry, combative, even violent.

To be called a true manic episode, the grandiose or irritable mood must last at least one week.

In addition, several of the following symptoms are present:

- inflated self-esteem
- decreased need for sleep
- more talkative than usual
- rapid proliferation of ideas, either spoken or imagined
- distractibility

- increased goal-directed activity (manic people can get a lot done!)
- excessive pleasurable activities that may prove to be self-destructive (e.g., gambling, spending money, finding inappropriate sexual partners, making risky business deals)

You can see some of the symptoms of ADD embedded in there, including distractibility, the proliferation of ideas, hyperactivity, and sleeplessness. However, mania in an adult is not easily confused with ADD. The mood is so hugely elevated or irritated in mania that symptoms like distractibility and hyperactivity are clearly secondary. The manic adult blows you away, while the ADD adult frustrates you.

Therefore, one good way to distinguish the two conditions in adults is to look at the major symptom. If the major symptom is a disturbance of mood, then think of mania and bipolar disorder. If it is a disturbance of attention, then think of ADD. Keep in mind, of course, that you may see both in the same person.

A second good way to differentiate between them is to look at the history. ADD is a long-standing, chronic condition that is not marked by cycling, alternating episodes of any kind. On the other hand, bipolar disorder is characterized by discrete episodes of mania, alternating with episodes of normal behavior or depression.

The problem becomes more difficult in children, however, because mania is not quite as clear as it is in grown-ups, at least not to the untrained eye.

Strictly speaking, the same criteria apply, but those who are most experienced in diagnosing and treating bipolar disorder in children and adolescents describe mania as a state that rarely lasts for one week. Indeed, the periods of mania in children can cycle in and out dozens of times throughout the day, even throughout a morning.

The hallmarks of childhood mania remain the same as in adults: elevated, expansive, or irritable moods, combined with the additional symptoms bulleted above. However, the periods of mania do not last nearly as long.

And while elevated or expansive mood is the most common form of mania in an adult, irritability is the most common in a child. However, the word *irritability* grossly understates the problem. These kids can be wild and crazed, spewing invective uncontrollably, hitting, spitting, attacking whomever gets in their way, screaming "I hate you!" at whomever offers help or comfort. You can understand why these kids were considered to be "possessed" in centuries gone by.

Irritability can certainly accompany ADD as well, but not the intense, otherworldly irritability of mania. The irritability you find in ADD usually derives from intolerance of frustration. Irritability can accompany childhood depression as well, but it is not the feral irritability of childhood mania. In childhood depression, the irritability comes out in whining, or being grumpy and unable to be pleased.

In mania, the irritability mounts a frontal assault. These kids are dangerous while they are manic. The episode can subside in a matter of minutes and ease into a period of depression, to be followed later by another period of mania, all in the same afternoon.

The picture is quite different from ADD. I spoke with Dr. Papolos and he said to me, "Once you know what childhood mania looks like, it is not that hard to diagnose." The history alone is usually sufficient to make the diagnosis.

Papolos estimates that 90 percent of all the children who end up getting diagnosed with bipolar disorder first received a diagnosis of and treatment for ADD. He believes this is a public-health crisis in the United States. The danger in making the wrong diagnosis is not only that stimulant medication will not help, *it might hurt.* He has found that stimulant medication can lead children who have bipolar disorder into mania or depression, even suicide. Furthermore, once stimulant medication has been tried, Papolos has found that the medications used to treat bipolar disorder become less effective.

Other experts, like Peter Jensen, disagree with Papolos on how dangerous it is to give stimulant medication to a child who has bipolar disorder. While no one would *want* to give stimulant medication to a bipolar child, the extreme danger of doing so is not well established. Indeed, studies from the National Institute of Mental Health support Jensen's point of view over Papolos's. However, almost all experts would agree that bipolar disorder is a real condition in childhood, that stimulant medication is not good for bipolar disorder, that bipolar disorder can be confused with ADD but should not be, and that the treatments for the two conditions are different.

In addition to the difference in symptoms between ADD and bipolar disorder, Papolos suggests two other sometimes helpful ways to distinguish between the two.

First, family history. You will often (but not always) find a history in one or both parents of bipolar disorder or alcoholism if the child has bipolar disorder. Second, there is a characteristic sleep problem in some children who have bipolar disorder. Some of these kids just can't be woken up in the morning. ADD kids can be like this somewhat, but the bipolar child will need to be literally dragged out of bed and stood up before he or she can get going. However, some ADD kids can be like this, too.

Once you diagnose bipolar disorder, the most effective medications are, first, the atypical antipsychotic medications and, second, the mood stabilizers. Stimulant medications tend to make these kids worse. The selective serotonin reuptake inhibitors, like Prozac, Zoloft, and Paxil, have no effect or make them worse.

Among the atypical antipsychotics, you might try Abilify first, because it does not cause weight gain. The one that Dr. Wozniak used first in her practice, Risperdal, is excellent in controlling aggressive symptoms, but it can lead to serious weight gain. Zyprexa is another atypical antipsychotic that can be quite effective. However, there is a risk of developing type 2 diabetes with these medications, and, perhaps, movement disorders.

Among the mood stabilizers, you might try Trileptal or Lamictal first, instead of the more standard ones, like lithium, Depakote, or Tegretol, due to a less offensive side-effect profile. However, this is a decision you must make only after you and your doctor review the various risks of all the possible medications. Lithium remains the "gold standard" mood stabilizer as it is the oldest one and has the longest track record, but its side effects can be severe. So far, there is no medication available to treat bipolar disorder that has a totally benign side-effect profile.

There is, however, an entirely new medication that was developed in Canada that some people are using in the United States for childhood bipolar disorder. This is a nutritional remedy called Empowerplus. It is composed of various vitamins, minerals, and supplements. If it seems unlikely that a simple mineral could alleviate a condition as complex and powerful as childhood bipolar disorder, remember that the medication that led to the great breakthrough in the 1950s in treating bipolar disorder in adults, the medication that is still the gold standard among mood stabilizers, is a simple mineral called lithium.

If you want to consider this new treatment, first keep in mind that there are no good studies to support it. However, I have spoken with doctors whom I respect a great deal who are starting to use it and get excellent results. I know of some adolescent patients who have told me how well it works and how glad they are to get off their old medications which caused so many side effects.

On the other hand, the recognized experts in the field are not recommending this as yet, at least not publicly. The best and safest course is to wait until—and if—more verification comes in. If you want to learn more, you can go to the company's website, www.truehope.com. Of course, you should discuss this with your doctor first.

If the diagnosis is bipolar disorder, make sure any additional conditions get treated as well. These kids may be depressed or anxious. The addition of an antidepressant—Dr. Wozniak suggests 5 mg of Celexa per day, or a low dose of another selective serotonin reuptake inhibitor—may help with both depression and anxiety. Furthermore, if ADD coexists with bipolar disorder, you may safely add a stimulant medication to the treatment once you have the manic symptoms under control.

All this is quite new. The work of Dr. Wozniak and Dr. Papolos has broken new ground for us all. We still have a lot to learn, but we have come a long way from when these kids were diagnosed as having, in Dr. Wozniak's words, "ADHD with a mean streak," or "wicked bad ADHD."

Experts still disagree about what is going on in bipolar disorder in childhood, but I have looked into it enough to know that this is a clinical reality. *Something* is going on, something unique and different from ADD.

It makes sense to me to heed the caution of those who have done the most work with these kids, experts like Wozniak and Papolos, and carefully consider the possibility of bipolar disorder before diagnosing ADD and certainly before starting a child on a stimulant medication.

But it also makes sense to heed the caution of an experienced clinician like Peter Metz and carefully look into the social history of the child. As I have mentioned elsewhere in this book, many kids—and adults—suffer from what I call disconnectedness. They don't have enough sustaining, supportive relationships with people who care about them, or groups who care about them, or even a dog or a cat who cares about them, to feel secure and good in this world. Over time, a disconnected child—or adult—can become a difficult child— or adult. Sometimes very difficult. So difficult, the bipolar disorder, or ADD, or conduct disorder, or oppositional defiant disorder, or the kitchen sink disorder, might be thrown at them, along with a handful of pills.

If you work with a doctor you know and you trust, you can sort all this out. It isn't as difficult as it sounds. But it does take more than ten minutes.

CHAPTER 16

ADD, READING PROBLEMS,

AND DYSLEXIA

L et me tell you about a first-grader who had trouble learning to read. He entered first grade in 1955 in a public school in a small town on Cape Cod. He had trouble with Dick and Jane and letters and sounds and words.

His teacher was a kindly old woman with white curly hair who wore lots of powder which sprinkled off her as she walked. She was like a human sugar doughnut. Her name was Mrs. Eldredge, and while she was firm in preserving order in the classroom, she never ridiculed or embarrassed anyone.

During reading period, while the students sat at round tables and took turns reading aloud—"See Spot run! Run! Run! Run!"—Mrs. Eldredge would go from table to table, listening and making corrections, sprinkling powder as she went. When it came time for the boy who couldn't read to recite, Mrs. Eldredge would pull up a little chair and sit down next to him, putting her arm around him and drawing him close to her prodigious, protective bosom. As he would stammer and stutter, unable to produce the right sounds, Mrs. Eldredge would hug him closer to her; none of the other children would laugh at his clumsy reading because he had the enforcer sitting next to him.

As you might have guessed, I was that little boy. By the end of first grade, I was still a poor reader, and to this day I am painfully slow getting through a book. I would have benefited from an Orton-Gillingham tutor; such an intervention would have made the rest of my life much easier.

But the intervention I needed most I got. It was Mrs. Eldredge's arm. Her arm took fear out of my learning to read. Her arm made it so I felt no shame in having the kind of brain I have. I have a disabled brain, a dyslexic brain, a disordered brain, a stupid brain—call it what you will. But I enjoy my stupid old brain, and I never would have had it not been for Mrs. Eldredge. My brain got through Harvard College as an English major (it had to read some books) and a premed minor (more books, science books!) and graduated *magna cum laude,* and it got through medical school (more of those books) and residency and fellowship (still more books), and now it writes books.

None of this would have happened had it not been for Mrs. Eldredge's arm. That arm has stayed around me ever since first grade. Even though Mrs. Eldredge resides now in heaven, perhaps sprinkling powder on clouds as I write these words, she continues to help me, her arm protecting me, and I continue to thank her for it.

If a person is born with a brain that has *dyslexia,* I would say, "Lucky her!" That person has untestable, unmeasurable potential. She is a surprise package; no one quite knows what she can do, including her. But, I can tell you from years of experience, she can do special stuff, and go to amazing places. She has talents that can't be taught, abilities that can't be bought, and a brain that eludes the predictive powers of all our wisest sayers of sooth.

But I would also say to that person, "Watch out!" She needs a good guide. She needs someone who has been down these trails before, who can tell when the bad guys are coming just by smell, who can show her how to get through the desert without much water and over the mountains even when it snows. She needs someone who will see to it that she never, ever gives up; someone who knows and can make her know that there is more to her than she can show or tell right now, that great things are acomin'.

She also needs a careful diagnostic workup. She needs to reap the benefits of the wonderful, effective treatments we now have for dyslexia. She is lucky to have dyslexia in 2004, because the process of diagnosis and treatment has advanced so dramatically of late.

Dyslexia may be defined as a difficulty in learning to read and spell your native language that can't be explained by lack of education, poor eyesight, or deficient mental capacity. If you have dyslexia, you may learn to read, but you will read with difficulty. You fail to develop what's called fluency, or the automatic quality reading takes on for people who do not have dyslexia. For them, reading becomes as automatic as riding a bike. They don't have to think about maintaining their balance. That's what it means to be fluent. But for the individual who has dyslexia, fluency never comes. He has to think about maintaining his balance every time he rides the bicycle called reading. He can do it, but only slowly and with effort and concentration.

Dyslexia is common, more common than ADD, affecting around 15 to 20 percent of the population. It is also common in people who have ADD. Exact figures are hard to calculate, but at least 20 percent of people with ADD also have dyslexia and vice versa. For a diagnostic workup and treatment you should consult a reading specialist. Many organizations train such specialists, including the International Dyslexia Society, the National Institute for Learning Disabilities, and the Lindamood-Bell Learning Processes Organization (see appendix for contact information).

Sometimes people confuse ADD and dyslexia, but in fact they are distinct and separate. Dyslexia refers to a reading problem. ADD refers to a problem with sustaining attention and organizing your life. When the symptoms of ADD are treated, the symptoms of dyslexia may improve, but this is only because everything that the person does, including reading, improves when he can sustain attention. While medication is an effective treatment for ADD, there is no medication that helps dyslexia.

What does help dyslexia is specialized tutoring. You need to develop phonemic awareness, the ability to break words down into the component sounds as symbolized by the letters. Sally Shaywitz, one of the great figures in the field of dyslexia, calls this breaking the code. But you also need to develop fluency. You can detect a nonfluent adult by asking him to read aloud. If he stumbles and stops and starts, he is not fluent, and he most likely has dyslexia. He can be treated, no matter what his age, although treatment is much easier in young children.

While Shaywitz, and many other experts, stress the importance of developing phonemic awareness, breaking the code, and developing fluency, Dr. Roy Rutherford, a British expert, offers a new, very interesting, but as yet unproven approach. Rutherford is one of the developers of the Dore method of treating dyslexia and ADD by stimulating the cerebellum by doing ten minutes of exercises twice a day. These exercises are tailored to the individual patient's needs based upon an initial assessment of cerebellar function. I discuss this promising—but still unproven, experimental—method in greater detail in chapter 29.

Rutherford and his colleagues believe that specialized tutoring, which is the standard, well-tested, and proven treatment for dyslexia today, doesn't produce better results because it doesn't get at the root cause of the problem. Rutherford says, "Phonological skill is only one part of the big picture we call dyslexia. Only training phonemic awareness is like only training the forehand in tennis. If you practice your forehand for a year, you will develop a superb forehand, but that doesn't mean you're a superb tennis player. If you only measure excellence at tennis by assessing forehand skills, you are obviously not addressing the whole game. So it is with dyslexia."

Rutherford recommends the cerebellar-stimulation exercise program as part of a comprehensive program to treat dyslexia. He advocates tutoring as well, with training in phonemic awareness, as does Dr. Shaywitz, but he would add to that the cerebellar exercise program to develop other skills such as fine motor control, attention, focus, working memory, balance and other postural skills, general coordination, hand-eye coordination, and visual-spatial skills, all of which have been found to be lacking in both people who have dyslexia as well as many who have ADD.

I should add that Dr. Shaywitz and the experts at the International Dyslexia Society do not recommend the method developed by Rutherford. They caution people to stick with what research has validated. On the other hand, I believe there is much that can be gained and little that can be lost by looking into cerebellar exercises as a supplement to tutoring in the treatment of dyslexia.

As in treating ADD, it is important in treating dyslexia to identify areas of interest and to build on talents and strengths. Otherwise, the child or adult will simply feel that he or she is stupid. You need to provide accommodations, like books on tape or keyboarding, to allow the individual to develop and express the creativity and dexterity with ideas that most dyslexics possess. The strength-based approach is vital. Whatever treatment a person receives for either dyslexia or ADD, promoting talents and strengths will invigorate the treatment and make it far more valuable.

The individual with dyslexia (or ADD) needs an optimistic (yes, optimism in a doctor or therapist makes a crucial difference!), well-trained guide who looks for the positive and sets up the conditions for the positive to emerge. He needs the Mrs. Eldredges and Sally Shaywitzes of this world, who will look at him as he writes funny or reads upside down or makes up words that hadn't existed before he discovered them and not cast looks of deep concern his way but smiles of knowing, radiant joy. He needs a guide who has been there and seen it. The dyslexic person needs a guide who knows that with an arm around him he can soar.

Soar where? That is for us to find out. But the dyslexic individual needs a guide who knows that as she misspeaks and gets flustered and underachieves and makes messes and misses the social cues she is so famous for missing and puts her shoes on backward, she has a zany angel alive inside her. If we can keep her from believing the bad things ignorant people say about her, she will help lead those ignorant people to a better world later on.

CHAPTER 17

GENETICS:

IF I HAVE ADD, WHAT ARE THE ODDS

MY CHILD WILL TOO? AND OTHER

INTERESTING QUESTIONS

Although ADD is highly heritable, no one actually inherits ADD. Environment plays a crucial role in the development—or nondevelopment—of ADD. All a person can inherit is a proclivity for developing the symptoms of ADD—a greater susceptibility to ADD than other people have. Life experiences determine how the genes a person inherits gain—or do not gain—expression. For example, if a toddler watches too much television, that increases the likelihood that the genes predisposing to ADD will be expressed and the child will develop ADD. However, if that same toddler does not watch television, he may never develop ADD, even though he inherited the genes that predispose him to it.

This is a crucial point in the genetics of behavioral and emotional traits. It is so important that a study proving the point was voted by *Science* magazine to be the second biggest breakthrough of the entire year in 2003. (The number-one breakthrough was proof that the universe is mostly made of what's called dark energy and dark matter, that the universe is expanding at a known rate, and that it has a fixed age: 13.7 billion years.)

If one parent has ADD, the odds of her children inheriting it are about 30 percent for each child. If both parents have ADD, the odds increase to more than 50 percent for each child. Keep in mind, those numbers also mean that *no* child may inherit it, or that *all* in a given family may. These are just probabilities. It's like flipping a coin and knowing that heads will occur 50 percent of the time—sometimes you will get three heads in a row even though the probability of heads each time you toss the coin is 50 percent. Looking at children already born, if one child has ADD, there is a 30 percent chance that each sibling has it too. Remember that these numbers reflect an increase over the probability of having a child with ADD if you were to just randomly sample parents in the population; that probability is about 5 percent. Because we see this increase in probability in families with an ADD parent or child, we say that ADD is familial, that is, it runs in families. Whether or not genes underlie this familiality requires further investigation.

That may be all you really want to know about genetics. If so, feel free to move along to another chapter. But if you want to know more, the plot thickens.

For example, the last probability cited, the 30 percent chance of another sibling having ADD if one sibling has it, rises to more than 40 percent if the siblings in question are adults. This suggests that the kind of ADD that persists into adulthood is more heritable than the kind of ADD that remits during puberty.

If you are thinking back to your high school biology class, you might be wondering where these numbers come from. If you were like me, you learned about a charming monk named Mendel who noted the traits of the beans and flowers he raised and worked out a beautifully logical system of dominant and recessive genes.

Do you remember drawing a square divided into four quadrants by which you could predict, say, the percentage of pink-petaled petunias you'd get if you crossed a pink petunia with a white petunia if pink were a dominant gene? You used notations like PP, Pp, pP, and pp, then you did the simple math.

I love Mendel. His life exemplifies that doing what interests you can benefit the world and make you happy to boot. His work refuted the idea that qualities acquired during life could be passed along to offspring. That idea, which at one point seemed as "obvious" to many people as the world being flat once seemed, has passed into the realm of the ridiculous, thanks largely to the sweet genius of Mendel.

But when it comes to qualities of personality, temperament, and behavioral tendencies, the genetics of Mendel need help. Much more than dominant and recessive traits, or sex-linked traits, or random mutations, combine to create the nature of a given human.

For example, identical monozygotic (MZ) twins who are given up for adoption at birth and then are raised in separate families almost always differ in many ways. They have identical genes; therefore, what differences they develop as they grow must be due to environmental influences. The extent to which twins share similar traits or conditions is measured by a statistic, either a correlation coefficient (if the traits are continuous, like height, weight, or IQ) or a concordance rate (if the traits are measured in a yes-or-no way, like diabetic or not diabetic, ADD or not ADD). A low correlation (or concordance rate) means no similarity and a high correlation (or concordance rate) means strong similarity. For example, the correlation coefficient for height among identical twins is about .9 (1.0 is the maximum possible), which can be interpreted as meaning that if you know the height of one twin, you can predict the other twin's height with extreme accuracy. Identical twins raised apart almost always grow to be the same height, with environmental factors like nutrition and exercise accounting for the difference. For fraternal twins, the correlation for height is about half of that for identical twins (about .4 to .5). We know that identical twins share 100 percent of their genes in common while fraternal twins share 50 percent of their genes in common. Because the twin similarity for height follows this pattern (fraternal similarity half that of identical-twin similarity), we can feel confident that genes are accounting for the similarities between twins.

Heritability estimates for traits and conditions in the behavioral sciences—like IQ, personality, and psychiatric disorders—are generally in the 50 to 60 percent range. The heritability estimate for ADD is about 70 to 80 percent, strong evidence for genetic influence in this condition.

But we must still use the term genetic influence, because environment also helps to determine outcome. Within the realm of what we do know, genes team with environment to influence personality, temperament, mood, cognitive style, and all the other qualities associated with the behavioral sciences, and the behavioral arts as well, for that matter. But how much does each do? The index just mentioned, heritability, tries to measure that contribution. Heritability is a number between 0 and 1, or between 0 percent and 100 percent, that tries to quantify how great the genetic influence truly is in a population at a particular point in time.

Because heritability is just an index of the relative importance of genes to environment at a particular point in time, and in a particular population, it can differ throughout the lifespan. For example, a sample of six-year-olds might lead you to believe that political persuasion is nearly 100 percent heritable. But a sample of eighteen-year-olds might make it seem nearly 0 percent heritable.

Based on numerous studies over the past fifteen years, the heritability of ADD averages out at about 75 percent. That is an exceptionally high number for a condition in the behavioral sciences.

Therefore, whatever ADD is, it is not a condition easily remedied by environmental forces. This is no delicate flower. No, it is a hardy sapling that will grow anywhere, even when opposed. All the more reason not to try to remove it, but to help it grow into the glorious, unusual tree it can be.

Although we know that ADD is strongly heritable, we still don't know for sure if a given child or adult will develop it. It would be helpful if we had a genetic marker or a biological test for it, or both.

We will, probably within this decade.

Perhaps the most promising line of research investigates the genes related to the neurotransmitter dopamine. In the brains of people who have ADD, dopamine is somehow out of whack. Dopamine levels may be too low in certain regions, or the effect of dopamine may be blunted in areas, or the molecules that transport dopamine from place to place may not be at the right level. One of the effects of stimulant medications, like Ritalin (methylphenidate), is to correct what's different with the dopamine systems in the brain.

Therefore it makes sense that if you could find a gene that regulated some part of the dopamine system, this could be a possible genetic marker for ADD. And, indeed, there is such a gene; in fact, there are several. A lot of research has focused on the dopamine 4 receptor gene (DRD4—and no, this is not a character out of *Star Wars*!). Studies have shown that the 7 repeat allele of this gene, known as DRD4-7 (don't worry about what that means, just think of it as a name tag), is associated with problems in the world of dopamine, which, in turn, can translate into the symptoms of ADD. There are several other genetic markers equally as promising.

Within a year or so, it is likely we will have commercially available tests for markers like DRD4-7. These tests will open up a whole new approach to diagnosis and treatment. We will be able to advise people about their genetic predispositions and vulnerabilities with much greater specificity than we can now. In technical terms, we will be able to counsel them about their genotype, i.e., which genes they have, not just their phenotype, i.e., what symptoms they have.

However, while the tests will be available, they will not be definitive; the genotype still cannot predict the phenotype. There are several reasons why. First, there are many, many genes involved in creating what we call ADD. Second, the syndrome of ADD is heterogeneous, inconsistent from person to person. Third, life experience influences the expression of the genes. Therefore, even though we can identify genes that are associated with ADD, we can't yet predict, based on genetic analysis alone, if a given person will develop ADD. For example, the DRD4-7 gene is present in a lot of people without ADD, so it increases one's risk of developing ADD only slightly; in fact, it increases the risk by a factor of 1.5. Just to give you a comparison, wearing a seat belt increases your health by a factor of 4.

Nonetheless, the development of genetic testing will help us counsel people, even if just about relative risk and what they might expect.

NeuroMark, one of several companies working to develop screening tests based on genetic assays, anticipates marketing both screening and pharmacogenetic diagnostic tests by the year 2005, possibly earlier. The first tests they plan to complete will be for ADHD and for depressive disorders. Following that will be testing for anxiety disorders, addictive disorders, and genetic risk factors for weight gain.

But remember, the genetic tests will allow us *only* to determine probabilities, predispositions, risks, and trends, not to reveal fixed outcomes.

The great advantage of being able to do such counseling, though, is that we can then advise people on how to modify the environment—by watching less television early on, or eating more family dinners—to reduce the chances of a child's developing a dangerous symptom—like drug addiction or violent behavior. We can help people set up environments that bring out the strengths of ADD, environments that provide structure, stimulation, opportunities for physical exercise, and other factors we know bring out the best in people who have ADD.

For example, if a child tests positive for the DRD4-7 gene and also tests positive for several other markers associated with ADD, a parent could begin to take steps that would reduce the toxic expression of the genes well before the diagnosis is made. Such steps could include all the steps we describe in the treatment section of this book, like adding structure to the environment; getting the child on a diet that is balanced, low in refined sugars and additives, and high in omega-3 fatty acids; encouraging lots of physical exercise; going out of your way to develop and reinforce good habits of organization, time management, and daily planning; making special efforts to educate the child about the excessive dangers drugs and alcohol present to such people, as well as their higher-than-average risk of auto accidents; and so forth.

Not only do these genetic markers promise help in how we counsel people, but the dopamine system may also give us a biologically based test for diagnosing ADD. The molecule that transports dopamine is called DAT, which stands for dopamine transporter. Don't ask me why dopamine has to catch a cab and can't travel on its own power; I'm sure there's a good reason because nature always has a good reason, but I don't know what it is. Using a brain scan and a radioactively labeled molecule called altropane, scientists have measured the concentration of DAT in adults who have ADD and adults who do not.

DAT turned out to be 70 percent higher in adults who have ADD than in those who do not. Once various technical problems get sorted out (you really do not want me to detail those here!), measuring the concentration of DAT by injecting a radioactive molecule into the bloodstream and then doing a SPECT scan might become a useful diagnostic test for ADD.

High levels of DAT are also associated with a high risk for developing addictions of various kinds. In addition, the A1 allele of the D2 receptor is also strongly associated with the development of a wide range of addictions or near-addictions. Therefore, measuring the levels of DAT as well as screening for the A1 D2 allele may be true godsends in helping to identify people who are at high risk for addictions of many kinds.

We have been unable to do this in the past. The family history alone usually gives clues. Most people who develop problems with addictions or near-addictions inherited the predisposition. But some-times it was not expressed in the lives of the parents or grandparents who carried the genes. It will be tremendously helpful when a sim-ple brain scan or a genetic test can give us data to support what the family history suggests, or even reveal what the family history failed to show.

CHAPTER 18

ARE WE TRAINING OUR

CHILDREN TO HAVE ADD?

As a society, we may be training our children—and ourselves—to have ADD to a far greater extent than we realize. Various new environmental factors may now be combining to induce not just attention deficit traits but true attention deficit disorder.

In discussing the genetics of ADD I emphasized that while ADD is heritable—i.e., genetically influenced—it is not inherited. All that can be inherited is a proclivity for developing ADD. To produce actual ADD, the environment must join forces with the genes. Our current environment may be doing that with preternatural power.

No one knows exactly what causes ADD, but we do know that we are seeing more of it now than ever before. The reason we are seeing such an upswing in the diagnosis of ADD today may be because our modern environment has become potently ADD-ogenic, much more so than it was, say, thirty years ago, or ever before.

That ADD is diagnosed far more frequently today than it was in 1974 is a matter of fact. The reasons why are matters of debate. Certainly one reason is that both the general public and the medical profession are more savvy and informed about ADD. People look for and recognize ADD more skillfully than they did three decades ago or even one decade ago. Some critics contend that another reason is that

ADD is a fad, a bandwagon excuse-makers love to hop on. I disagree with that point of view, but I accept it as a possibility in some areas.

However, it strikes me that the major reason ADD is diagnosed so much more frequently today than ever before could be that the true incidence of ADD is rising dramatically. Our modern world could be the driving force. Distinctive elements of modern life, arising from quite disparate sources, could conspire to create a sort of cultural "perfect storm," perfectly designed to induce ADD.

The world has never before seen the cultural typhoon that has swept us all up in the past thirty years. We are flying in its winds right now, so it is difficult to gain perspective and measure what it is doing to us. We do know that it is exciting. We also know that it is new, unique in the history of the world. Those who would look back in history for an era like ours could not find one. That's another reason it is hard to know what to make of it.

What makes life unique right now comes from our greatest achievements in the sciences. Physics and chemistry have blessed us with labor-saving and lifesaving discoveries. But some of these discoveries have infiltrated our lives so intimately that they may be causing us serious harm.

First of all, electronic-communications technology, the progenitor of the Information Age, has commandeered our attention to an alarming degree. Television, cell phones, Walkmen, the Internet, video games, Game Boys, faxes, e-mail, Blackberries, and all the rest of the electronic means and devices we love have wound their way so possessively into our lives that we spend less and less time with one another, face-to-face. The electronic moment is supplanting what I call the human moment. Without meaning to, we are losing touch with one another.

In 1986, Neil Postman foresaw the damage that the electronic culture could do in his book *Amusing Ourselves to Death*. Raised on a diet of sound bites and electronic stimulation, children can lose the ability to carry on an extended conversation or listen to one, whether or not they have ADD. Jane Healy elaborated on this theme in her books *Endangered Minds* and *Failure to Connect*. The trend only continues: a recent study showed that toddlers who watch more than two hours of television per day are 30 percent more likely to develop ADD later on.

The more children channel-surf and find entertainment in passive, watching ways, the less they learn how to tolerate frustration, bear the tension of not getting what they want, or develop deep imaginative skills.

The second blessing of science that may inadvertently be harming us comes from chemistry. When we learned how to preserve our crops with pesticides and add shelf length to our food with preservatives, we also started to introduce a wide range of environmental pollutants, the impact of which we cannot comprehend.

As much as we live in a brave new electronic world, we also live in a deeply chemically dependent world. Never before in history have we been so saturated with chemicals: the air we breathe; the clothes we wear; the cosmetics we use; the detergents that wash our buildings and our bodies; the medicines we take; the foods we eat; the waters we bathe in, swim in, and drink—all of these teem with chemicals we use to make life better, safer, cheaper, faster, tastier, softer, and even, ironically, cleaner.

The extent to which all these chemicals may be joining forces with genes to create ADD is anybody's guess. My guess is that it's a large extent, much larger than we like to think.

It is not just ADD that is mysteriously on the upswing. We have seen a dramatic increase in the diagnosis of asthma over the past decade, from around 7 million in 1980 to around 25 million today. And we have seen an equally dramatic increase in the diagnosis of autism-spectrum disorders, including classic autism and the increasingly prevalent Asperger's syndrome.

Four A's—ADD, asthma, autism, and Asperger's—are on the rapid rise for reasons unknown. Various factors in the modern environment may be poisoning us. I can't claim to know exactly what they are. But the two I named above—electronic superstimulation coupled with interpersonal disconnection and chemical intoxication—seem particularly worth monitoring as they are so pervasive and under our skin.

ADD—as well as asthma, autism, and Asperger's—may be canaries in the mine shaft of modern life. They may be telling us to watch out and to change our ways. They may be telling us to spend more time with one another and not get addicted to electronics. They may be telling us to watch carefully what we eat, drink, breathe, bathe in, touch, and ingest as medicines.

It would not be terribly difficult to make some changes in our individual lives. Of course, we need help from the government to clean up global pollution. But we can begin by taking the simple steps of watching less TV, surfing and e-mailing on the Net fewer hours, and spending more time with one another, face-to-face, making friends a priority, taking in the positive energy of the human connection.

And we could try to eat a healthier, less chemically dependent diet; try to use less toxic fluids when we clean our houses; pay more attention to the quality of the air we breathe and perhaps invest in a filter if we live in an area of bad pollution; consider getting more exercise so we will need fewer medications; and in general steer clear of chemicals unless we know for sure that they will help us without causing us—or our children—any harm.

CHAPTER 19

ADD, ADDICTIONS, AND A

NEW USE OF THE 12 STEPS

What if nothing in life gives you true pleasure except substances or activities that are bad for you? And what if you have a problem controlling impulsive behavior? This is the dilemma that the adult with ADD faces who also struggles with an addiction or a near-addiction.

I have already cautioned that addictions are common in adults who have ADD, and that near-addictions and intermittent substance abuse are more the rule than the exception. This may be because of an in-born physiological problem that makes finding pleasure in ordinary ways much more difficult for the person who has ADD than for the person who doesn't have it.

One way of dealing with the problem of addiction—and certainly the safest way—is to abstain from alcohol, drugs, and addictive behaviors like gambling or indiscriminate sex. You then must search for other, safer ways of finding pleasure. This is the method that AA recommends, as do most organizations devoted to helping people recover from addictions to substances or to dangerous activities.

But what are you to do if nothing provides the pleasure that alcohol, gambling, or some other dangerous substance or activity provides?

No one has the "right" answer to that question because there is no right answer. How do you achieve moderation or abstinence when your body seems set against it? And why are people willing to suffer the ravages of an addiction for only fleeting moments of pleasure?

The most succinct answer to that question that I have ever read came from Samuel Johnson, the great eighteenth-century literary genius and commentator on human nature. When asked why the men in a pub were drinking to excess and "making such beasts of themselves," Johnson replied, "They drink in order to forget the pain of being a man."

We have learned since Johnson's time that nature equips some people with fewer tools than others for forgetting the pain of being a man and finding pleasure in safe and healthy ways. Ironically, many who are so limited are also gifted with great talents. Many also have ADD. They must somehow limit their addictive activities in order to develop their considerable talents.

But how? Although the question has moral dimensions, it is not solely a moral choice—even though many people try to reduce it to one. It is as much a physiological decision based upon a person's capacity to exercise choice and control—capacities that have as much to do with physiology as with morality and strength of character.

Alcohol and drugs can cost a person everything of value in his life. In return, they give him brief moments of pleasure and peace. The decision to abstain would be obvious, and enacting it would be easy were it not for the power of physiology and the fact of genetic variations.

Millions who face this choice choose the moments of pleasure and peace, even at the cost of everything they value and love. Such is the desire to "forget the pain of being a man," if only for a few hours, that people will throw away everything for those few hours.

The people who choose to drink—or gamble or do drugs or whatever the self-medication may be—are not so much weak as they are desperate. Not wired to feel pleasure in ordinary ways, they contend every day with a curse they inherited. They contend every day with relentless pain. They must struggle to find a better way to relieve that pain than addiction.

I believe the best "better way" lies through human connections: friendships, memberships, involvement in relationships and groups where you are deeply valued and understood. Fellowship is the best and safest "drug" we have. Twelve-step programs offer this, but they are far from the only way.

Medications can also help. We have come a long way in our ability to prescribe medications that treat the subtle kinds of desperation, depression, and anxiety that can lead to self-medication. Exercise can help a great deal. Exercise is one of the best tonics we have for the mind and soul. Diet and nutritional interventions can also help. There is good evidence that omega-3 fatty acids help stabilize moods. Beyond that, there is ongoing research into various nutritional interventions to treat addictions.

But the best program must include some means of developing connectedness and group support so that the person never feels *alone* no matter how rotten he feels. Most people who have ADD and most people who develop addictions share secret feelings of unworthiness, shame, and a fatalistic, nihilistic foreboding that lead them to withdraw from others when they are in distress. Some kind of group program—be it through a 12-step program or group therapy or membership in a close organization—offers the best antidote to these toxic feelings.

MORE ABOUT 12-STEP PROGRAMS IN TREATING ADD

For anyone bound to an addiction or a compulsion or a dangerous habit that you can't break, a 12-step program might set you free. Give it serious thought before you dismiss it as "just not for you."

A 12-step program can also help people with ADD who aren't addicted in the conventional sense of that word, but in whom ADD generates a state that *resembles* an addiction. Some of the negative symptoms of ADD—like inconsistent attention leading to underachievement, danger-seeking, disorganization, and poor time management—can create recurring, habitual negative feelings. Over time, these negative feelings can capture a person like a recurring nightmare. He returns to the negative feelings the way an addict returns to his crack house, as if he were bereft without the negative feelings, painful and destructive though they clearly are.

Let me give you a few examples of how having ADD can operate like an addiction:

- Some adults with ADD can't let go of their sense of unworthiness. No matter how much they achieve, they can't believe the achievements are their own. They continue to disown what they have achieved, feeling instead that they are fundamentally worthless. These people behave as if they were addicted to feelings of shame, guilt, and unworthiness.
- Some adults with ADD are addicted to conflict. Wherever they go, they instigate an argument. They have insight into the problem, but they can't stop doing it, even though it costs them relationship after relationship or job after job. They seem addicted to the negative feelings associated with interpersonal conflict.
- Some adults with ADD can't stop procrastinating. They can hire coaches and buy all sorts of equipment to combat their procrastination, but they still find themselves getting things done in a frenzy at the last minute. They seem addicted to the pain of the last-minute crisis.
- Some adults with ADD can't keep promises. The moment they make the promise they fully intend to keep it, but then they forget about it. No matter how many strategies—from a coach to a reminder system to rewards and punishments—they set up to make sure they keep the promise or fulfill the commitment, time and again they fail. They seem addicted to the bad feelings they receive from others and from themselves when they fail to keep a promise or meet an obligation.

Usually, we don't think of the kinds of problems described above as *addictions*. But what we have learned about addictions may point toward a solution.

I have often been asked what a person can do if she has tried everything I recommended in *Driven to Distraction* but still is not making the progress that she should be. I have suggested various answers to that question throughout this book—from new nutritional remedies like grape-seed extract, omega-3 fatty acids, or other specific dietary supplements; to new movement therapies like the cerebellar stimulation program; to new medications such as the long-acting stimulants Concerta or Adderall XR, or the new nonstimulants amantadine, Wellbutrin, or Strattera; to my five-step method of developing strengths and talents that begins with connectedness and play. A 12-step program is one more possible item on that list.

Whether a person suffers from a true addiction—to alcohol, other drugs, food, sex, gambling, shopping, work, exercise, or whatever—or behaves *as if* he were addicted to some of the negative feelings created by the symptoms of ADD, he may find that a 12-step program allows him to let go of whatever it is he has been unable to let go of so far.

The 12 steps are not for everybody. But I urge people to think twice before they dismiss this program. Almost everybody whose life has been changed by a 12-step program began by saying, "That kind of program may be good for certain kinds of people, but it's not for me," or "I don't like groups," or "Those programs are for alcoholics and bums, and I'm not that bad off."

I am not trying to convert anyone to a 12-step way of life. I simply want to offer it as a serious option, one that *can* perform miracles. It has done so for millions of people—almost all of whom thought it was not for them when they got started. I should also add that neither John Ratey nor I have ever been part of a 12-step program ourselves; we are not concealed converts trying to sneak our cause into this book. However, we have treated many people who benefited tremendously from "working the program," as the saying goes. For addictive behaviors, these programs offer the best help for the least amount of money.

Of course, AA is the best known of the 12-step programs, but there are many others. There are 12-step programs for people addicted to food, to gambling, to narcotics, to sex, to spending and shopping, to self-destructive relationships, and more.

An innovative model of how a 12-step program can help someone with an addiction to negative feelings—an addiction many people with ADD suffer from—was developed by Melody Beattie in her work with codependency. Her book *Codependents' Guide to the Twelve Steps* brilliantly—and practically—explains how to work the 12 steps if you suffer from an addiction to feeling overly responsible for other people. I might add that many spouses of people who have ADD get into codependent patterns that are not good for either member of the couple.

WHAT MAKES THE 12 STEPS WORK?

While I have never joined a 12-step group or even attended at 12-step meeting, I have talked to hundreds of people who have, and I have treated many as my patients. As I listen to their accounts, I marvel at the results, and I often wonder what makes the difference in these programs. Whatever it is, it works wonders in places where we doctors often fail. These programs can remove shame, develop confidence, alleviate guilt, promote trust, activate dormant talents, and instigate lasting joy, all in a context of humor, humility, and fearless truth-telling.

I will never forget what one man said to me, a man who had both ADD and an addiction to narcotics. After he joined a 12-step program he was able to give up his addiction. He has been clean and sober for more than twenty years. He explained to me that abstinence was only one part of the program. "Most people think of the 12 steps in terms of what you give up. But the truth is, you get back much more than you give up."

"Okay," I argued, "but you still did have to give up something you used to like an awful lot, something that had given you bursts of pleasure, even though it was also killing you. How did you give up the drugs? What did you turn to instead for the high they used to give you?"

"Fellowship," he replied instantly. He didn't have to think for even a fraction of a second. This was not a man who would parrot what he'd been taught. He had truly discovered a better high in fellowship than he had found in drugs.

I sense that fellowship is the core force in all 12-step programs. It is not easy to work the program—that's why they call it work—but it can lead to deep and lasting pleasure, a much better pleasure than an addiction or dangerous habit can supply.

For those of you who are not familiar with the 12 steps, here they are, as originally written for AA.

THE 12 STEPS OF ALCOHOLICS ANONYMOUS

1. Admitted that we were powerless over alcohol—that our lives had become unmanageable.

2. Came to believe that a Power greater than ourselves could restore us to sanity.

3. Made a decision to turn our will and our lives over to the care of God *as we understood Him.*

4. Made a searching and fearless moral inventory of ourselves.

5. Admitted to God, to ourselves, and to another human being the exact nature of our wrongs.

6. Were entirely ready to have God remove all these defects of character.

7. Humbly asked Him to remove our shortcomings.

8. Made a list of all persons we had harmed, and became willing to make amends to them all.

9. Made direct amends to such people whenever possible, except when to do so would injure them or others.

10. Continued to take personal inventory and when we were wrong promptly admitted it.

11. Sought through prayer and meditation to improve our conscious contact with God *as we understood Him,* praying only for knowledge of His will for us and the power to carry that out.

12. Having had a spiritual awakening as a result of these steps, tried to carry this message to alcoholics, and to practice these principles in all our affairs.

Let me now show how each of these steps can be "worked" in life with ADD.

Step 1—"Admitted that we were powerless over alcohol—that our lives had become unmanageable." If you have ADD but do not suffer from an addiction, it is not alcohol or some other substance that you are powerless over. But you are powerless over other matters that have rendered your life unmanageable. You can substitute your own word or words for the word *alcohol* in step 1. Let me give a few examples of how people I have treated for ADD have filled in that blank:

- We admitted that we were powerless over piles and procrastination—that our lives had become unmanageable.
- We admitted that we were powerless over shopping, spending, and impulsive decision-making . . .

- We admitted that we were powerless over disorganization and chaos . . .
- We admitted that we were powerless over forgetfulness, lapses in attention, and failure to follow through . . .
- We admitted that we were powerless over negative self-talk, feelings of being a loser, and regrets over blown opportunities . . .

Step 2—"Came to believe that a Power greater than ourselves could restore us to sanity." People sometimes stumble over this step, thinking they are being coerced into some kind of religion or faith they don't subscribe to. However, faith and religion need have nothing to do with it. We adults with ADD know all too well about powers greater than ourselves that exert a negative influence. We can feel powerless before the power of piles, for example, or the power of procrastination. If we know about negative powers, why not acknowledge a positive power greater than ourselves?

Furthermore, most adults with ADD do have a deep spiritual inclination. They intuit the existence of a higher power. Why not use that power?

Step 3—"Made a decision to turn our will and our lives over to the care of God *as we understood Him.*" There is no coercion here. You either feel ready to do this sort of thing or don't.

However, let me explain in secular terms how this decision can make sense for people with ADD, even if they do not believe in a conventional God. I will pick an example from my own life, and I will intentionally choose a homely, nonspiritual example.

The example is organization. I remain organized by using habits I learned long ago, in fifth grade. But more goes into my organizational process than that. At its core, my organizational process is an act of faith. I *believe* I will stay well enough organized, and so I do. That is the only way I can persuade myself not to get so terrified that I micromanage every little detail and fret over every single potential mistake. I allow the process to carry me, which frees me up to do my creative work. You could say I allow God to carry me, or I allow my prior school training to carry me, or my unconscious, or good luck, or an angel.

The point that can assist people with ADD is simply this: it can help a person to trust some force outside of herself instead of feeling that she has to oversee everything alone, without assistance.

Step 4—"Made a searching and fearless moral inventory of ourselves." For most adults who have ADD, part of the value in this step is finding out what they have done *right,* as they typically give themselves no credit at all. Of course for those people who have been in denial, the moral inventory can unearth some unpleasant items as well.

Step 5—"Admitted to God, to ourselves, and to another human being the exact nature of our wrongs." I would quickly add to that "and our good parts as well," because, as I have said, most adults with ADD do not admit to their strengths and talents. Of course, it also helps to admit the wrongs. To yourself. To God (or the higher power, or your angel, or your bedpost). And, most important, *to another human being.* This is where a person begins to feel how formative fellowship is.

Step 6—"Were entirely ready to have God remove all these defects of character." I'm not crazy about the language here, but who am I to argue? These steps have helped so many people that I have no business changing them. If I were to change the wording, which I wouldn't presume to do, I would rephrase it "Were entirely ready for love to fill us up."

Step 7—"Humbly asked Him to remove our shortcomings." For people with ADD the key here is the process of reaching out. Ask God, or the higher power, or the group, to remove whatever is wrong. Usually, the adult with ADD feels that he must remove them himself. When he can't do it himself—and no one can—he feels he has failed. Step 7 says, No, you can't do it yourself; humbly ask for help, and you'll be amazed at what may happen.

Step 8—"Made a list of all persons we had harmed, and became willing to make amends to them all." This is a dangerous step to do alone. You need someone, or a group, to help you from falling into a chasm of guilt. Adults who have ADD usually have harmed a lot of people—not intentionally, but they've harmed them nonetheless. They also have helped a lot of people. Still, it is good to take stock of the people you have disappointed, angered, or otherwise hurt, and to feel willing to do what you can to make things right. As you do this, you will find that you can start to forgive yourself.

Step 9—"Made direct amends to such people whenever possible, except when to do so would injure them or others." This continues the process of healing and forgiveness that the previous step set in motion. Once again, you should not do this without the support of another person or a group, as you could tip into a terribly despondent place.

Step 10—"Continued to take personal inventory and when we were wrong promptly admitted it." One of the beauties in this step is that the more you do it, the better it feels. No longer do you have to pretend that you are on top of everything. No longer do you have to try to satisfy that imaginary fifth-grade schoolteacher. You can accept the human inevitability of messing up and not feel devastated by the sinking feeling of here-we-go-again. Instead, you say, "I messed up. I apologize. Let me make it right." And that's an end to it! Amazing!

Step 11—"Sought through prayer and meditation to improve our conscious contact with God *as we understood Him,* praying only for knowledge of His will for us and the power to carry that out." If you need a secular version of this step, let me offer this: "Sought through prayer and meditation to improve our conscious contact with positive energy as we understood it, praying only for a knowledge of its presence in us and the power to act upon its direction."

If there is one single force that can change a life with ADD from a sour one to a sweet one, it is finding a way to connect with positive energy. It is present within all of us and outside all of us. We just need help finding it, connecting with it, and following its light.

Step 12—"Having had a spiritual awakening as a result of these steps, tried to carry this message to alcoholics, and to practice these principles in all our affairs." The "spiritual awakening" lies at the heart of the most dramatic changes in the lives of adults who get diagnosed with ADD. Some call it an "aha" experience. Others call it a revelation. Others call it "finding the key that had been missing for so long."

But at the heart of the transformation from a life of frustration and underachievement to a life of creativity and fulfillment is an awakening to the possibilities in your life, possibilities that adults with ADD long ago gave up on. You don't need to call this a spiritual awakening. Just let it happen.

Then help others do the same. One of the best ways to consolidate the gains you make in treatment is to take what you have learned and teach it to others—to schoolteachers, to friends, to grandparents, to your family doctor, to whomever is interested or you can get interested. After all, how a life can change from sour to sweet makes for a very interesting story.

The 12-step method evolved in an effort to help alcoholics, and then to help people with any kind of addiction. I have shown here how it can help when the negative feelings associated with ADD operate like an addiction.

PART FOUR

◆

Mastering the Power and Avoiding the Pitfalls:

The Treatment of ADD

CHAPTER 20

THE TREATMENT OF ADD:

WHAT WORKS BEST

W hether for children or adults, the treatment of ADD should be comprehensive and include a wide range of possible interventions, certainly more than medication or some other single step. Assistance should also be provided over the long-term, as ADD generally does not go away. The person being treated may not need to go see the doctor very often, but he should always know that help is just one telephone call away.

I divide a comprehensive plan into the following eight steps. Each step need not be implemented, but each step should be considered. The program was outlined in chapter 1, "The Skinny on ADD," so I will offer only a few additional words here. Subsequent chapters will expand upon specific points that our patients have found particularly helpful.

1. Diagnosis, which should include identification of talents and strengths
2. Implementation of a five-step plan that promotes talents and strengths (detailed in chapter 22)
3. Education

4. Changes in lifestyle
5. Structure
6. Counseling of some kind, such as coaching, psychotherapy, career counseling, couples therapy, family therapy
7. Various other therapies that can augment the effectiveness of medication or replace the use of medication altogether, such as an exercise program that stimulates the cerebellum, targeted tutoring, general physical exercise, nutritional interventions, and occupational therapy
8. Medication (only if desired)

Step 1—Diagnosis, which should include identification of talents and strengths. Making the diagnosis opens the door to treatment. You should make sure your diagnosis is both accurate and complete, taking into account the likelihood of coexisting problems. Your diagnosis should delineate potential strengths and talents, because you will build your confidence and self-esteem on these.

Diagnosis is also therapeutic in itself. When you diagnose ADD, you break all those moral diagnoses that had plagued you for years.

Step 2—Implementation of a five-step plan that promotes talents and strengths. See chapter 22 for a description of this method.

Step 3—Education. The way you make the diagnosis therapeutic is by learning about your own mind and about ADD. You need to learn what ADD is and what it isn't. You need to teach other members of your family about it. You need to explain it to teachers and to all others who deal with your child, or whomever has the ADD. Family therapy sessions can help with this. So can couples therapy.

There are various organizations that put out educational materials that can be quite helpful in bringing the truth about ADD to a wide number of people. There is a listing of educational resources at the end of this book.

Step 4—Changes in Lifestyle. There are five major elements here:

1. *Sleep.* Most people who have ADD do not get enough sleep. They stay up too late on their computers or watching TV, and then they have enormous trouble getting out of bed in the morning. In fact, various sleep disorders, such as delayed sleep latency or sleep apnea, may be associated with ADD. You should consult a sleep

specialist if you do not wake up each morning feeling refreshed from your night's sleep, or if you do not get enough sleep. "Enough" sleep is that amount of sleep it takes for you to wake up without an alarm clock. A sleep clinic can diagnose sleep disorders and prescribe proper treatment.

2. *Diet.* The whole field of diet and the brain is taking off. What you eat is as powerful, if not more so, than any medication. See the chapter 25 for some basic suggestions.

3. *Exercise.* One of the best treatments for ADD is physical exercise. Never deny children recess; they need that exercise. You can use exercise to wake you up when you are working or studying and you start to feel logy or distracted; just stand up and do a few jumping jacks and stretches. And if you get regular physical exercise every week, your mind will be better focused throughout each day. Ten minutes of physical exercise offers the same benefits—without the side effects—as a dose of Prozac combined with a dose of Ritalin.

4. *Prayer or meditation.* We now have a large body of evidence show-ing that daily prayer or meditation helps to focus and calm the mind. Children as well as grown-ups can do this. For example, my eight-year old, Tucker, learned some basic yoga in his second-grade class. One day when he was arguing with his mother he said, "Wait a minute." Then he went into his bedroom, where Sue saw him sit-ting cross-legged in a meditation pose intoning, "Ohmmmmmm, Ohmmmmm." After a few minutes of that Tucker came out and said, "Okay, Mom, I feel much better. Now let's keep talking."

5. *Positive human contact.* Most people with ADD, in fact most peo-ple, period, don't get enough positive human contact these days. This is especially true for the people with ADD as they have to deal with so many reprimands, reminders, remediations, and re-proaches. Try to make sure you get some positive moments every day as well.

Step 5—Structure. This refers to any habit or external device, like a list or a filing cabinet, that you create or set up outside the brain to make up for what's missing inside it. ADD brains don't have enough filing cabinets. They don't naturally acquire the habit of being on time. They lose things. The more you put your imagination to it, the more you can think of various structures—reminder systems, habits that you train into yourself—that can dramatically help. In later chapters we offer many specific tips about structure and other nonmedication interventions.

Step 6—Counseling of some kind. Various kinds of counseling can help, depending upon your needs. Family therapy and couples therapy can be extremely helpful. Group therapy for adults with ADD is one of the best interventions I know of. And coaching—working to help a person get organized and make plans to achieve goals—is one of the most practical and efficient treatments for adults who have ADD as well as adolescents who are mature enough to want to be coached.

Step 7—Various other complementary or alternative treatments. We propose a wide variety of other therapies in this book. Some, like targeted tutoring programs such as Orton-Gillingham for dyslexia, are standard. Others are new and as yet unproven, like cerebellar stimulation or nutritional therapies. We will discuss these in subsequent chapters.

Step 8—Medication. According to the most up-to-date and reliable research that we have, no treatment is as safe and effective in treating ADD as medication. One medication or another will work 90 percent of the time, and with minimal or no side effects. Medication should not be used alone. It should always be used as part of a comprehensive treatment plan. And you certainly should not take medication if you don't want to. Alternatives can work well. However, you should know that according to the best research we have, medication is the single most effective treatment for ADD that has been developed so far.

CHAPTER 21

THE KEY TO TREATING ADD:

FIND THE BURIED TREASURES

To find joy in life, a person needs to find something he likes to do and is good at.

Helping someone create a better life begins, therefore, in identifying what is or what might potentially be positive and worth building on in the person's life.

Accordingly, the treatment of ADD should begin with an effort to find what's good in a given person. "There's gold in them thar hills." So there is in *every* brain, ADD or otherwise.

The refrain of this country's great gold rush should be the refrain of every treatment plan for people who have ADD. We're living in what amounts to a great brain rush, which we should all take advantage of. As scientists discover more and more golden nuggets about the brain, people have a better chance than ever to discover the treasures buried in their brains or their childrens'.

Most treatment focuses on what goes wrong in the world of ADD. To be sure, a lot can go wrong, and that must be attended to. But, if treatment is to be as transformative as possible, it must look for the treasures. It must ferret out the hidden strengths, the potential talents, in every child who has ADD, and in every adult. It must discover where the brain lights up.

By the time my children have children, a detailed profile of the mind/brain will be a standard part of every child's pediatric evaluation and school progress report. It will highlight strengths and offer specific methods on how to develop those strengths, as well as outline vulnerabilities and offer specific ways to overcome them as well.

If you learn nothing else from this book, learn this: no matter how old a person is, if she has ADD she has more talent than she thinks she has. Don't shudder at this diagnosis. Take it for what it is: an opportunity to make life better.

Some diagnoses—like cancer or heart disease—herald the beginning of hard times, but the diagnosis of ADD should mark the end of the worst times and the start of better times. Especially in adults, by the time the diagnosis finally gets made, a lot of bad years may have piled up, misery may saturate the person's life, many opportunities may have disappeared, huge mistakes may have ruined a once-good reputation, and life may look as bleak as a beach in winter. The diagnosis of ADD tips all that to the good. When this diagnosis is made, right on that very day, right at the moment of diagnosis, the diagnosis shifts the bad that has happened into the light of science and out of the darkness of moral condemnation.

Once the diagnosis is made, the next step is to find and develop your talents. People often ask me, "What are ADD people good at?" My answer is, "You never know. But whatever you do, don't stop looking." You can't predict what your talent will be. Maybe it's in being creative with investing online. Or maybe in working with motors and engines. Or maybe in inspiring people to buy some product. Or maybe just in inspiring people. Whatever the talent, the goal of treatment is to bring this talent to light and put it to work. Maybe we should call it mining, rather than treatment.

Whatever you call it, the development of talent is a crucial but often neglected goal of the process. You build a life on your talents and strengths—what is right and good about you—not on your weaknesses, however skillfully they might be corrected.

When you first receive the diagnosis, you may feel afraid. This diagnosis may sound ominous, containing the words *deficit* and *disorder*, but you need not be afraid.

You may fear the term ADD. I don't like it myself. In *Driven to Dis-*

traction we suggested that it be called attention variability syndrome. But ADD and ADHD are far better terms than their predecessor; this condition used to be called minimal brain dysfunction, or MBD. Imagine being told you or your child has that! I qualify for that diagnosis, and I have often imagined what it would be like to go into a job interview and say, "Hi, I'm Ned Hallowell, and I think I'd be able to make a great contribution to your company. You'll also be glad to know that I have minimal brain dysfunction." I doubt that the interviewer would say, "Oh, come right in. Our company is looking for people just like you!" Saying you have attention deficit disorder, or, worse yet, attention deficit hyperactivity disorder, may not be a whole lot better, but those terms are at least somewhat less offensive.

All the diagnostic terms that have ever been used suffer from one serious flaw: they all emphasize what's wrong and state nothing about what's right. This is the tradition in medical diagnosis, of course. In psychiatry we often make the huge mistake of building our treatment plan without first explicitly identifying the strengths and talents the person has. In so doing we miss one of the most powerful tools a person has to get better: his strengths.

Because we use the medical model in psychiatry, we make diagnoses as other specialties do. We diagnose depression or bipolar disorder or schizophrenia or anxiety, and then we begin to prescribe remedies for what's wrong.

However, when we do that we leave the patient without her most powerful remedy: the healthy part of her mind, the talented part, the successful part, the harmonious part.

I have sat on the other side of the desk—the patient's side—and listened to myself be diagnosed, and I have felt my heart sink as my problems and weaknesses or my children's were enumerated without any mention of what we did well. At those times it felt as if my greatest allies were being taken away, leaving me and my kids alone to fend for ourselves without our best troops at our side. I wanted to say, "But what about the good stuff, the stuff we do well?" but I didn't. Like most patients, I didn't speak up. I just listened quietly as the doctor did his job, which was to tell me what was wrong. The more he told me what was wrong, the weaker I felt, and the less able to get better. The more I sank in my chair, the gloomier I got, the sicker I became.

Try to counteract that if you can by asking whomever makes your diagnosis to point out the strengths in you or your child. If he does not do that, do it yourself, or speak to someone who will.

It is important to get into a positive frame of mind. Without positive energy, treatment fails. This might sound like a minor point, but in fact it is crucial. I set a goal when patients come to see me: I want them to leave my office feeling better than when they walked in. I know that if they do, then they will make the best use of whatever suggestions I have given them in the office and they will be most likely to come up with useful strategies of their own.

CHAPTER 22

HOW TO FIND THE BURIED TREASURES:

FIVE STEPS THAT LEAD TO LASTING JOY

L ifelong joy is within the grasp of most people. It is within the grasp of everyone who is not mired in poverty or trapped in horrific situations—and even many of those people have found lifelong joy. However, most people don't know how to use the magical tools that reside in their minds, tools that can turn almost any life into a joyful one.

What separates greatly satisfying lives from less satisfying lives is one glaring difference. People who feel deeply satisfied with their lives and find enduring joy are people who do what they love and love what they do.

People who are not satisfied gave up long ago on the possibility of doing what they love. They decided that it was impractical to try, or that they had no passion to pursue. They decided, usually somewhere in their twenties or maybe their thirties, that happiness was not in the cards for them, and so they set about trying to make do.

But it is never too late to find joy. Whether you have ADD or XYZ, you can create a joyful life—at any age. There is always, always hope.

Virtually every book ever written about long-term happiness and joy includes one central piece of advice: do what you love. The advice appears so often that it becomes cliché: follow your bliss; do your own thing; build on your passion.

To thrive in life you need to find out what you're best at, then build upon those talents and skills. I have offered ideas in this book on how to fix up what's wrong in life if you have ADD, but if you want to find joy, you need to do more than just fix what's wrong. You need to find and build on your strengths. Put differently, you need a plan not just to avoid misery but to promote joy, even ecstasy.

There are many guides on how to avoid misery, or what to do about misery when it grips you, but there aren't many guides on how to create and sustain joy. So I wrote one, a book called *The Childhood Roots of Adult Happiness,* published in 2002.

I discovered that it isn't money or fame or even good health that correlates most strongly with enduring joy in adulthood. Instead, what correlates statistically with joy most powerfully are internal qualities like optimism, the ability to reach out to others, a feeling of being at least somewhat in control of your life, and a can-do attitude coupled with a want-to-do attitude.

I then researched what most commonly leads to those inner qualities. Part of the answer is genetics, and we can't control that. But genetics do not provide the whole answer. Far from it. Indeed, life experience strongly influences how the genes a person is born with find expression in life.

So then my research had to answer the question, What kind of life experiences are most likely to lead to the inner qualities that most closely correlate with enduring joy in life?

Based on the wide range of empirical data that has become available in the past two decades, and based on hundreds of conversations with experts in diverse fields, I developed a five-step method that can be used in childhood or adulthood. This method helps lead a person to a deeply satisfying, joyful life.

Originally, I recommended it for parents, teachers, and coaches to use with children. But then I realized it is equally applicable to adult life.

While not originally designed for people who have ADD, it is perfectly suited for us. In retrospect, I can see I followed it in my own life. Of all the adults I know whom I would deem happy in their lives, all but a few incorporate the basic steps outlined in this five-step method into their own lives. If you can incorporate it into your life, it will give you a way to find and promote strengths, not just remediate weaknesses.

The five steps constitute a cycle, one step naturally leading to the next. Then the entire cycle repeats itself. Once started, it can continue for a lifetime, like a giant flywheel of joy, feeding off its own momentum. Here is how the cycle looks:

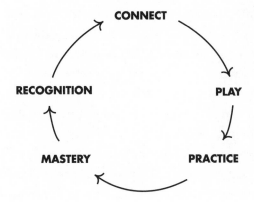

As you set this cycle in motion in a child's life, or in your own, you will see positive developments immediately, and they will grow in strength and depth over time.

The starting point is the feeling of connectedness. This is the most important part of the cycle. You want to create a feeling in the child— or in whomever you are hoping to help find joy—of being a part of something positive, something larger than himself. Creating a connected life is the key to happiness and health.

You can develop a connected life at any age. Current research reveals that people who live connected lives are not only happier and more joyful most of the time, they are also physically healthier and they live longer. There is no more significant single step you could take to make your life healthier and more joyful than to develop a connected life.

But what do I mean by a connected life? The elements of a connected life can include all of the following points of connection. You don't need to have them all, and, in fact, you should guard against having too many. Think of your points of connection as a garden. With careful tilling it will grow and thrive, but if you overplant it will suffer.

1. *Family.* This is the core connection for most people. But don't worry: if you don't feel connected there, you can find connectedness elsewhere. And remember, connection and conflict go hand in hand. If you have conflict in your family, that means it is connected. The opposite of connection is not conflict; it is indifference.

2. *Friends and community.* For many people, their circle of friends becomes like an extended family.

3. *School or work.* If you feel welcomed and treated fairly at school or at work, and if you have one or two friends there, you will do much better than if you don't. Recent studies have shown that the kids who get into trouble are the ones who feel disconnected at home and at school. On the other hand, the feeling of connectedness at home and at school conveys powerful strength and protection from trouble.

4. *Activities.* If you can find a few activities that you really love to do, chances are that you can build joy, confidence, and self-esteem by doing them, even if they do not relate to school or work.

5. *The arts.* Music, painting, literature, movies, dance, sculpture—all these and more. The arts offer a connection that almost everyone can derive great joy from.

6. *Groups, teams, organizations.* Whether it be a club or a team or a committee in an organization that you believe in, these kinds of connections convey a feeling of purpose and being needed.

7. *Pets.* Some of the deepest feelings of warmth and positive energy come from our pets.

8. *Nature.* This connection offers strength, joy, and inspiration—as well as places to play—all our lives.

9. *Ideas and information.* What matters here is that you feel comfortably connected in the world of ideas and information. Fear and shame are the great disconnectors here. Make sure shame and fear do not contaminate any learning environment. They are the truly dangerous learning disabilities.

10. *The spiritual world.* Whatever your connection might be to what is beyond knowledge, it is worthwhile to cultivate it, in whatever way your beliefs or traditions suggest.

11. *The past.* By developing an awareness of your heritage, your traditions, and the stories of your ancestors, you gain a clearer sense of

why you are here now, which in turn connects you to the deeper meanings of life.

12. *Yourself.* A comfortable connection to yourself naturally follows from connectedness in the previous areas. People who have ADD often feel quite uncomfortable with themselves. The best remedy is to bolster their connections outside of themselves.

Creating a connected life takes time, and it requires work to maintain it over a lifetime. But if you tend to it regularly, you will find that many of the stresses that afflict other people do not affect you nearly as severely. A balanced, connected life leads to a sturdy kind of joy that hard times cannot easily strike down.

The connected individual—of any age—naturally feels safe and secure enough to go to step 2 in the cycle, which is play. By play, I mean something deeply and profoundly formative—any activity in which you become imaginatively involved. The opposite of play is doing exactly what you are told.

When you play, your brain lights up. This is where you could find joy for the rest of your life, so take note when it happens. You will not be able to play at everything you do. But when you do find an activity you can play at, an activity where your brain lights up, you have found the gold I was referring to in the preceding chapter. The best way to mine the gold in the ADD brain—or in any brain—is to play.

When you play, you are likely to enter a state that one of the foremost researchers into happiness, psychologist Mihaly Csikszentmihalyi, has named *flow*. In flow, you become one with what you are doing. You forget who you are and where you are. Your brain glows.

The more activities you try, the more likely you are to find one where your imagination kicks in and you play, and maybe even enter into flow. Perhaps for you it is in gardening. Or for your child it is in skiing. Or for your spouse it is in tracking stocks.

Once you find some activity in which you can play, you want to do it over and over again. This is called practice, which is step 3. Practice that emerges out of play is practice you want to do. You don't have to be hounded to do it; you want to do it. Here is where habits of discipline develop that will last for a lifetime.

As you practice, you naturally achieve mastery, which is step 4. By mastery I do not mean that you are the best, just that you are getting better. This feeling of making progress is the key to self-esteem and confidence, as well as motivation.

People with ADD often suffer from low self-esteem, lack of confidence, and little or no motivation. The best remedy for that is to lead them through these steps to mastery. It is on these islands of competence, as psychologist Robert Brooks calls them, that self-esteem, confidence, and motivation take root and grow.

As you gain mastery, other people notice and value what you're doing. This is step 5, recognition. Recognition not only consolidates the feelings of self-esteem and confidence that mastery engendered, it connects you to the people who have recognized you. This is the root of moral behavior.

People who steal, vandalize, or commit other immoral acts usually do so out of a feeling of being disconnected from the wider group. If you feel connected to a wider group you naturally do not want to do wrong by it because you feel a part of it. Kids with ADD often break rules, and even laws, and develop what we call a conduct disorder, or, when they grow up, an antisocial personality disorder. One of the best antidotes for this is to go through the five-step cycle, and end up feeling connected to a larger social group.

As you can see, these five steps naturally generate many of the qualities we so dearly hope people with ADD will develop: security, enthusiasm, a passion for some activity, discipline, confidence, self-esteem, motivation, and moral behavior.

This cycle will develop talents and strengths, as well as naturally provide the desire to achieve—without resorting to fear or nagging as motivational tools.

The most common mistake people make is to jump in at step 3 and demand practice. That may work in the short term, but over the long haul it usually peters out. You should put your most concerted efforts into steps 1 and 2. The rest will "flow."

CHAPTER 23

HOW TO FIND THE BURIED

TREASURE IN SCHOOL:

ONE SHINING EXAMPLE THAT

ALL SCHOOLS SHOULD FOLLOW

In the previous chapter I outlined a method for promoting lifelong joy that can be used by people of all ages whether they have ADD or not. But it is particularly important that children, and especially children who have ADD or other learning differences, connect, play, and find interests and strengths early on.

Far too often schools identify flaws and weaknesses but do not identify interests and strengths. In the schools that can afford to provide support services, the child who has ADD receives tutoring, organizational help, and various other forms of remediation, all of which can help. But if that is all she receives, the child can start to feel very early in life that she is a walking disorder, a defective person, who must dutifully give up fun time for remediation time. The cure can be worse than the disorder.

People build joyful, fulfilling lives not on remediated weaknesses but on developed strengths. However, when I propose to schools and even to parents that they devote more energy to identifying and promoting the interests and strengths children have, I usually receive comments about how nice that idea sounds but how impractical it is.

Of the many examples I could give to refute that sad and incorrect stance, let me offer the story of the Rye Neck Union Free School District in Mamaroneck, New York, where Peter Mustich is superintendent of schools.

A public-school system in an affluent area does not always equate with excellent education. In the case of Rye Neck the difference is not the affluence of the area, it is the wisdom, passion, persistence, and creativity of the professional learning community.

Fourteen hundred students attend kindergarten through twelfth grade. Four hundred are in the high school. One philosophy unites the entire system: *build on strengths* and include *every* child and adult in the community of learners. They have adopted education-expert Joseph Renzulli's school-wide enrichment model, or SEM, to fit their particular district's needs.

Before SEM, the school system had a program for "gifted" students. A student qualified for this program by scoring high on an IQ test and being well behaved. It was limited to about twenty kids in the elementary grades, the so-called G-kids, or gifted kids. Their very vocal parents jealously guarded the program against non-G intruders. When I asked Peter Mustich why he started the SEM program he told me it was because it was important to acknowledge the giftedness of every child, not just the designated twenty. He had to make a change.

At first, he just wanted to expand the number of G-kids. But the more he thought and read, especially the work of Joseph Renzulli, the more he believed in the giftedness of *all* children. So he determined to set up a program that would treat every student as a gifted child. The parents of the G-kids were resistant, but that did not deter Mustich.

He brought in Valerie Feit, a former ballet dancer who had "reinvented" herself through a master's in gifted education, to help develop the program. Far from lowering standards to include everyone, they raised standards, making the entire high school a Regents school, which meant students had to satisfy an even higher set of academic requirements. "We believed all the kids could do it," Mustich said. "We just had to figure out how, for each student."

Mustich and his team created a curriculum that aimed to make learning apply to real-life situations. They had observed that many students lost interest and motivation when the subjects lost relevance to the lives they lived. So the teachers learned to search for what each student was interested in, and propose projects accordingly. The teachers learned to differentiate their instruction based upon a student's needs and abilities, thus freeing the curriculum from a rigid, one-size-fits-all approach.

For example, a fifth-grader named Bernie was having trouble with both reading and writing. He was also quiet and introverted and was socially isolated and lonely. Normally, even in the best public and private schools, a student like Bernie would be referred for a neuro-psychological evaluation and then would be given tutoring and other support services in a resource room or in a one-on-one setting. If the school or parents had additional resources, they might pay for psychotherapy to work on the social problems.

But not at Rye Neck. Diane Santangelo, administrator for Special Services, referred Bernie to Valerie Feit for the purpose of identifying his strengths. Valerie tried to get to know him before doing anything else. As they chatted and Bernie began to feel comfortable, he started to open up and tell Valerie what he was interested in. One subject he mentioned was solar-powered automobiles. Upon learning this Valerie researched the topic and found a kit, which the school system bought and gave to Bernie. His project that semester became building a small solar-powered car from the kit—which he did. In the process he gained acclaim from his peers and teachers, and saw his lagging reading skills improve. Over a few months this shy boy nobody knew became a leader in the class.

Most schools follow procedures driven by lines like the one I was given by a superintendent of schools when I objected to the rigid approach his system was taking with a student who was a patient of mine. "This is how it says to do it in the policy manual," the superintendent said to me, "and you've got to have standard policies in any large school system. I don't expect you to understand that, but that's reality."

By rejecting the standard, bureaucratic model and instead building a proud, professional learning community, Mustich has proven that superintendent—and the thousands of others like him—to be dead wrong. By allowing Valerie to get to know Bernie, instead of subjecting him to a standard, one-size-fits-all, far more expensive evaluation, the Rye Neck school system could invest the money it saved in a therapy that really worked: a solar-car kit. I am not implying that a standard evaluation is useless, just that the decision of when to use it should be open to discussion among parents, administrators, and teachers.

Discussion among teachers is usually useful. A sixth-grader named Tom was in a project group but was refusing to do a project. His stance was that he found nothing interesting or anything worth doing. He rebuffed the efforts of different teachers to draw him out or suggest topics that might catch his eye.

The leader of the projects group decided simply to appoint Tom editor in chief of a newspaper, Tom's own newspaper. It was up to Tom to create it. Suddenly Tom came to life. He persuaded other students and teachers to write articles. He organized the whole project with little outside help. He made school-wide announcements over the loudspeaker when he needed more material or when he wanted to get some information. He actually succeeded in producing a newspaper.

Of course, it was a lucky stab appointing him editor in chief of a nonexistent newspaper, but I am sure the school would have found some other project if that one failed. They succeed with so many different and disparate students that even a skeptic might start to agree with their contention that all students are gifted.

A student named Henry had been tested as gifted in elementary school, but his grades started to slip as he got older. By eleventh grade he said to Valerie, "I used to be gifted." He had become socially isolated and felt empty at school. While he had loved school as a little boy, as a young man it held nothing but boredom and pain for him.

Enter Valerie. As she got to know Henry, she found out he was interested in making films, so she suggested he make one about eleventh grade. The projects budget gave him the little money he needed—he already had a camera and other supplies—and Henry set to work. Making the film became a central part of his eleventh-grade curriculum. Suddenly he got attention and began to regain self-respect. As he found that the school valued his talent, he started to value the school—again. And he found out that he was still gifted.

No matter what the age of a child, or the learning style or so-called disability, the first priority in this school system is to look for talents and strengths. If none can be found, they catalyze their development.

For example, a first-grader named Louis had dyslexia, and learning to read and write was a struggle for him. He was despondent. He did not have many outside interests, but he did like to talk. The school suggested that Louis's parents buy him a tape recorder and let him dictate stories. Within a month Louis had written a "book" that was five pages long. A first-grade novel. It is safe to say Louis may be on the best-seller list one day, thanks to the efforts of this innovative school.

About 10 percent of the students at the school are, like Louis, "disabled" in various ways. Some have physical disabilities, while the rest have various learning differences like dyslexia or ADD. Diane and her Special Services team have worked hard to foster collaborative relationships with the general-education staff, and as a result these children are mainstreamed as much as possible. They are all expected to take and pass the Regents exams.

This school celebrates progress and success. One highlight of the year is the Special Education Awards ceremony at the end of the year. Each child gets an award for some real achievement. One year I was privileged to be the guest speaker at this event. Each kid was genuinely proud and excited. Most ran to the stage to accept their awards—except the girl who had cerebral palsy and couldn't. But she beamed as bright as a lighthouse lamp when her name was called and walked to the stage to receive her award. These kids—and their teachers—are heroes of mine now.

Children who no one thought could pass not only pass but do well. The teachers say, "We say you can do this, we expect you to do it, now do it," and the students do it! This is not a punitive model, but proof of what high expectations coupled with an imaginative, flexible system can do. The school makes sure the students get the correct diagnoses and treatments that are based in solid research, but they then take the process several steps further, providing a sterling example of the effectiveness of the five-step model I outlined in the previous chapter. The school and I had not collaborated; we simply found each other prescribing the same program.

My first principle in working with all learners is to expel fear and shame from the learning environment. They do this in the Rye Neck schools at every turn. No one is embarrassed that he or she is different. Teachers buy into the notion that all kids are gifted—and the few teachers who don't are encouraged to explore other job opportunities. The faculty is proud of what they do, and they work hard to continue their own education. These educators believe in the possibility of a better future for their school. The entire school hums with a feeling of excitement. This is what education should be everywhere.

CHAPTER 24

MAJOR DANGER ALERT:

COLLEGE AND ADD

I have a friend whose son, Eric, has ADD. When Eric went off to college he felt he was on top of the world. At last, he could leave home, be on his own, do what he wanted to, escape his mother's supervising eye and his father's predictable advice, and begin his life as an adult. He loved his parents and his four siblings, but he had had enough of them. He loved his hometown, but he had had enough of it. And he had liked his high school well enough, but he had had way too much of it. The adventure of college loomed in his imagination the way Disney World had loomed when he was a little boy.

Eric had no idea what he wanted to major in, but he knew what he didn't want to major in: anything that required writing term papers and reading long books. He would stick with math, science, and computer courses, and see what else struck his fancy. He would live in a frat house and stay up as late as he wanted to. He hoped he would find a girlfriend soon, and he relished the idea of finally being able to have some privacy in his love life. College seemed like paradise.

When he came home for Christmas vacation he didn't know how to tell his parents what had happened in his first semester. Whenever they had called him during the fall he had told them everything was great—and in many ways it was. Much to his delight—and somewhat to his surprise—he had found a girlfriend right away. In fact, there were more girls interested in him than ever before. And his frat brothers were awesome. Really good guys, down-to-earth, fun-loving, not a jerk in the group. The drinking was heavy, but it never got out of hand. No *Animal House* antics. At least, not often.

All that was missing that semester was going to classes. Eric had gone to orientation and picked courses out of the course catalog. He actually went to classes the first week or two. But once pledging got started and he hooked up with that whole new world, it was hard to make it to every class. Pretty soon, it was hard to make it to any class. Some of his frat brothers got on him and told him he'd better be careful, but he laughed off their advice, figuring he could rely on the note-taking service and cram for exams. For now he could focus on his social education.

When his parents called early in the semester he told them about the courses he was taking and he told them how much he loved the college. He told them about the great friends he was making, about the several girlfriends he had, and he reassured his mother that if he ever had sex it would be safe sex—of course, she had asked. Little did his mother know that sex should have been the least of her worries.

When exams rolled around, and Eric thought of cramming, he kept putting off actually opening the books or looking at the notes. There was just too much else to do! He did manage to show up for the exams. But, as he left exam after exam, he knew what had happened. Bombs away.

The only question was how bad it would be. When he got home and his parents asked about his grades, he said he didn't know, he had to wait until a card came in the mail.

The card arrived two days after Christmas. Of course, his mother spotted it. Eric opened it in private. He took a deep breath, not quite believing what he saw. How could he explain this?

Eric's grade-point average after the first semester was 0.00. He had failed every course he had taken. Good parents, good family, good kid. None of that is guarantee that what happened to Eric won't happen to any student who has ADD when he goes off to college.

When he told his parents—and being the basically honest, good-natured person he was, he just walked into the living room and told them—they were, of course, flabbergasted. How could this be? Hadn't he told them whenever they'd called that everything was just great? Why had he lied? How could he have done this? Didn't he understand the consequences? What had gone wrong? How could this possibly have happened? How could the college have let it happen, let alone Eric? It seemed an impossible, freaky nightmare. But it was real.

Eric and his parents suffered for days, steeping in anger, guilt, fear, and despair, until, characteristically, they stopped all that and began to make constructive plans. Since they didn't know what to do, they sought help from people who did. Eric went back to college, but this time he had a plan that made sense. With advice from a specialist in ADD, supervision from a coach at college, and Herculean effort on Eric's part, he followed a daily routine and gradually pulled his 0.00 GPA up, even though those zeroes constantly pulled down on it like an Antaean anchor. He graduated with a GPA over 3, and is now a happy man. Married, with two little daughters, he holds a high-level job at Fidelity and is doing well. His nightmarish freshman year far behind him, he laughed when I reminded him of it and shook his head. "Can you believe that happened?" he asked me. "Yes, I sure can," I replied. "I see it happen all the time."

I offer his story here so that others don't have to learn what Eric and his family learned the hard way. If you don't have ADD, it is difficult enough to make the transition from home to a college or university. If you do have ADD, it is perilous far beyond what most people imagine. If you do not prepare in advance, the chances are good that you will stumble.

But if parents and the soon-to-be college student take some basic steps, they can drastically reduce the chances of a disaster like Eric's befalling them. Usually, no one warns parents—or prospective students—about the dangers of college in advance, nor proposes specific steps to avoid those dangers. All the effort goes into getting into college. Once the acceptance letter arrives, everyone heaves a sigh of relief. Months of work and worrying at last come to an end. Families pop open the champagne to toast the future college grad. But if as a parent or a student you are not careful, your worries may not be over; they may have just begun.

To avoid the dangers of college, information and preparation make all the difference. First of all, parents and teenagers alike should know in advance how *totally different* a college or university is from home.

The most glaring difference is that in most homes there is someone, like a mom or a dad, who deeply loves and checks up on the high school student every day. No one loves you at college, and not many people check up on you ever, let alone every day. At home, someone makes sure you don't watch TV or surf the Net all day and all night. Someone makes sure you get physical exercise. Someone makes sure you eat right and don't abuse drugs or alcohol (more or less). At most colleges, no one sees to any of this.

At home, many people care about you. Parents, siblings, extended family, friends, parents of friends, neighbors, teachers, coaches, and various others take notice when something is amiss and they speak up. For example, these people make sure that weeks do not go by during which a student does not attend school; they make sure that vast quantities of beer do not get consumed without anybody noticing; they make sure that personal hygiene does not totally disappear; and they make sure that emotional problems get taken seriously, even if they can't always be solved.

At most colleges and universities, little of this happens. Most have weak student-advising systems and even weaker systems for the delivery of mental-health care. The services that do exist provide crisis counseling, brief psychotherapy, and the dispensation of medication. A student who is not suicidal, not in crisis, not severely depressed, and not in need of medication but who "merely" feels lost, confused, unhappy, and is not making much of the college experience will not receive the support he needs until serious damage has been done, as in Eric's case and thousands of college students every year. The ones who make the headlines commit suicide—colleges and universities have seen a rash of suicides over the past decade—but the great majority do not do anything nearly that drastic. They do veer off course, stop taking good care of themselves, cease to get physical exercise, get into drugs and alcohol, have sexual experiences that upset or traumatize them, lose their excitement for life, fall under the influence of friends or even teachers who undermine their best intentions, and lose ground in life at a time when they should be gaining ground, building confidence, skills, friendships, and enthusiasm.

Parents and students should know in advance that going from home to college means going from a place of dependence and high supervision to a place of independence and low supervision. It is a jarring, albeit longed-for transition, one that students who have ADD are particularly ill-equipped to handle.

Parents and students ought to prepare for this transition methodically, instead of simply letting the student jump into the college environment literally overnight, hoping she can swim.

I remember wasting my freshman year of college. That I had ADD but didn't know it only made matters more difficult. I went from a boarding school where there were rules, structure, and a faculty who cared about me and watched over me to college, where there were few rules, little structure, and no faculty I could find to guide me. So I slept late, drank too much, skipped classes, played bridge late into the night, and changed from being the enthusiastic, engaged, achieving twelfth-grader I had been to a lackluster, underachieving, lost freshman in college.

Some people call this a rite of passage. I call it a waste of time—at best. At worst, this "rite of passage" leads to tragedy. Kids entering college, especially those who have ADD, are not prepared for the freedom they suddenly acquire. They are not ready for the abrupt withdrawal of adult supervision and guidance, as much as they say they want to be free of it. They are not prepared, overnight, to run their own lives. So, they regress. They create *Animal House*. Happily, most survive the experience and years later look back fondly on what fun they had.

But a closer look reveals many stories of serious setbacks, and some lost lives. In order to thrive, most students need more guidance than they receive at college. Without such help, they can make bad decisions.

What saved me were members of my family really pressing me on what I was doing, what my plans were, what I wanted to do after I left college, and how I was spending my time. Oddly enough, it wasn't my parents who did this for me, but a cousin named Josselyn, who was a few years older than I was, and her husband, Tom, an orthopedic surgeon. Josselyn wouldn't leave me alone, pestering me and pinning me down, forcing me to look at issues I wanted to avoid—like what I was going to do with the rest of my life.

I also found a teacher who helped me, William Alfred, a professor of English. All students were required to do an independent study in their field of concentration with a person the college called a tutor. The department assigned tutors to students, or a student could ask a specific faculty member if he would be willing to be his tutor. William Alfred was a beloved and revered professor. As an English major I was eligible for Alfred to be my tutor, but I didn't think I stood a chance of getting him. Josselyn kept on me to ask him anyway. So, after one of Alfred's great lectures, I went up to him and blurted out, like a smitten teen asking for a date, "Professor Alfred, would you be my tutor?"

"Oh, yes," he said. "Come by my house at five and we'll talk about it. Thirty-one Athens Street." And he breezed out of the lecture hall, his fedora cocked forward on his head. That man was to change my life.

I met with him one-on-one in his cozy den once a week for the next two years. I read more than a hundred plays under his guidance and discussed them with him. With his help, I wrote my undergraduate thesis on the religion of Samuel Johnson. I studied as hard as I ever have, trying to live up to the great privilege of studying English literature under this legendary professor.

Between the lines, Professor Alfred was teaching me life. Even though he was well acquainted with sadness, Alfred loved life, and he encouraged all his students to go at it full force, not holding anything back. When I considered going on to graduate school in English he quickly interjected, "Oh, no, don't do that. You'll end up hating literature." Unlike some professors, he didn't want me to follow his path. He wanted me to find my own. When I told him that I dreamed of becoming a doctor, he lit up. "Yes, a doctor! You would be a very good doctor. I will come to you in my old age!"

William Alfred and Josselyn and Tom provided exactly what I needed, what I had not found in my freshman year: structure, guidance, accountability, and inspiration.

Research done by Richard Light at Harvard shows that one of the key determinants of a successful undergraduate career at any college or university is the student's finding a senior faculty member she can make a close, mentoring relationship with. Doing this requires luck or boldness or both. Most undergraduates are intimidated by the senior faculty. They need encouragement—as I got from Josselyn—to approach these august figures.

Especially if a student has ADD, it is also important that someone at home—a parent, other relative, former coach, *someone*—remains closely involved, keeping tabs on what is going on at college day in and day out.

If a parent, or some other person, can remain involved, that greatly reduces the chance of a surprise like Eric's arriving in the mail over Christmas vacation. Since the colleges really do not act *in loco parentis,* in the place of parents, parents should not assume that the college will keep a close eye on their child.

Even if your child does not have ADD, I recommend that you begin during senior year of high school to prepare your child for the transition to college. If your child does have ADD this is crucial. Once your child gets to college, you should then assist him to organize and run his life. You should not stop supervising his life. Of course, you will not have the degree of close supervision you had at home. But you ought to have more contact than an occasional phone call.

Here are steps I suggest taking:

1. During senior year of high school, begin to talk with your child about what college will be like. As you visit colleges, anticipate what surprises the coming year will hold as you tour campuses, check out dormitories, look at dining facilities, and drive around the cities or towns. Not only can you anticipate the wonderful surprises of new friends, new courses, a new city, and treasured freedom, you should anticipate other, less welcomed developments. This is a natural time to begin to ask questions like, "Who will wake you up in the morning?"; "How will you get to breakfast?"; "Where are you going to do your laundry?"; "What are you going to do for spending money?"; "How much do you think you should set aside for books and clothes?" Your twelfth-grader may not welcome this line of questions, rebuffing you with comments like, "Oh, Mom, get off my back. I'll handle it on my own!" The problem is, if he has ADD, he probably won't—at least not without planning and preparation.

2. Now you need to bring the discussion out of the realm of nagging

and into the realm of realistic planning. Reassure him that you are not going to go to college with him. He *will* be on his own, far more than he has ever been before. But ask him to reflect on how much he depends on you for such necessities as laundry, wake-up calls, and money. You are simply offering to help him plan how to live life without you. (Ouch!)

3. Once you establish yourself not as a nag but as an assistant in organizational matters, you can begin to get down to specifics. Decide for yourselves what plans to set up, but whatever you agree upon, try it out at home in advance. Starting around February, begin to withdraw your daily supervision and support, in anticipation of life at college. Of course, don't do this without warning. Make it part of an organized, get-ready-for-college routine. Think of these last six or seven months at home as training camp for college, a time to get ready for freedom, to learn the practical skills required to live a much less supervised life responsibly and successfully. Practice everything from learning how to self-monitor bedtime to learning how to do laundry to learning the task of money management to learning how to seek medical help without Mom around to take your temperature and call the doctor. The closer college gets, the more prepared a student should become to live on her own—emotionally prepared as well as practically prepared. The last few months at home can serve as a critical time of training—as well as a time to relish being together. It is a time of emotional upheaval for student and parent alike. But it also ought to be a time of growth in the skills of self-sufficiency.

4. Use your imagination and experience to work with your son or daughter on developing strategies for the demands of daily life—without you. Address key areas like:
   - How to get up in the morning without Mom's wake-up service
   - How to get to bed at night without Mom to tell you to
   - How to continue to get physical exercise without the required sports schedule of high school (For example, taking a sport like tennis or squash, which can easily be planned into the week, or taking an intramural team sport. In general, trying to take exercise that requires him to show up for someone else, like a tennis partner or a soccer team. That way he will be less inclined to blow it off.)

- How to get enough sleep (log off the computer by midnight; don't get drunk; avoid caffeine after dinner; sleep in a bed; and other bits of applied common sense)
- How to do laundry
- How to set aside time for studying every day without Mom to tell you to
- How to eat a healthy diet (college students can do this!)
- How to make breakfast or know what to eat for breakfast if someone else makes it for you
- How to manage a checking account and credit cards
- How much discretionary money the student will have and where it will come from
- How to seek help when help is needed
- How to drink alcohol safely (limit yourself!)
- What about sex?
- How to apply for support services for ADD if the student needs them
- Where the office for support services is located at the college or university
- What to do when the student has ignored all these well-laid plans and feels too guilty to call for help (We'll call you! Just tell us the truth. There is no problem we can't solve as a team, but we have to know what the problem is to solve it.)

5. Once you know what college your child will attend, call and find out exactly what its requirements are to qualify for whatever accommodations your child needs, like untimed testing, a single room, or a language waiver. Often the requirements are stupefyingly complicated and difficult to obtain. Most colleges require, at the very least, a complete neuropsychological evaluation done within the past three years. You need to get started early in making an appointment with a neuropsychologist, as they tend to be overbooked, and in doing whatever else you need to do to satisfy the college's requirements. Don't wait until the last minute, assuming that because your child's high school allowed the needed accommodations the college automatically will. It probably won't. Some colleges and universities, like the University of Pennsylvania and the University of Arizona, have excellent support services for students with learning differences. But most do not. However,

you can turn any college into a good college for your child if you apply the suggestions in this chapter. In most cases, you do not need to send your child to a college or university that specializes in learning differences.

6. *Find someone who can serve as a coach for your child while he is in college.* This is crucial. By a coach I mean some person who can make friends with your child, get to know him, and then check in on him three or four times a week to assist him in planning and organization as well as in getting what he wants to get out of college. You will first need to have persuaded your child of the advantages of having such a person in his life. Then you can begin the task of finding the person. It could be a relative who lives near the college. It could be someone who works in the learning differences department at the college or at a local high school. It could be a graduate student at the university who wants a part-time job. You might put up a notice on bulletin boards around the campus advertising for a part-time assistant, since few people will know what the term "coach" means in this context. The coach does not have to have any special training. You and your child can explain the job. The coach should know something about the ins and outs of the university, but he need not have an advanced degree. The only essentials are that your child likes him and that he is reliable. You should pay the coach a reasonable fee, but certainly not the higher fee you would pay a tutor or a therapist. A good book to help the coach help your child is *ADD-Friendly Ways to Organize Your Life,* by Judith Kolberg (an expert on getting organized) and Kathleen Nadeau, Ph.D. (an expert on ADD).

7. If you need additional help in securing accommodations, finding a coach, or preparing for college in other ways, three good books on the subject are *ADD and the College Student,* edited by Patricia Quinn, M.D.; *Survival Guide for College Students with ADD,* by Kathleen Nadeau, Ph.D.; and *Coaching College Students with ADHD,* by Patricia Quinn, M.D., Nancy Ratey, and others.

8. Once college begins, stay in touch closely with your child and with the coach. You should have agreed in advance on how you are going to do this so there will be a minimum of conflict around it. If your child continues to resist the idea, use bribes. Do whatever

you need to do to establish permission for your supervision. The stakes are too high not to do this. I suggest regular phone calls and periodic visits. If this seems like too much, as if I am recommending that parents not let go of their children or that parents be intrusive and overly protective, that's because our custom is one of dangerous neglect. By following my suggestions you are helping your child, not encumbering him with assistance he doesn't need. As he becomes more and more independent and shows that he can handle the demands of daily life without you or the coach, you can pull back gradually. But don't expect to be able to do this for at least several months.

9. Make sure that through your efforts and the efforts of the coach, specific goals are being met. You can make your own list, but it ought to include the following:
   - Reasonable selection of courses
   - Regular attendance at class
   - Reasonable number of hours studying
   - Papers handed in on time
   - Decent amount of sleep
   - Exercise every day (very important!)
   - Healthy diet
   - Absence of alcohol or drug abuse
   - Development of friends

10. Encourage your child to look for a senior faculty member he finds inspiring and to try to make a close relationship with that person. Ask the coach to give advice on how to do this as well as encouragement. Such a mentor can help shape your child's life profoundly.

These steps, while not foolproof, will drastically reduce the chances of the disaster that befell Eric befalling your child, or of your child's wasting time, flirting with danger, as I did freshman year. Looking back, I shudder at what trouble I could have gotten into, at what bad decisions I could have made, decisions that would have haunted me for the rest of my life, had Josselyn and Tom not intervened and Professor Alfred not agreed to take me on. I lucked out. It is best not to rely on luck.

I am not suggesting that college shouldn't be a time for fun, nor am

I proposing that college students be goody-two-shoes. I am simply pointing out the real dangers of college for students who have ADD— as well as for other students. If these dangers can be avoided, a student can much better enjoy and make good use of the rambunctious, stimulating, formative years that college ought to be.

CHAPTER 25

NUTRITION AND ADD:

A CORNERSTONE OF GOOD TREATMENT

The most potent medication we have is also our most dangerous and abused drug. It is called food. Consumed properly, food can aid in the treatment of all diseases and prevent many of them from developing in the first place. But consumed improperly, food directly leads to our most common killers, like heart disease, diabetes, stroke, obesity, and high blood pressure—and it influences the course of ADD.

Food rarely comes up when we talk about the mind and brain, which is a mistake, because what you eat determines how effectively your brain operates. It is such an obvious point that it usually goes overlooked. The most common errors, like skipping breakfast or self-medicating with food, can sabotage the best of treatment plans.

If you do not eat properly, you can become distracted, impulsive, and restless, not to mention develop all sorts of other symptoms. You can look like you have ADD, even if you do not. Therefore, the treatment of ADD—as well as any effort to lead a healthy life— must now consider diet as an essential component of a proper regimen.

I offer here a guide, but also a sympathetic voice. Even though I have expert training, I often feel as confused as a novice when I try to sort out which advice about nutrition to follow and which to ignore. Let's dive in together in this chapter.

The whole field of nutrition and the brain is blossoming beautifully—but at times it is also exploding chaotically. So many experts make so many plausible, sometimes evidence-based recommendations that it is difficult to know which to follow. For example, when I wrote to a friend complaining of jet lag that I was suffering from, she sent me back an e-mail which I excerpt here:

> Drink lots of water on your next flight. And we must talk about your food allergies when you get home. Rotation diet really is important. The foods that are most often repeated in our diets are usually the bigger culprits. Limiting wheat and milk products to only once every four days is a good place to start. When you are allergic and stop consuming wheat each day, for instance, you actually don't feel great. Your need for dopamine from carbohydrates may be to blame. Also, Candida likes to have its sugars to eat and if denied them, dies. When dying, Candida gives off 97 different neurotoxins (I am told). So, you feel not so good to downright awful. If you take some carbohydrates or simple sugars, and then feel immediately better, you know you were experiencing Candida die-off. It is fierce for some folks. Still, gradually, you might think of moving in the direction of consuming only one item from each food family every four days.
>
> Some families: poultry and eggs, fish, beef, crustaceans, grasses (wheat and carrots), grains.
>
> Also, a little baking soda in water after a meal reduces the allergic reaction. Careful about blood pressure, though.

Whew! What am I to do with that? It would be easy if the woman who sent me the e-mail were a crackpot, but she isn't. Far from it. She runs a scientific company and she keeps up with all the latest developments. I trust her. But am I supposed to realign all my eating habits, and those of my family, based on this e-mail? Should I read a book about food allergies? I don't have the time. Should I just trust my friend? Or go see a specialist? Which specialist? These are the kinds of decisions we face every day, thanks to all the new knowledge that surrounds us. Not enough time has passed to test what we know, sort it out, and make general recommendations. But it might be a serious mistake to ignore it until we do.

Another friend told my wife, Sue, and me about a product she was taking, called Juice Plus+. When she told us she was also selling this product and was a distributor for it, I felt simultaneously obliged to buy it, since she is a good friend, and skeptical that it would prove to be valuable. What is valuable is recommended by our physicians, right? Since when do we get our medical needs met by door-to-door salespeople or friends?

Since now, it seems. In this Information Age, it is impossible for any doctor to keep up with everything that is known. It is hard enough for doctors to read all the journals in their own specialty. Increasingly, valuable advice can come from nonprofessionals who have taken the time to learn a lot about some product or technique that most physicians have not yet heard about.

As my friend told me about Juice Plus+, and answered all my skeptical questions, I got more and more interested. I called the company and managed to speak to one of the executives as well as one of the chief scientists there. Juice Plus+ is a capsule containing powder derived from the juice of fresh fruits and vegetables. Using a special method the company invented, the juice is reduced to a powder using low heat quickly. The scientist at the company told me that using low heat and doing it quickly are the keys to making sure that the powder provides almost the same nutrients as the juice itself would.

Since my family has a difficult time eating enough fruits and vegetables every day, we need help. Juice Plus+ makes up for what we miss, or so its makers claim, a claim that is backed up by some solid scientific research.

The product is rich in antioxidants, which are vital in reducing the toxic effect of free radicals on our systems. If the articles I have read are correct, taking this supplement will improve our immune function, reduce the risk of developing cancer, perhaps reduce the risk of Alzheimer's, and do other good things that the nutrients in juices do.

Am I crazy? Am I gullible? Should I just take what my doctor prescribes and scoff at all the rest as snake oil, proffered by good old American profiteers?

This is both the dilemma and the opportunity the Information Age creates. Obviously, in the case of Juice Plus+, Sue and I have come down on the side of believing in the product, even in the absence of an endorsement from the American Medical Association or the surgeon general. If you write to the company, they will send you a packet of articles from reputable journals that convinced me and might convince you too.

I also take a product called Reliv. Reliv is the brand name for a powder that you dissolve in water. It is a dietary supplement, rich in vitamins, minerals, and other "proprietary" ingredients. I am the only member of my family who takes this product. You may be laughing at me by now, wondering if there is anything on the market that I *don't* take.

I take Reliv because a woman approached me after a lecture I gave and told me about it. She was so convincing that I thought it was worth a try. Once again, I read the literature she gave me that supported its value, and it seemed to have merit. When I asked her about Juice Plus+, she told me that Reliv was better because it is dissolved in water, which allows it to be absorbed from the gastrointestinal tract better than capsules like Juice Plus+. Of course, I then called the people at Juice Plus+. They told me that their product was better than Reliv because it contained key ingredients, like antioxidants and phytonutrients, that Reliv didn't have.

How did Dr. Hallowell, an expert in his field, resolve this dilemma? I take both. If nothing else, I am sure I have the most expensive urine in the Boston area.

Of course, I also take omega-3 fatty acids—in the form of fish-oil gel caps—which I discuss in the next chapter, and Empowerplus, which I discuss in the chapter on bipolar disorder. I also take spirulina (blue-green algae), vitamin E, saw palmetto (for my prostate), Lipitor (for my previously elevated cholesterol, which is now in great shape), and hydrochlorthiazide (for my previously elevated blood pressure, which also is now in great shape). I used to take a multivitamin supplement, but there are more than enough vitamins in the supplements I have added and I don't want to overdose on vitamins. That can be highly toxic.

In addition, I exercise regularly, try to get enough sleep, and go to church every Sunday I can. I also keep up with my friends, have dinner with my family every night I am in town, and try to lead as connected a life as I can.

I offer all this embarrassing detail to share with you the blessing and the curse of the times we live in. We know so much, it is hard to know what to use and what to forget about, and how to sort out what has good evidence from what seems plausible but is unproven. I am sure of the value of some of what I do. I am convinced that family dinners, keeping up with friends, exercise, and going to church make me healthier.

As for the dietary supplements, I can't say for sure. Some people may scoff at my multiple ingestions, and I can understand their ridicule. On the other hand, I have been unusually healthy since I started this regimen in early 2003, as well as mentally more alert than ever. I have not had my usual colds and flu, my prostate has shrunk, and my PSA (prostate-specific antigen) has dropped.

What is the cause of my improvement? My Reliv lady says it is Reliv. The Juice Plus+ people say it is Juice Plus+. Barry Sears, whose company makes the omega-3 fatty acids I take, claims credit for his product. The folks at Truehope, who make Empowerplus, believe they have a hand in my doing better. I am sure the people who make the saw palmetto would take credit if I spoke to them. However, Professor Arnold, an authority in alternative or complementary treatments, told me that a placebo-controlled study has shown no benefit in taking saw palmetto.

The truth is, I don't know exactly what is happening with all that I ingest. If I weren't an adventurous soul, willing to try anything as long as it is safe and legal, I am sure I wouldn't have tried as many of the supplements as I have.

What I will suggest in the rest of this chapter includes some old advice and some new, but it is all well enough established for me to recommend as scientifically sound, and based on solid evidence, not mere speculation. As for the rotation diet, taking steps to counteract food allergies, trying Juice Plus+, Empowerplus, or Reliv, you can decide for yourself. I believe they all have merit, but I cannot recommend them as medically proven. Far from it. We will have to wait for more scientific studies to sort it all out for sure.

However, everyone should follow some proven bits of advice, like eating a balanced diet. Of course, the meaning of *balanced* is evolving the more we learn. It is safe to say now that no one should overeat carbohydrates, as it creates a heavy glycemic load, which in turn drives the release of insulin, which over time the body resists, developing insulin resistance, which leads to diabetes and other chronic disorders. Whenever you eat carbohydrates, be sure to eat some protein in an equal (and not very large) portion.

The role of supplements is evolving. One supplement that medical science has proven worthwhile is omega-3 fatty acids, which I discuss in the next chapter.

I owe the suggestions that follow to my consultation with a true scholar in the field of nutrition named Helen Rasmussen, senior research nutritionist at the Jean Meyer USDA Human Nutrition Research Center on Aging at Tufts University. She knows enough to avoid fads, but she is not resistant to new ideas. However, as with all supplements and medications, you should talk to your doctor to decide what is best for you.

1. Eat lots of vitamin C. I say *eat* because the vitamin C in pills is not as good as the vitamin C you get from eating fruits and other foods that contain vitamin C. Vitamin C helps modulate the synapse action of dopamine, a key neurotransmitter needed in treating ADD.
2. Make sure you get vitamin B-12 and folic acid, either in your diet or as a supplement. They improve cognition and help prevent cell death in the brain.
3. Both vitamin E and selenium improve brain function. Make sure you take in enough in your diet or take a daily supplement.
4. Some research suggests a possible correlation between low levels of zinc and high levels of magnesium and the symptoms of ADD. However, you should not add zinc or restrict magnesium without the supervision of a doctor. Adding or subtracting these indiscriminately from your diet could lead to dangerous problems.

5. You may consider taking a daily multivitamin supplement that contains vitamin C, vitamin B-12, folic acid, vitamin E, selenium, and others. But be careful not to overdose on the fat-soluble vitamins, which are A, D, E, and K. They can accumulate in your body and cause toxic damage. Make sure your doctor supervises what you are taking.

6. A safe way to address the issue of vitamins and minerals (like the aforementioned zinc and magnesium and fat-soluble vitamins) is simply to take a multivitamin every day that contains the recommended daily allowance of all the vitamins and minerals mentioned above, as well as all the others that humans need.

7. Recent findings suggest that blueberries and grape-seed extract are very good for the general health and for the brain. They are rich in antioxidants, and may help improve memory as well as prevent Alzheimer's.

8. Super blue-green algae may be even better than blueberries for cognition and memory. Actually, the blue-green algae in the ocean are the source of the omega-3 fatty acids in fish oil.

9. Drink lots of water. This is good for you in many different ways. Eight glasses a day is a good amount. As long as your kidneys are working well it is hard to drink too much water. However, old people sometimes do this, and it can be dangerous, as sodium levels can drop. So make sure your kidneys are working well.

10. Current evidence does not support the use of ginkgo biloba as a regular supplement, although it is in widespread use as a "brain enhancer" or "smart pill." It may cause blood dyscrasias. It can also increase the risk of stroke and interacts with Coumadin.

11. Take a daily supplement of omega-3 fatty acids (see next chapter for more detail).

12. Eat a balanced diet, of course. The meaning of *balanced* changes as we learn more. Omega-3's will soon be part of a balanced diet, as the food pyramid itself undergoes reconstruction. Most authorities recommend less starch and flour-based foods than they used to, and more fruits and vegetables. Protein ought to be included in every meal—especially breakfast—if possible. Avoid junk foods. Try to eat fresh foods, and avoid foods that come in boxes, bags, wrappers, packages, or tubes.

13. Beware of elimination diets unless you have an actual sensitivity to one or more food components, as a small minority do, as such diets can unbalance your metabolism. One of the most famous of the elimination diets was developed by Dr. Feingold for the treatment of hyperactivity and ADD. The Feingold diet eliminated all additives and refined sugars, which was harmless; but it also eliminated some foods, like berries, cherries, and grapes, which are nutritionally useful. The main problem with the Feingold diet, however, is that it is so difficult to follow.

14. Sometimes a food can actually treat a particular condition. For example, if you have a prostate problem or are concerned that you might develop one, it makes sense to eat lots of tomatoes; tomatoes are rich in lycopene, which is good for the prostate. To give another example, some people who suffer from macular degeneration are prescribed eggs laid by chickens who have been fed a diet rich in marigolds. These eggs are totally yellow, including the white. They are rich in lutein and vitamin B-12, which when ingested go to the eyes and help repair the problem. We don't know of a food specifically good for ADD as of yet. However, omega-3 fatty acids may prove to be more beneficial than we had thought. This is under investigation right now.

15. Avoid foods with ingredients you can't pronounce, those long words that usually end in *ite* or *ate*.

16. Avoid foods that contain trans-fatty acids. You can find them in peanut butter, candy, cakes, cookies, potato chips, Crisco, stick margarines, and many other foods. The trans-fatty acids are listed among the ingredients, usually under the phrase "partially hydrogenated vegetable oil." They will probably be outlawed by the FDA soon, but in the meantime, don't eat them. Trans-fatty acids act like saturated fats, only worse. They suppress good cholesterol and they accumulate in arteries.

17. Stay away from potato chips and other foods that contain any ingredient that begins with "partially hydrogenated." That can be a code term for trans-fatty acids.

18. Don't self-medicate with food. Avoid binging on carbohydrates.

Eating a pint of ice cream at midnight is not a good way to elevate your mood. Carbohydrates give you a squirt of dopamine, but there are other ways to do this: exercise, making love, meditation. You can do any of those at midnight instead of getting the ice cream fix.

CHAPTER 26

OMEGA-3 FATTY ACIDS:

A NUTRITION-BASED TREATMENT FOR ADD

The discovery of the importance of omega-3 fatty acids in our diet may be the most important discovery in nutrition in the past fifty years. Indeed, it may be one of the most important medical discoveries of our era. Omega-3 fatty acids may hold the key to preventing and treating such disparate and devastating diseases as diabetes, heart disease, Alzheimer's, depression, and cancer.

Most people are aware that starting in the 1950s the modern American diet began to drift away from whole foods toward processed foods and fast foods. Once the TV dinner (are you old enough to remember that?) became popular, it soon led to McDonald's and Burger King. No one waited for food. We bought what we could eat right away. Opting for convenience, we forgot about healthy diets.

Soon, doctors began to warn us that our unhealthy diets were contributing to if not causing the diseases that were killing us—most notably heart disease, high blood pressure, stroke, cancer, and diabetes. Nutrition began to find its way back onto the map.

Beyond recommending a balanced diet, doctors began to make use of the discoveries from the nutritional sciences and make more specific recommendations. Vitamins C and E became standard supplements. High-protein/low-fat diets came into fashion, followed by low-carbohydrate/high-protein diets.

Gradually, we started to take nutrition seriously and see food as the remarkable "drug" that it is, carrying with it enormous potential to make us well—or make us sick.

One of the most important specific recommendations doctors are starting to make today is to supplement the daily diet with omega-3 fatty acids. Most Americans do not eat nearly enough of these essential fatty acids. Current estimates are that the average American eats 125 milligrams of omega-3 fatty acids per day, only about 5 percent of what the average American ate a century ago. The consequences of such a deficiency in omega-3 fatty acids are dire.

Low levels of omega-3 fatty acids leads to chronic inflammation throughout the body, which in turn increases the risk of our most notorious diseases, from cancer to heart disease to diabetes. Correcting these low levels by taking a daily supplement of omega-3 fatty acids can reduce inflammation and so reduce the risk of these killers. When research determines the right dose for a given individual, and determines the best means of administering the supplement, omega-3 fatty acids may prove to be the next wonder drug.

But we know enough already to act now. Aside from the general health benefits of correcting an omega-3 fatty acid deficiency, we know that omega-3 fatty acids increase the levels of dopamine in the brain. Dopamine is the neurotransmitter that the medications we use to treat ADD also act to increase. Therefore, although not proven, it is logical to speculate that omega-3 fatty acids may provide a specific nutritional treatment for ADD.

There are various ways to add omega-3's to your diet. They can be found in certain fish, like wild salmon, sardines, and tuna, or in fish-oil supplements, as well as in flaxseed, flaxseed oil, and certain other plant sources. The reason we must ingest the omega-3's regularly is that we are unable to synthesize certain fatty acids, the omega-6 and omega-3 fatty acids, on our own—and they are essential for life, especially the life of the human brain. Most Western diets are rich in omega-6's, but low in omega-3's, leading to widespread deficiencies in omega-3's. This is creating a disaster in public health. "Our epidemic of heart disease and cancer may be the result of a fish oil deficiency so enormous that we fail to recognize it," said Dr. Evan Cameron from the Linus Pauling Institute.

Not only do we need omega-3's but the balance between the omega-6 and the omega-3 concentration in our systems is crucial. More specifically, the important balance is between one particular omega-6, arachidonic acid (AA), and one particular omega-3, eicosa-pentaenoic acid (EPA). Most people eat far more food containing omega-6 than omega-3, thus unbalancing the ratio. Soon, people will be able to get a standard blood test to measure their ratio of AA to EPA. It should be from 1.5:1 to 3:1. You can get the blood test now, but it is not readily available. To find out how to get it, go to Dr. Barry Sears's website, www.DrSears.com. You could then follow your blood levels and adjust your dosage of omega-3's accordingly.

However, if you do not get the blood test, it is safe to advise that a child take up to 2.5 grams per day of an omega-3 supplement like fish oil, and an adult take up to 5 grams per day, as long as the fish oil is free of toxins. You can buy fish oil at health-food stores or order it over the Internet. Make sure that what you get is pharmaceutical grade and free of contaminants. You can be sure that it is free of toxins by going to www.ifosprogram.com, an independent website that analyzes fish-oil products. (IFOS stands for International Fish Oil Standards.) The dosages I suggest may sound high, but keep in mind that one table-spoon of cod liver oil, Grandma's standard, contains 2.5 grams of omega-3 fatty acids.

Since we need research to validate this approach to treatment, I am in the process of doing a study at my center in Sudbury, Massachu-setts, in collaboration with Barry Sears on the effect of treating ADD with fish-oil supplementation. The early data shows that people with ADD are especially low in omega-3's. The outcome of the study should help us determine dosing guidelines based on monitoring blood levels of the essential fatty acids.

But even before the research is complete, because of the good chance that omega-3 fatty acids will help ADD, and because they are good for you in many other ways, I recommend that they become a daily dietary supplement for people who have ADD—as well as every-one else. Barry Sears has researched the effect of omega-3 fatty acids on health and written a guide to their use called *The Omega Zone Diet*. Dr. Andrew Stoll of MacLean Hospital and Harvard and his wife, Dr. Carol Locke, manufacture a brand of omega-3 called OmegaBrite, and it is available over the Internet at omegabrite.com. Stoll also wrote an excellent book about omega-3's called *The Omega-3 Connection*. Dr. Sears also sells his brand, and it is available at his website, www.Zonediet.com. I take Sears's fish-oil gel caps every day myself, and I recommend them to all my patients as well, while John takes OmegaBrite capsules and recommends that brand to his patients.

Although we do not yet have a study to prove that omega-3 supplementation will effectively treat the symptoms of ADD, there is good reason to believe that it will, based on the existing research literature on the use of omega-3 fatty acids in other neurological conditions—not to mention based on Grandma's common sense.

CHAPTER 27

PHYSICAL EXERCISE:

A GREAT TREATMENT FOR ADD

AND A MAGIC TONIC FOR YOUR BRAIN

I hate to floss my teeth. It's boring, it takes more time than I want to put into such an unsightly task, and it's difficult for me to do because my teeth sit very close together. When I asked my dentist if I could stop flossing he said, "Sure. From now on just floss the teeth you want to keep."

Physical exercise is sort of like flossing. It can be boring if you do it alone (I really cannot believe that some people *enjoy* swimming laps), it takes more time than most of us want to set aside for it, and it can be difficult to do, especially as we get older. I am fifty-four and had a total hip replacement due to arthritis last year. My old forms of exercise, squash and tennis, while not forbidden, are now restricted, so I have taken to riding an exercise bike and lifting weights. Boring, time-consuming, and difficult.

But it is one of the best gifts I can give myself. When patients ask me if they can stop exercising now that they are getting older, I reply, "Sure. Just exercise the parts of your body and brain you want to keep."

You do not have to become a bodybuilder to get the amount of exercise you need. Thirty minutes a day will suffice. And you don't have to go to a gym. Brisk walking will do the trick. Everyone should exercise. The only people for whom exercise is contraindicated are those who have anorexia. Not only is exercise good for people's health in general, it is good for the brain in particular, and specifically good for ADD.

The general health benefits are well known. Exercise improves cardiovascular health; it builds bone strength; it reduces bad cholesterol and elevates good cholesterol; it tones muscles and cuts away flab; it reduces the risk of developing adult-onset, or type 2, diabetes; it helps curb high blood pressure and lowers the risk of having a stroke; it bolsters immune function; and it helps build physical endurance.

The benefits exercise confers to the mind and brain are less well known, but they are extensively documented in the scientific literature. When a person exercises, she sets in motion a cascade of events that her brain loves. She sends more blood to her brain. With more blood comes more oxygen. Exercise also stimulates the release of a plethora of nutrients, hormones, chemical precursors of neurotransmitters, growth factors, and cleansing agents that bathe the brain in precisely what it needs to function at its best. Exercise also stimulates the production of brain-derived neurotropic factor (BDNF), which is important in stimulating the growth of new neurons. We think of exercise, therefore, as not only giving our hearts a good workout but also giving the brain an equally useful dose of nourishment as well as a cleansing bath.

You might think of BDNF as a mason arranging the bricks in the brain. Exercise calls out the mason. But even the best mason needs bricks. The bricks—the building blocks of brain cells which the mason will assemble—come from what you eat. More specifically, the building blocks for your brain come from omega-3 fatty acids, in which the average American diet is woefully low. Therefore, it is important to supplement the diet with omega-3 fatty acids to maximize the brain-building effects of exercise. (See the previous chapter for a discussion of how to do this.)

Regular exercise also acts as an antidepressant and an antianxiety agent. It protects against the development of dementia, including Alzheimer's. It enhances cognitive function—which is to say it makes you smarter. In an era of false claims, exercise is one of the true "smart pills" we have.

Especially important for those who have ADD, exercise also promotes mental focus, making it an excellent treatment for ADD. Regular exercise promotes sustained attention, the ability to stay alert and remain on task. Regular exercise builds mental endurance and reduces mental fatigue.

Not only does physical exercise provide preventive maintenance against ADD, it also is an excellent treatment in an ADD emergency—what I call a mental meltdown. Let's say you are paying your bills and you are starting to get spacey, or you are working on an important presentation and you are starting to daydream, or you are studying for an exam but you are starting to forget what you are reading. In all of these acute situations, exercise will help. Instead of going to the refrigerator or grabbing a cup of coffee, first try getting up from your chair and doing twenty-five jumping jacks or running up and down a flight of stairs a few times. A quick burst of exercise is like pushing the reset button on your brain. It totally changes your brain's chemistry and leaves you feeling refreshed and focused.

Children and adults alike who have ADD should think of physical exercise as a mainstay of their treatment program. Parents should make sure that holding a child in from recess or sitting in a detention period is not part of their child's school's discipline regimen. If a child must pay a penalty, let it be in doing something physically active and useful, like raking leaves or running errands. Parents should also make sure that a child is not denied sports because of poor academic performance. This would be like being denied academics because of poor performance in sports. Sports and academics are both essential for proper development. A student may be denied extra time in sports due to poor academics, but all students should be allowed their minimal daily requirement of sports and exercise.

Adults should have a minimum daily requirement as well. Of course, employers and others in authority do not hold adults in from recess or give them detention periods. Instead we adults hold ourselves in from recess and force detention upon ourselves. We don't schedule exercise, which is like an adult form of recess, into our daily routine. And we force ourselves to waste time sitting in pointless meetings or lectures, in what amounts to adult detention periods, when we could be out getting the exercise that we so desperately need.

The message is clear, simple, and strong. To treat ADD, to maintain optimal brain function, and to maintain good physical health, all people should get regular physical exercise.

Of course, you don't have to bother exercising any part of your body or brain you don't want to keep.

CHAPTER 28

POWERFUL EXERCISES FOR THE

BRAIN THAT IMPROVE ATTENTION

E xercising your brain keeps it young and fit, much as exercising your body keeps your body fit. Of course, you can overdo mental exercise, just as you can overdo physical exercise; this leads to exhaustion, either mental or physical. But as a general principle of mental hygiene, stretching your brain every day is an excellent way to stave off the mental ravages of aging.

Mental exercise can be quite specific. Just as physical exercise can target specific muscle groups, mental exercise can target specific mental activities. The following exercises were designed to improve attention and organizational abilities. They were developed by experts on physical training in Russia, where there is a great tradition of emphasizing the mental contributions to physical well-being. The exercises were given to me by Simon Zaltsman, a physical trainer I work with. Simon grew up in Russia, where he became a world-class athlete, and emigrated to the United States as an adult. As a trainer, he stresses that the most significant limits we have are the mental limits we impose on ourselves. If I ever tell him that I can't do a certain exercise, he smiles and says in his rich Russian accent, "Do it. You can. You'll see." If I persist, I always end up being able to do the exercise.

These exercises will challenge you. Don't be surprised if you get angry or frustrated and don't complete them the first time. But, as Simon tells me, you can do them! Just persist. If you try the exercises once a day, you should soon find that your attention span is lengthening and your ability to stay on task is growing stronger. Also, the quality of your focus should sharpen.

1. Position one blank sheet of paper to your right and another to your left; then take a pencil in each hand. Simultaneously, draw a vertical line on the right sheet and a circle on the left sheet. Repeat three times, alternating figures on the right and left sheets.
2. Draw a triangle on one sheet while drawing a square on the other. Then switch: draw the square on the first sheet and the triangle on the other.
3. Draw a circle on one sheet while drawing a triangle on the other. Switch figures and do it again.
4. Draw two circles on one sheet while drawing one square on the other. Then switch.
5. Draw two squares on one sheet while drawing one triangle on the other. Then switch.
6. Draw a triangle on one sheet while drawing a square on the other and also tracing a circle on the floor with one leg. Then switch hands (and switch to the other leg).
7. Draw a circle with one hand and a triangle with the other while tracing a square on the floor with one leg. Then switch all.
8. Draw a triangle with one hand and two squares with the other while tracing a circle on the floor with one leg. Then switch all.
9. Draw a triangle with one hand and a square with the other while tracing a circle on the floor with one leg and nodding your head twice forward and twice backward.
10. Draw a triangle with one hand and a square with the other while tracing a vertical line with the leg on the same side as the hand that is drawing the triangle, and a horizontal line with leg on the same side as the hand that is drawing the square. Then switch all.

These are extremely difficult, aren't they? But don't despair. Keep Simon's words in mind, and do as many as you can in ten to fifteen minutes. Just like when you go to the gym, the key is to keep at it. Gradually you will see results. Your attention will improve. In addition, it is likely that your organizational ability will improve as well as your ability to control your impulses. You may also see marked improvement in your coordination.

CHAPTER 29

CEREBELLAR STIMULATION:

A SPECIFIC KIND OF PHYSICAL EXERCISE

THAT CAN BE USED TO TREAT ADD

L et me tell you an amazing story about my son Jack.

Jack was born on May 12, 1992. He inherited from me ADD as well as my reading problems. In addition, Jack is immensely creative and possesses a certain unpredictable, often zany sense of humor. For example, one day when he was about ten, I asked Jack what he wanted to do when he grew up. Without a moment's hesitation he replied, "Breed chickens."

I have *no idea* where that response came from. But that is typical of Jack. He comes up with ideas out of nowhere all the time. One morning all five of us were asleep in a motel along the New Jersey Turnpike. We'd stopped there late the previous night and collapsed into bed, all five of us in two beds and a cot. Clothes littered the room. When dawn broke, Jack woke. He then woke me up and asked if he could turn on the television. I said no, it was too early, and I asked him to go back to sleep. Later I felt someone pushing on my shoulder. When I opened my eyes I saw Jack standing over me. "Look what I've made!" he proudly proclaimed.

When I looked up I saw a shadow stretching from the door clear across the room to a fixture on the window. As I looked more closely I could see that it was not a shadow but a rope made of the bits of clothing we had strewn across the floor. Jack had tied our clothes together and strung them from one end of the room to the other. "It's a clothes-line!" Jack announced with great pride and glee.

We undid the line, but I was proud of Jack's creation and did not get angry with him for having knotted and wrinkled our clothes. After all, whatever was powering his brain as he thought up and fashioned his "clothesline" was the same force that has led to all the inventions throughout history.

As much as I love the way Jack's mind works, and want to do all I can to promote his strengths, I have worried about one problem: Jack always hated to read. He loved to be read to. Although he learned how to read with no problem, he never liked it. And the more he had to read, the less he liked it.

For years, we would have battles in the evening, as by sixth grade Jack's school required that he read for at least thirty minutes every night. Getting him to do it could be an ordeal. Sometimes he would start to cry. I hated the idea that he would associate such pain with reading, but, on the other hand, Sue and I wanted to make sure he progressed in his education.

I turned to my dear friend Priscilla Vail for advice. Priscilla, who passed away in 2003, was one of the wisest people ever in the field of learning differences. She was a short woman with a heart that filled the world, a spunky critter (she loved words and would have loved that I called her a critter) who spread loving energy everywhere she went. Priscilla transformed what I had thought in medical school was a dull subject—learning difficulties—into one of my life's passions. She wrote the book that first got me interested in the field in the early 1980s, a classic book called *Smart Kids with School Problems*. She knew, before most people did, that kids with school problems often were the most talented kids of all. She devoted her life to helping them develop those talents.

Priscilla coined a term for smart kids with school problems, and it is one of the most apt diagnostic terms I know. She called them conundrum kids. Rather than sticking a label on them that sounded more precise—but really wasn't—she humbly allowed the mystery to remain, and then set about finding the talents embedded in the particular conundrum each child presented.

She succeeded gloriously. I recommend all her books for their wealth of practical suggestions, their clarity of prose, their verve, and their unalloyed hope. One of her best, *Emotion: The On/Off Switch for Learning*, states in the title alone a profound truth many parents and teachers forget, if they ever learned it.

So when I turned to Priscilla for help with Jack, I knew I was turning not only to one of the best in the field but also to someone whose heart—not just mind—I deeply trusted and loved. This is important. Experts are not that hard to find, particularly if you know where to look, but wise and loving experts are.

When I told Priscilla about Jack, she referred us to Dr. Lynn Meltzer, another leading expert whose office was near to us. Her team evaluated Jack and prescribed tutoring at her center in Lexington, Massachusetts. The tutoring worked. It helped Jack get better organized, write more fluently, and read more efficiently. But efficiency did not bring joy; Jack still hated to read.

The evaluation also identified Jack as having ADD. At Dr. Meltzer's suggestion we started Jack on Ritalin LA (a long-acting form of the stimulant medication Ritalin). The medication further improved his organizational abilities, his comprehension in reading, as well as his participation in class and his relationships with peers. As so often happens, once he could pay attention better, he could do just about everything else better.

However, he still hated to read. My heart sank when I saw how dismal Jack felt when asked to read. I have struggled all my life with my own reading problem. Like Jack, I love stories and words. I have been writing ever since I can remember, and making up phrases and epigrams in my mind. I majored in English in college and got top grades, but reading was always like driving on square wheels for me.

At the core of my struggle lurked a problem that I could see Jack was developing himself. While I loved stories and characters and essays and ideas, I labored at the process of getting anything off a page and into my mind. This problem has dogged me my whole life, and I prayed that Jack would not have to contend with it too. But there he was, plagued with the same square reading wheels that plagued me.

Not only was this upsetting to Sue, Jack, and me, it was puzzling. Why should this creative, highly verbal boy hate to read, even after he received the best treatments available, treatments that were not available for me when I was a child? We had taken the steps for Jack that should have solved his problem and rounded out his wheels. What else could we do? Maybe Jack was simply going to have to go through life like me, loving the content of books, but having to struggle to dig it out.

Then something happened that I now consider to be one of the luckiest moments in my life—and in Jack's. I met Wynford Dore, a British businessman-turned-learning-specialist. A woman who was helping him bring his new method to the United States brought him to meet me, to see if I thought his ideas made sense.

Along with his partner, Dr. Roy Rutherford, Dore came to visit me while I was on vacation with my family at a cottage on a lake in northwest Connecticut. There, on a sunny August morning, as the lake mirrored the sky and the kids splashed and swam, Dore and Rutherford explained their innovative, new method of treating ADD, dyslexia, and dyspraxia through cerebellar stimulation, and they told me of the outstanding results they'd been getting at their clinics in England.

I liked those two men, and I could see they believed strongly in what they were doing. Both Dore and Rutherford did the little things that make me trust someone: they were straightforward, they made eye contact, they didn't use a lot of big words, and they could laugh at themselves.

I listened carefully to what they said. They didn't know I was concerned about Jack. They just knew me as a person who was involved in treating ADD and learning problems.

They told me that the exercises they prescribed were simple, but that they did something specific that standard physical exercise does not do as vigorously. They specifically stimulated the cerebellum. If they did the exercises for ten minutes twice a day, in about six months to a year most people experienced major improvement. Not only did reading, organization, and attention improve, but confidence and self-esteem also grew. Withdrawn children became more outgoing. Quiet children began to speak up and participate in class. Clumsy children became better coordinated. Overall, children—as well as adults who did the exercises—grew to enjoy their lives more fully and make much better use of the talents they had.

The exercises included such activities as balancing on a wobble board, a flat board with a curved bottom; juggling; moving your eyes from side to side; standing on one leg; and a host of other exercises that draw upon the ability to balance, coordinate alternating movements, and perform actions that cross the midline of the brain and back again.

"What? You're telling me that if you do these exercise for ten minutes twice a day, you'll see improvement in reading problems as well as ADD? That sounds ridiculous! But I guess you've heard that before!" I said to Dore and Rutherford. They laughed and nodded, yes, they had.

As ridiculous as it sounded, I was intrigued. When we said goodbye, I told them I wanted to learn more, to visit their center, to read up, and to talk to other experts. After they left, I felt as if I might have just encountered something important.

I thought about what Dore and Rutherford had told me. I had heard for several years about the neglected importance of the cerebellum. And, as I began to explore, I learned that other people had devised methods similar to Dore's long ago. There was a doctor named Frank Belgau who developed the "Belgau balance board," which sounded just like the wobble board the Dore method employs. A group called the National Institute for Learning Disabilities had developed a method called rhythmic writing, in which the subject draws a figure eight on a chalkboard, crossing the midline of his body (and brain) in doing so, while responding orally to problems in arithmetic computation. I read about another program in which subjects were asked to walk on balance beams. All these programs were using techniques similar to the Dore method, but not exactly the same. But none of these methods had passed sufficient muster to be widely accepted. Perhaps Dore was simply rediscovering old, discarded ideas, ideas that were sometimes useful but not nearly as revolutionary as he hoped.

I soon discovered there was a panoply of techniques that stimulated the cerebellum and often led to improvements in cognition, mood, physical sensitivities, and coordination. While not a cure, they sometimes provided help in ways tutoring or medication did not. I began to see there really was an empirical base to what Dore and Rutherford had developed. I felt that I was getting on more solid ground—ground that others had trod upon before. But I also could see that these techniques were far from proven to be useful.

I learned about a program called the Brain Gym, which is based upon what its creators call educational kinesiology. The methods of

the Brain Gym—similar to, but not the same as, Dore's methods—
draw upon movement, balance, and sensory integration to enhance
learning as well as to treat specific disorders, like ADD. Using physical exercises to promote learning and emotional health, Brain Gym
has enjoyed some success. Many teachers and parents have told me
about it in glowing terms. But again, that is only anecdotal, not scientific evidence.

Using exercise and movement to help solve problems with reading,
problems with attention, or even emotional problems, which had
seemed like a radical if not nonsensical idea to me only a few months
before, was making more and more sense to me the more I looked
into it.

As I stressed in chapter 28, we have known for decades that physical exercise is good for the mind and the brain. It is an excellent treatment for ADD, depression, anxiety, and just about any mental ailment
you can think of except anorexia. But psychiatry has tended to segre-
gate physical exercise from mainstream treatments, which is a terrible
mistake.

Ironically, it is parents—and not we professionals—who have
started to bridge the gap. Out of love and desperation, parents learn
about *everything,* while we professionals tend to know and keep up
with only what our respective disciplines tell us we ought to know and
keep up with, what has passed the gold standard of the controlled, randomized, double-blind study.

But a parent is not constrained by the guidelines of a guild or
blinded by the zeal of a "true believer." A parent just wants to find help
for her child. The more I listened to parents, the more I was roaming
outside the usual boundaries of child psychiatry or child psychology in
my search for help for Jack.

Where was I? I was where the people who most desperately seek
help find themselves: looking everywhere, even outside the box, without a definitive guide, being given all sorts of conflicting opinions by
knowledgeable, dependable people. I was trying to stay open-minded
but skeptical, not wanting to get fooled, but not wanting to overlook
something that might help. And if I, an expert, felt confused, imagine
how someone with no special knowledge or training must feel!

My search next brought me *The Out-of-Sync Child* by Carol Stock

Kranowitz, a book I briefly mentioned in chapter 9. Based upon research done by Dr. A. Jean Ayres as well as Kranowitz's extensive experience and review of scientific literature, *The Out-of-Sync Child* gives a broad understanding of how movement relates to learning and emotion. It is an important book and an excellent one. Many people think of it as the bible for sensory integration disorder, or SI. The treatments it recommends are usually provided by occupational therapists.

There is some overlap in the symptoms of ADD and SI. If you go to see a child psychiatrist you would likely get diagnosed with ADD, while if you go to see an occupational therapist you would most likely get diagnosed with SI—even with the same set of symptoms. No one is right here. It depends on what lens you look through and what training you had.

By now I was swimming hard to stay afloat in all this new information. Since it was Wynford Dore who set me on this search, I decided to get more involved with him. I could easily do this because he had a branch office in Wellesley, Massachusetts, near where I live. I went and had myself evaluated, and found that, yes, indeed, I fit the profile of someone who had cerebellar problems. This was consistent with my ADD, as well as with my dislike of reading. But I went to the Dore center more to get a feel for how his operation worked rather than to learn about me. I liked the feel of it.

My next step was to ask Sue how she'd feel about sending Jack to the Dore center. She was skeptical at first, but when I told her of all that I'd learned and the good results Dore had been getting in England, and when I pointed out that there was a plausible theoretical basis for why the program worked, and when we both considered that we were already using all the standard treatments and that this new one could do no harm, we decided to give it a try. We had Jack evaluated, and he started doing the exercises at home each morning and evening.

The people at the clinic gave him a toggle board, a round board with a rounded bottom, as well as a notebook in which he was to record his daily exercises, and a bag of other paraphernalia, like beanbags, that were to be used in some of the exercises. Each day he would stand on the toggle board and try to balance himself; he would toss the beanbags in assigned ways; he would memorize short groups of letters and numbers; he would perform eye movements that were prescribed by directions in the notebook; and he would do an assortment of other exercises, all of which he actually enjoyed.

At the end of every ten-minute session he was supposed to record how difficult each exercise was. When he went back for his six-week checkup, the clinic would increase the level of difficulty based on how he had rated the exercises.

What happened? Jack now likes to read. Actually, that is an understatement. He loves to read. After doing ten minutes of exercises— exercises that he enjoyed doing—twice a day for six weeks his attitude about reading started to change. Three months into the program, he looked forward to reading at night. Now, if there are tears, they are tears he sheds at having to close his book and turn off the light.

Of course, you must bear in mind that this is only one case. From a scientific standpoint it is useless and proves absolutely nothing. However, it is true and, to my mind, amazing.

I can't explain what happened. The best I can figure is that Jack's hatred of reading stemmed from difficulty in keeping his eyes scanning smoothly across a line. This talent—which comes naturally to most people—does not come naturally to everyone. If you have trouble with eye-tracking, you will not enjoy reading. It will feel like you're reading while riding in a car that has square wheels. The words will jump around.

When I tried to pin Jack down as to what reading used to be like, he did describe what sounded a bit like problems with eye-tracking. Cerebellar stimulation could definitely help with that. Whatever the reason, I was elated that we had found a treatment that worked, and found it while Jack was still so young.

When I have time, I am going to go back and have the exercises prescribed for me. They tell me it is not too late for me to change. The oldest patient the Dore clinics have treated was an eighty-six-year-old woman. She had never been able to read or write. After six months of doing the exercises, she was reading. She said, "People say that life begins at forty. I feel that life began at eighty-six for me."

But the story poses many questions and doubts. I have spoken to world-renowned experts, experts whom I know and respect, who remain highly skeptical. When 60 Minutes did a segment explaining the good the Dore method can do, the International Dyslexia Society

(IDS), an extremely reputable and authoritative organization that for decades has been researching and treating dyslexia, issued a statement decrying the report, emphasizing that the Dore method is unproven by solid research. The IDS urged people to get the treatments that are tried and true, like the proper sort of tutoring, rather than risking their time and money on an unproven treatment.

I felt torn. On the one hand, I didn't want to foolishly fall for some treatment that was offering false hope. On the other hand, I saw Jack. His exercises worked where tutoring and medication had failed. But we are not stopping the tutoring or the medication, as each of those treatments is helping in its own way. However, the cerebellar exercises were able to help in a way that no other intervention had.

I realized I needed to learn more, as did the whole medical community. I knew how hard it is to get new ideas accepted, but I also knew how common it can be for desperate people to accept uncritically any treatment offered them.

I knew that the Dore method was not going to do any overt damage. But I wanted people to avoid covert damage, like spending money foolishly or neglecting standard treatments that were proven to work.

So I studied and learned and thought and talked. The one study that had been done and been published in a refereed journal—in *Dyslexia* in 2003—supported the validity of the Dore method. But to establish a treatment as effective requires many studies. And many studies take many years.

I felt that since the treatment was so safe it would be all right to tell other people about it, as long as I cautioned them that they should also get the proven treatments first. If those didn't work, or didn't work completely, then perhaps one might try the Dore approach in addition to, not instead of, the standard treatment.

The whole idea of gaining access to emotion and cognition through physical movement seemed strange to me at first, but the more I learned about it, the more sense it made. For example, often we think better when walking than when sitting down. Physical disciplines like yoga and tai chi lead to emotional and intellectual improvement. Dance has long been recognized as a useful form of psychotherapy— not to mention a way to access powerful feelings.

But why target the cerebellum? Because recent brain science is showing us how much more involved in global brain function the cerebellum is than we used to believe. Brain-scan studies have shown connections between parts of the cerebellum to the prefrontal lobes and other areas of the brain that govern what goes awry in ADD and dyslexia.

The more I read and learned, the more evidence I discovered supporting the importance of cerebellar stimulation in treating such conditions as dyslexia and ADD. I knew about Jack, but now I was finding a whole lot more. I reviewed once again the study that was published in the journal *Dyslexia* in 2003 by David Reynolds and others, entitled "Evaluation of an Exercise-Based Treatment for Children with Reading Difficulties." In this study, conducted by an independent, unbiased set of investigators, thirty-five children from a middle school in England who were screened by the Dyslexia Screening Test to be at risk for literacy difficulty were divided into two groups. One group did the cerebellar-stimulation exercises, while the other group did not. After six months, the group that did the exercises showed significantly greater improvement than the nonexercise group in dexterity, reading, verbal fluency, and semantic fluency. The exercise group also achieved significant improvements on the national standardized tests of reading, writing, and comprehension.

Soon after reviewing that study I met with Trevor Davies, the head of the school attended by the children in the study. A fifty-five-year-old man with thirty-four years in education, twenty-two of those as head of a school, Trevor is a highly respected authority in education. He is an inspector in what the British call the Office for Standards in Education. "In all of my career," Trevor said to me, "I have never seen anything that has had as massive an impact on children's ability to learn as this method, nothing that even approaches the impact on their learning or their ability to learn."

I asked him about the standard methods of treating reading problems, like developing phonological awareness. "They are successful," he replied. "They help children cope. They give them little strategies which they can use, but they don't get to the root cause, while the Dore program does. The tutoring programs don't have anywhere near the kind of impact on the many dimensions of a child's life that the cerebellar exercise program does. We've had fifty kids go through the program now, and all but two have had positive results."

He then offered me words of caution that reminded me of what

Nancy O'Brien's doctor had said to her way back in the 1970s, when he diagnosed her with ADD but warned her that no one would believe the diagnosis and also that other experts would call the treatment dangerous and faulty. Davies said to me, "I fear that other heads of schools will be afraid of using this for their pupils, afraid of their school being labeled as a school for slow children—even though our test scores have gone up amazingly. It will take a lot of work to break down the prejudices that exist right now."

After talking with Trevor Davies I believed more than ever that there was real merit to cerebellar stimulation. I also felt frustrated knowing how long it will take to produce the studies we need. Although I knew we needed a lot more research to evaluate this treatment, I had read enough and learned enough and seen enough to recommend that people give it a try, even before it became a standard treatment, validated by extensive research.

But I also wanted to promote the research. To help with that, I went to a school near my office and spoke to the head. It is a special school for kids who have learning problems. The woman who runs it is a genius at finding the talents in all children, and she also has an open mind. When I told her about the program, she lit up with interest.

She now has seventeen students at her school doing the cerebellar exercises. They started in January 2004. In six months to a year, we will be able to evaluate their progress.

By now I was so involved in this effort that I wanted to tell the world about physical exercise and cerebellar stimulation. I became a consultant to the Dore clinics and was paid a fee to offer advice and help develop research. Therefore, I am biased. The more I see, the more a biased supporter of this kind of treatment I become. I see it now as a potentially powerful adjunct to standard treatment for people of all ages.

To learn more, I went to England at the end of 2003 to visit the centers there. I wanted to talk firsthand to children and adults who had completed or nearly completed the program.

Many reported benefits at least as powerful as Jack's. Janice Coleman, a lovely British mom, told me about her son's experience. "When Simon was five and six, he picked up math easily, but he had trouble with reading. His school said he didn't have dyslexia, so he bumped along, until we took him to the Dyslexic Institute [a chain of private centers in England, similar in structure, if not in practice, to centers like Lindamood Bell or the Sylvan Learning Centers in the United States], where he was diagnosed with dyslexia and found to have an IQ of one hundred twenty. His reading, spelling, and comprehension were all one and a half years below grade level.

"Unfortunately, this was not bad enough for us to qualify for help at school, so we paid out of pocket for private tutoring for a year and a half [four thousand dollars per year], but made no progress. Simon learned good strategies, which he memorized, but he was unable to apply them. So he basically got nowhere. Actually, he lost ground. His confidence hit bottom. His teacher would make comments like, 'We've gone over this material already. Why don't you learn it?' Finally, when he was ten, the head of the school came up with a new idea. He suggested we try Dore.

"Although we agreed to try it, my husband was very skeptical. He said to me, 'There is more chance of a proven landing of an alien on this planet than there is of these exercises helping Simon.' And, in fact, at first Simon got worse. He became disruptive and couldn't concentrate at all. But, over time, we began to see positive changes. Gradually, he started to do better, and he gained a lot of confidence. He went from being a child you had to pull words out of to one who spoke up easily in class.

"After nine months," Janice went on, "tests of comprehension went from one and one half years behind to one and one half years ahead of grade level. His class rank out of one hundred twenty has climbed from one hundred ten to fifty. And when he got an A in English, his dad proclaimed, 'An alien just landed and we have proof!' "

I gathered many similar stories while I was in England. For instance, at the clinic in London, I interviewed Dawn Purdom, who is in charge there. She told me of a boy who had recently completed the program. "He used to walk around the perimeter of the playground during recess just picking up little sticks because he had no friends. Now, he just made the football [soccer] team, and he is in seventh heaven."

Next she told me of a woman who came for treatment because she was a poor reader and speller and had no confidence in herself. Now, six months after starting the exercises, she has quit her job, where she had been repeatedly harassed and taunted. She felt confident enough to look around for something she really wanted to do, and she just landed a position in the United States. She will be leaving next week to work for the man on whom they based the movie *The Horse Whisperer.* "Did you see it?" Dawn asked.

"Yes," I replied. "That will be a perfect job for someone with dyslexia. It's just great that she felt confident enough to go for it."

Dawn nodded and said, "Often people don't realize what a close connection there is between a person's confidence level and their academic challenges. But if you can't read or if you can't pay attention, you are always going to feel left out and your confidence is going to go down. You are going to withdraw and not want to speak up. A mother was in here the other day in tears telling me what it was like to watch her son sing in the Christmas service at school in front of a big crowd. Before he got treatment he wouldn't speak up at all, let alone sing solo in front of a crowd."

I asked Dawn about the problems she's seen with the treatment. "The biggest one," she told me, "is keeping the kids on the program. The positive changes are gradual. It usually takes six months to get the full advantage. Day to day, you tend not to see any improvement. When they come in here for their six-week checkup, and we do the assessments, we can see the changes, but that's because we're comparing them to how they were six weeks before. It takes a lot of encouraging to keep them doing the exercises day after day. Even though it is only ten minutes twice a day, that takes a pretty big commitment on the part of a child and the parents. The ones who do it are glad they did, but we lose some as well."

I could feel Dawn's dedication to this work. I asked why she felt so committed. "Because I see the good it does," came her instant response. "One boy we treated was staying awake as long as he could into the night, not wanting to fall asleep. His mother would find him lying in bed fully awake at three or four in the morning. She asked him why he was having trouble sleeping, and he said he didn't know. Then, one night, he finally told her the truth. He wanted to be awake so he could have more waking hours at home. Since he was being bullied so badly at school, his time at home was the only time he was happy and he wanted to extend those hours as much as he could. After treatment here, he got a new best friend. That's why I love this work."

Of course, these stories are only anecdotal. The positive results people tell of may be due to extraneous factors, like the positive attention the subjects received in the six months of treatment. After all, there is only one study published in a refereed journal, the study in *Dyslexia,* and respected authorities have even criticized the design of that study. Obviously, we need more research. Several studies are under way.

There are grounds to speculate that the studies will validate this method. Until now, we have underestimated the importance of the cerebellum, so we have not often turned to it as a lever of therapy. A walnut-shaped clump of neurons situated at the back and base of the rest of the brain, the cerebellum has been an afterthought—literally— until now. But consider this: small as it is, the cerebellum is highly convoluted, winding in upon itself. If you spread it out flat, its surface area is the same as each half of the rest of the brain. Even more striking, the cerebellum contains 50 percent of the neurons in the entire brain, and receives one-half of the entire brain's blood supply. Why all that blood and all those nerves in that little walnut? Nature doesn't waste.

It must be that the cerebellum, so long thought merely to regulate repetitive movements and assist in balance, actually does much more. Two top researchers in neuroscience and major figures in their fields, James Bower and Lawrence Parsons, wrote a review article in the August 2003 issue of *Scientific American* in which they stated that "the cerebellum may play an important role in short-term memory, attention, impulse control, emotion, higher cognition, the ability to schedule and plan tasks, and possibly even in conditions such as schizophrenia and autism."

Stimulating the cerebellum, therefore, might lead to all sorts of positive changes in brain function, including improvement in reading and attention as well as coordination and movement.

Whether or not the Dore method of cerebellar stimulation will prove to be as good as it seems in its initial trials is an unanswered question. Further studies may conclude that it is no better than a brisk walk for the treatment of ADD. We must remain critical, even skeptical, until we have a full body of research to give us a definitive answer.

But Wynford Dore, Roy Rutherford, and their colleagues deserve credit for developing an innovative method of tapping into the untapped power of the cerebellum. How well it will stand up under scientific trials and scrutiny remains to be seen. I believe their method—

and the other methods based upon similar principles, like the Brain Gym and the Interactive Metronome—offer potentially worthwhile complementary treatments for ADD.

These treatments should be *offered* as part of a standard treatment program. While they do not have the proven track record of medication for ADD or tutoring for dyslexia, they have helped enough people for new patients to be able to be told about them by mainstream professionals. The professional can then offer the critical appraisal and cautions so the patient doesn't scrounge around without guidance looking for *something* that will work. The patient can then decide, in conjunction with the doctor rather than the Internet, whether or not to pursue any such complementary treatment.

Cerebellar stimulation can be done in conjunction with, not instead of, the standard treatments like medication or tutoring. We need to apply all the treatments that work—as long as they don't conflict with one another or become repetitive—in order to get the best results.

Cerebellar stimulation is a treatment that might help you or your child profoundly, perhaps getting to the root of the problem instead of merely treating the symptoms.

Whenever I see my son Jack happily reading a book, I feel glad I gave this treatment I had never heard of a chance. Of course, I can't say for sure cerebellar stimulation is what helped Jack. But I do know that it did no harm and that now he loves to read.

CHAPTER 30

TO TRY MEDICATION OR NOT:

SOME REASSURING GUIDELINES

By far, the decision patients who come to see me agonize over most once their ADD has been diagnosed is whether or not medication should be a part of their treatment. The decision is even more difficult when a parent must decide for a child.

My wife, Sue, and I went through this with the two of our three children who have ADD, so I know how it feels to be on the other side of the desk, so to speak. Even though I am a doctor and have expert knowledge about these medications and more than twenty years of clinical experience, I felt inexpert and inexperienced when I had to decide about the treatment for my own children. Sue and I had several conversations with each other and with various doctors before we decided to go ahead with medication. I am glad we did, as medication has enormously helped the two of my kids who have ADD. They would have suffered unnecessarily without it. Still, it was not an easy decision to make.

From a parent's standpoint, the decision is difficult partly because you are considering using a medication you know little about—and about which you may have heard some terrible things—to treat a condition you barely understand in someone you love more than life itself—your child. But the difficulty goes deeper than that. After all, the decision was difficult even for me, and I possess expert knowledge.

But from a medical standpoint, it is not a difficult decision. Stimulant medications, the main group of medications we prescribe to treat ADD, are as safe as penicillin or aspirin when they are used properly. First used in 1937, they have been around for more than sixty years, so we have extensive research data on them and decades of clinical experience. Furthermore, the most detailed, extensive study to date, a huge, multicenter study comparing different treatment plans for ADD, showed that medication is the single most effective treatment for ADD. That is not to say that there aren't other effective treatments, just that medication emerges as the single treatment proven to be most effective now. Medically speaking, these medications are safe and effective. That's good news.

However, a lot more than medical science goes into the decision a parent—or any individual—must make when it comes to taking medication, especially medication that influences how you think. We all have deep feelings about this, feelings that must be brought to the surface, expressed, and respected.

I urge you to sit down with your spouse or some other person who is close to you and discuss these feelings. But before you do so, make sure you get the medical facts. Speak to a doctor who knows the research on the medications used to treat ADD. Don't trust an Internet search. There is so much misinformation and biased information on the Net about stimulant medications that a nonexpert can't separate fact from fiction.

If you can't find a doctor who knows about these medications, call the nearest medical school to you and ask for the department of psychiatry. Someone there should be able to help you.

You can also turn to books. However, be careful. There are quite a few biased books on this topic, books masquerading as objective, but in fact packing an antimedication polemic. If you are already inclined not to use medication, which is how most parents feel, these books will simply reinforce that feeling.

The best book I know about medications used to treat children is by Dr. Timothy Wilens from Massachusetts General Hospital and Harvard Medical School. The book is called *Straight Talk About Psychiatric Medications for Kids*.

As you gather the facts and mull them over, I want to offer some basic principles and information to help you when you must make this difficult decision for yourself or for one of your children.

Most important, never forget that you are the one who has control. Do not take medication—of any kind—until you feel comfortable doing so. Talk about it, learn about it, think about it, sleep on it, do whatever you do when you face a difficult decision. But never go against your basic feelings or beliefs. Don't let anyone bully or pep-talk you into taking medication or giving it to one of your children. It can take weeks, months, even years, before you want to give medication a try. You may never want to give it a try. That's fine. That's much better than doing it against your will, or compelling your child to take it against his will.

If you do take a medication when you really don't want to, or if you compel your child to, the medication won't work as well, and you or your child won't take it for very long. In addition, you will feel angry inside, and you will resent the people who made you do something so personal against your wishes. Such an attitude makes for bad outcomes.

That said, let me reiterate the good news. The medications we use to treat ADD, primarily the stimulant medications like Adderall, Concerta, Ritalin, and Dexedrine, along with the nonstimulants Strattera and Wellbutrin, are *very* safe when they are properly used.

You must be sure you are seeing a doctor who has experience in treating ADD to make sure the medications will be prescribed properly. And then you must make sure that you, or your child, takes them properly, according to the directions given when prescribed.

Most of us share a particular fear about medications: we wonder what might be discovered later on about a given medication that we don't know now. There have been notorious medications—thalidomide a generation ago, and fen-phen more recently—that were approved for use, only to create disastrous side effects later on that had not been detected in the clinical trials.

But remember, stimulant medications have been in use in this country since 1937. Most people don't realize what a long track record we have with this specific category of medication. If this group of medications were going to create some kind of unforeseen problem, they probably would have done so by now. On the other hand, we do not have studies of people who have taken stimulant medication for many years, since we used to discontinue the drug during puberty, believing that ADD went away as you passed through those years. Now that we know that ADD often persists into adulthood, we may fear that some unforeseen side effect will develop from the long-term use of stimulant medications.

It remains to be seen if that will happen. It is unlikely, however, because we do have long-term experience with another potent stimulant, namely caffeine. Whatever side effects caffeine is going to create tend to happen right away. Of course, even with caffeine, some studies have suggested that long-term use is associated with the development of cancer in rats, and maybe in humans. The same has been said about Ritalin, Concerta, and the other stimulant medications. Whatever this risk might be, it is extraordinarily small.

Moreover, if you look at the side-effect profile of an over-the-counter medication most people consider to be the epitome of a safe medication, namely aspirin, you will see that its track record shows more dangers than that of stimulant medications. Thousands of people suffer strokes or gastrointestinal bleeding every year due to side effects of aspirin, and many of these people die or become permanently incapacitated. Hundreds of people commit suicide by overdosing on aspirin every year. And yet, we rightly consider aspirin a safe medication, an extremely valuable part of our pharmacopoeia.

There is no totally safe medication. Every time you take a pill or a potion you should do the following calculation: do the potential benefits of this medication outweigh the potential risks? You can pose the question in another way after you learn about the side effects of the medication by then asking: what are the "side effects" of *not* taking the medication?

That's what convinced Sue and me with our daughter. We knew that stimulant medication was safe, but still, we didn't want to give any medication to Lucy if we didn't need to. However, she was having real trouble keeping track of what was going on in her classroom, even though she attended an excellent school, had a great teacher, and was in a small class. Between the school's efforts and ours, everything that could be done had been done, short of medication. Sue and I decided that the damage done to Lucy by not knowing what was going on in the classroom much of the time far outweighed the small risk of giving her stimulant medication.

The reason I say "small risk" brings me to another point many people overlook. It is that all the effects of stimulant medication are immediately reversible by stopping the medication. Depending upon which stimulant medication you take, the effect of the medication lasts from four to twelve hours—then it's gone.

In other words, giving one of these medications is not like doing surgery. Surgery is irreversible. And yet, many people think of taking medication as an irreversible event. "What if it takes away my creativity?" many of my adult patients ask, for example.

"Well," I reply, "in that case your creativity will come back in a few hours." Whatever the medication does—good or bad—it will not last more than twelve hours. In a worst-case scenario, if it makes you so agitated that you become manic, that is treatable with other medications. This does not happen often, but it can happen, and if it does, there is a satisfactory and safe remedy.

There are other worst-case scenarios. You could, theoretically, have an allergic reaction to the medication, go into shock, and die. This can happen when you ingest anything for the first time, from a pill to a peanut. You could have a seizure. Stimulant medications have been known to lower the seizure threshold. The pill could somehow obstruct your airway, cause laryngospasm, and you could die from that. Any pill could do that. These are the reasons why most people rightly do not want to use medication unless they need to.

In the vast majority of cases in which stimulant medication is prescribed by a competent doctor, all the side effects can be controlled by reducing the dose or discontinuing the medication. The goal is to get target symptom relief with minimal side effects. By "minimal," I mean mild appetite suppression without weight loss, and sometimes a transient headache without blood pressure elevation or elevation of heart rate. If anything more severe occurs, I suggest lowering the dose or stopping the medication altogether. Then you can try another stimulant, or switch to one of the nonstimulants, either Strattera or Wellbutrin.

In addition to side effects, people understandably fear that since stimulants are a controlled substance, and since they can be sold on the street as a recreational drug, taking them might lead to an addiction or open the gateway to other drugs of abuse.

The medical facts here are also reassuring. Studies have shown that children who take stimulant medication have a *lower* rate of drug abuse than kids with ADD who do not take stimulant medication. Far from opening the gateway to drug abuse, stimulant medication helps close it.

However, the potential to abuse stimulant medication does exist. If you grind it up and snort it, you will get a buzz. If you want to sell it on the street, you can. This is not true of aspirin. In this sense, stimulant medication is more dangerous than aspirin. Accordingly, we must carefully educate those who take stimulant medication, and closely supervise its use.

You must weigh the pros and the cons and then decide. The risk/benefit analysis must always take into account the risk of not taking the medication, as you pursue nonmedication treatments. Right now, the clinical research supports a trial of medication if the diagnosis is ADD.

Just don't lurch into it. Learn about the research. Don't proceed until you feel comfortable. You must do some homework. Don't let fear or unwarranted bias make the decision for you.

If you do decide to go ahead, I want to caution you about one more problem. The greatest danger associated with stimulant medication relates to *how* it is prescribed. It is crucial to present this medication to a child or an adult with care. If the person—of any age—believes she is taking a "stupid pill," a "smart pill," or a "shut-up-and-be-quiet pill," then taking the medication will do great harm. The harm will not be physical but psychological.

I explain to kids and grown-ups alike that this medication is like wearing eyeglasses. It doesn't make you smarter, and it doesn't make you quiet. It just allows you to focus better on what's going on. That often results in your performing as if you were smarter, or behaving in a quieter, more organized way, just as eyeglasses can make you perform at a higher level and behave in a quieter, more organized way.

Finally, you should know, as a parent or as an adult considering taking medication, that there is no single treatment that has been shown to be as immediately and dramatically effective as medication in treating ADD, and that it is most effective when it is part of a comprehensive treatment plan that includes education, structure, lifestyle changes, coaching, and a focus on talents that need to be developed.

When used properly, one medication or another will help 80 to 90 percent of people who have ADD. That means that 10 to 20 percent will not benefit or will have to discontinue it due to side effects.

With all these facts in mind, you should be able to decide for yourself, or with your child. Remember, you are in control. Until you feel comfortable, do not take any medication. But if and when you do decide to go ahead, keep in mind that what you are doing is reversible if you don't like it, and has put up an excellent track record over the past sixty years.

CHAPTER 31

IF YOU CHOOSE TO TRY MEDICATION,

WHICH SHOULD YOU CHOOSE?

The goal in using medication to treat ADD is to reduce or eliminate the symptoms that bother you—so-called target symptoms—
while inducing no side effects. You should work with a doctor who
understands the subtleties of the medications so that you can achieve
this goal, or at least come close.

There are many medications and combinations of medications that
can help in treating ADD. If you are considering a trial of medication,
try not to think of doing so as a drastic, last-ditch intervention. These
medications are so safe and effective that the logical time to use them
is at the beginning of treatment, not later on, at a last-ditch, desperate
stage.

Think of medication as eyeglasses. You wouldn't try a year of squint-
ing or doing eye exercises before you tried eyeglasses. Why wait before
trying medication? If it doesn't work or if it causes side effects, you
simply stop it; if it does work, it will make every other aspect of treatment all the more effective.

Indeed, there is no single intervention in treating ADD that is as
immediately and dramatically effective as medication. However, as I
stressed in the previous chapter, that certainly does not mean you

must use medication. You should not until you feel comfortable doing so. However, the medical facts are on the side of giving it a try.

The two basic categories of medications we use to treat ADD in both children and adults are the stimulants and the nonstimulants. The bulk of the research has been done with the stimulants.

STIMULANT MEDICATION

People often wonder how a stimulant can help someone who has ADD. After all, people with ADD often seem *overly* stimulated. But the term stimulant is misleading. A good way to think of what a stimulant does is that it stimulates the brakes in the brain. It stimulates the inhibitory circuits. People with ADD tend to have trouble inhibiting incoming stimuli—hence they are distractible. And they have trouble inhibiting outgoing stimuli—hence they are impulsive and restless or hyperactive. Stimulant medication helps them curtail both distractibility as well as impulsivity and hyperactivity by stimulating their braking system, their inhibitory neurons. Like the brakes in a car, stimulant medications allow the brain to slow down enough to gain control.

When stimulants work—when any medication used to treat ADD works—they improve mental focus and bolster executive functions (e.g., planning, prioritizing, organizing). They sharpen mental focus the same way eyeglasses sharpen vision. With improved mental focus comes improved performance, greater patience, reduced irritability, better organization, more effective use of creativity, and a host of other benefits. If properly monitored, the side effects should be minimal.

Many patients are surprised that the medication for their ADD has a positive effect on their mood, their anxiety, and their aggression. Most of the time we warn patients we start on stimulants about how the medications might make them anxious or tense or prone to temper outbursts, but in fact the majority of people feel calmer, more relaxed, and less driven.

Anxiety and tenseness are tools we have evolved to help us prepare for danger. We are in a mild form of danger when we are not engaged, when we are not focused. We startle more quickly and more often and are generally more anxious when we lack focus, and stimulants help people to focus.

There are two basic categories of stimulants: those made from methylphenidate (known to most people by one of its trade names, Ritalin), and those made from amphetamine (known to most people by two of its trade names, Dexedrine and Adderall). We have a lot of research to document their effectiveness, and a great deal of clinical experience to guide us. If you are going to use medication to treat ADD, it therefore makes sense to start with a stimulant.

If one stimulant doesn't work, another one might. So, if you try a methylphenidate-based stimulant like Ritalin, Concerta, or Ritalin LA and it doesn't help, you might then try an amphetamine-based stimulant like Adderall with excellent results.

The most important difference among the various stimulants lies in how long they last. When we wrote *Driven to Distraction,* there were no good long-lasting stimulant medications. That meant you had to take a stimulant medication two or three or even four times a day. This posed major problems. First of all, it was difficult to remember to take the additional doses during the day. As one of my patients said to me, "How am I supposed to remember to take the medication that's supposed to help me remember to take the medication?"

Even more of a problem was how embarrassed many children felt having to go to the school nurse and line up to get their medication. Whether or not they should have felt embarrassed is another matter; the fact is that most did. Therefore, they didn't want to take the medication no matter how much it helped them.

A third problem related to how rapidly the medications could wear off. As the therapeutic effect dropped off, many people felt a sudden resurgence, or rebound, of their original symptoms. This rebounding was often worse than the problems that led the person to take medication in the first place.

One of the most significant advances in the treatment of ADD has been the development of effective, long-acting stimulant medications. The big revolution came with Concerta, which is an extended-release form of methylphenidate. Concerta operates with an innovative push-pump technology developed at MIT. Due to the mechanism of release of the drug, it can't be ground up and snorted, so it can't be abused in that way. As the capsule is swallowed, the outer shell of medication is released into the bloodstream, and then, over time, as moisture enters the capsule, a piston begins to push the medication out. Blood levels are maintained for eight to twelve hours, depending upon individual variability. (There is not much consistency among individuals in the world of psychopharmacology.)

After Concerta appeared, other long-acting stimulants came out: Ritalin LA (for long-acting, not Los Angeles), Adderall XR (for extended release), and Metadate.

Ritalin LA is similar to Concerta, but a greater proportion of the active ingredient, methylphenidate, is released immediately, thus providing an initial boost that many people with ADD need at the start of the day. This is called bimodal release, in which 50 percent of the active drug is released immediately, and the other 50 percent is released four to five hours later.

Ritalin LA uses a new technology called SODAS (spheroidal oral drug absorption system) to create a beaded formulation that cannot be ground up and abused. When crushed, the beads break into shards that are extremely painful to the nasal passages when inhaled. If you inhale it once, you will never inhale it again!

Furthermore, the beaded formulation affords an advantage that Concerta lacks: the capsule can be opened and the beads sprinkled on cereal or applesauce for children who can't swallow pills.

Adderall XR also is a beaded, bimodal release formulation with the same advantages as Ritalin LA. Choosing between the two is simply a matter of choosing between methylphenidate and amphetamine. Both work well, but for some people one works better than the other. The only way to find out which works best for a given person is to try each.

These long-acting stimulants dramatically improved what medication used to offer in the treatment of ADD. Now you could take one pill that would last all day. You didn't have to remember to take the pill that was supposed to remind you to take the pill. Now, if you were a child, you didn't have to go to the school nurse for medication. And now you could take a medication that did not create the jarring ups and downs that the short-acting medications did.

This last point is particularly important because one of the most upsetting aspects of having ADD is the inconsistency that plagues whomever has it. This is no minor point, as ups and downs of arousal, vigilance, attention, focus, and mood can make you ineffective and unreliable. People can't count on you, and you can't count on yourself. You can miss opportunities, lose faith in yourself, and gradually even lose your resolve to try. For instance, adults with ADD will often say that they do not attempt activities or take classes that require much consistency because they fear that they may not be able to do it.

But with long-acting medications, you can get what you seek: the even and balanced states of attention, vigilance, mood, and arousal. This allows you to feel that you will be the same you from hour to hour and day to day, that you are, as one of my patients put it, "a continuous flow of energy, not a random firing of arbitrary neurons." In that state, you can count on yourself to be essentially the same person throughout the day.

Rebound of original symptoms with longer-acting medications can still be a problem, but much less often and much less severely. It does not even compare to the rebound with the short-acting medications.

Pemoline (brand name, Cylert) is a medication that used to be widely prescribed for ADD and worked well. It is not a controlled substance, but it is a stimulant and has a track record comparable to the other stimulants, like methylphenidate and amphetamine. However, a few years ago the Food and Drug Administration became concerned about the possibility of liver toxicity associated with the use of Cylert. Experts debate whether this concern was justified, but once the FDA put out what is called a black box warning on Cylert, which one might think of as the FDA's equivalent of a hex sign, Cylert all but disappeared. It is still available, but it is rarely prescribed. Practically speaking, that is all right, as there are many other excellent alternatives.

NONSTIMULANT MEDICATIONS USED TO TREAT ADD

Many people simply do not want to take stimulant medication. If stimulants are not for you, you have excellent options.

Amantadine

Originally, amantadine was developed as an antiviral agent, but when a doctor gave it to a group of patients who had Parkinson's disease, the symptoms of the Parkinson's disease got better. Thus, serendipitously, it was discovered that amantadine is what pharmacologists call a dopamine agonist. That means amantadine stimulates the production of dopamine. Stimulating more dopamine helps alleviate the symptoms of Parkinson's disease.

More dopamine *also* helps alleviate the symptoms of ADD. But when doctors tried giving amantadine to people who had ADD, the side effects were so severe that the medication was abandoned by most doctors for use in ADD.

However, "most doctors" did not include William Singer, M.D., a pediatric neurologist at Harvard Medical School and the Center for Developmental Neurology in Wellesley, Massachusetts, or his colleague Dr. Roger Cohen, a neuropsychologist. Working with Cohen and a team of other clinicians, Singer developed a way of administering amantadine that avoided the side effects.

He found that the doses given previously had been too high. Using the liquid form of the medication, he was able to give doses as low as 25 mg. He would start a patient at 25 mg and then go up gradually, increasing the dose by 25 mg each week until he saw a therapeutic benefit.

He has now treated four hundred patients—all children—with amantadine and obtained excellent results. There are some distinct advantages amantadine has over stimulant medications as well as the other medications used to treat ADD. According to Singer:

- Amantadine produces a therapeutic effect that is smooth and even. It doesn't wear off the way stimulants do. It lasts twenty-four hours, as long as you take it every day.
- Amantadine helps with executive functioning. It helps people get started instead of procrastinating. It helps people get organized and manage time more effectively.
- Amantadine has absolutely no abuse potential.
- Amantadine is not a controlled substance. Therefore, unlike stimulant medications, which are controlled substances, amantadine can be called in by your doctor to the pharmacy, and your doctor can allow for refills without your having to get a new prescription.
- Amantadine has fewer side effects than the stimulant medica-

tions, as long as it is dosed properly. When it is given in the correct dose, there are almost always no side effects at all: no appetite suppression, no increase in blood pressure, no insomnia.

- Amantadine helps with symptoms related to sensory integration disorder, which often occur in people who have ADD.

You might wonder, if amantadine is this good, why isn't everyone prescribing it? That's because Singer and his colleagues are more interested in treating patients than in writing articles for medical journals. Singer has simply never gotten around to writing up his extensive, positive experience in prescribing amantadine for ADD.

But he is a totally credible witness. Dr. Singer has an outstanding reputation in the Boston area. I completely trust his anecdotal report. Perhaps our inclusion of his experience in this book will prompt a double-blind, randomized study of amantadine followed by a written report in the *New England Journal of Medicine*. If that happens, people should give credit to Bill Singer and his colleagues.

Bupropion

The atypical antidepressant bupropion goes by two trade names: Zyban and Wellbutrin. It is effective in helping people quit smoking or chewing tobacco and in curbing other addictions.

It can also be used to treat ADD, but its track record is not as good as that of the stimulants. However, when it does work, it is excellent. Think of it as a second- or third-choice medication. Side effects can include anxiety, tantrums, sleep difficulties, and, rarely, seizures.

Strattera

A new medication called Strattera came out from Lilly pharmaceuticals in the winter of 2003. A norepinephrine reuptake inhibitor, Strattera generated huge enthusiasm in its clinical trials prior to its being released due to its efficacy in treating ADD in both children and adults. Indeed, it is the only medication approved by the FDA for treating ADD in adults. Although we doctors routinely prescribe other medications, like Concerta and Adderall, for ADD in adults, those prescriptions are "off-label." While legal, they are not officially sanctioned by the FDA to be used in adults to treat ADD.

Strattera has certain advantages. It is not a controlled substance, so it is easier to prescribe than the stimulants, which are controlled substances and therefore carefully regulated and supervised by the Drug Enforcement Agency. When you go to the pharmacy to get a prescription filled for a controlled substance you may have to produce various forms of identification, report your address, and sign certain forms. In addition, you can get suspicious looks from other people, even pharmacists, which have made some people feel as if they were committing some kind of crime by getting their prescription filled. In addition, many doctors do not like to prescribe controlled substances because doing so can lead to questions and audits from regulatory agencies such as the DEA or the state Board of Registration and Discipline in Medicine. While it is certainly legal to prescribe controlled substances to treat ADD in children and adults, it can prove distressing for both patient and doctor.

Strattera has other advantages. Unlike the stimulants, its effect is smooth and even, and it lasts all day. Stattera is associated with an increase in dopamine activity in the pre-frontal cortex but not in the striatum or the nucleus accumbens. This means that, like the stimulants, it helps with executive functioning—decision-making, time management, and the like—but, unlike the stimulants, it has no abuse potential or any propensity to cause tics or muscle twitches. Also, it can be stopped abruptly without causing symptoms of withdrawal.

One problem with Strattera is that it takes much longer to reach a therapeutic dose than with the stimulants. Stimulants are the perfect ADD medication in that a person does not have to wait long for results! Not so with Strattera. Indeed, one reason people do not get good results with Strattera is that they increase the dose too quickly or do not go to a high enough level, ideally 1.2 to 1.5 milligrams per kilogram of body weight. According to Dr. Len Adler of New York University, who has had a great deal of experience in prescribing Strattera, a good dosing schedule is as follows: week one, 25 mg per day; weeks two and three, 50 mg per day; week four, 75 mg per day; week five, 100 mg per day. The dose can be increased in week six if the person's weight so indicates and if there have not been side effects or sufficient symptomatic improvement. The medication can be taken in one dose after breakfast.

Side effects may include nausea. Dr. Adler suggests ginger tea as a good antidote, and he finds that the nausea passes after a week or so. Strattera can also cause dry mouth. It is important to stay hydrated while on the medication, and also to have mints available. It can be sedating; if this is a problem the medication can be taken at bedtime. On the other hand, it can also cause insomnia in some people. It can suppress the appetite; therefore, it is important to maintain food intake so as not to lose weight. If insomnia and appetite suppression are both a problem, Dr. Adler recommends one-half tablet or 15 mg of Remeron at bedtime; this helps with sleep and also with appetite suppression. Finally, Strattera can sometimes cause urinary hesitancy as well as erectile dysfunction.

Hopes ran high when Strattera first appeared. We all hoped that this new medication would make the stimulants obsolete. However, that has not happened yet. In some instances, Strattera would be a first choice—for example, in an adult who has a propensity to abuse drugs or who has a tic disorder—and it is a medication to consider for all people who have ADD. As we learn how to prescribe Strattera more effectively and build up a bank of clinical experience, it may surpass the stimulants as a first choice, but for now it is still too new to be deemed the best.

Modafinil

Modafinil (trade name, Provigil) was developed and approved for the treatment of narcolepsy—a syndrome in which you fall asleep involuntarily—and other states of excessive fatigue. Some doctors see Provigil as a replacement for the stimulants. But we see it as a drug to be used in combination with other medications, usually not by itself.

It can help to smooth over periods when the main medication is not quite effective. Lasting eight to ten hours, it can help keep the level of arousal and vigilance steady. Many people for whom we have prescribed Provigil reported being calmer and less impulsive. It is also useful in treating addictions.

It appears to work on the histamine system in the brain. Histamine wakes up the brain. Most people have experienced the drowsiness caused by antihistamines they may have taken for colds. Provigil operates in the opposite direction; it is "prohistamine," hence it leads to alertness. By promoting histamine, it improves frontal-lobe function: decision-making, organization, time management, prioritizing, and the like; indeed, it has been shown to raise scores on tests of frontal function.

John Ratey describes Provigil as a "Zen drug," in that it allows a person to feel awake without the feeling of being pushed, revved, or directed to a certain task. That rushed feeling can be a drawback of the stimulants.

This may be because the stimulants act by increasing dopamine, especially in the limbic region of the brain. The subjective feelings of pressing toward a goal, striving, or seeking something seem to be mediated by dopamine, especially in the limbic system. (I say "seem to be" because we really don't know exactly what does what in the brain, yet.) While those striving, pumped-up feelings can be useful at times, at other times they can be stressful and disadvantageous. Provigil allows a person to feel alert and on top of things without that push that the stimulants sometimes exert.

Provigil works well in combination with the stimulants or Strattera, smoothing out the effects of both. An additional benefit is that for almost everyone Provigil has no side effects.

Clonidine and Guanfacine

Clonidine (trade name, Catapres) and Guanfacine (trade name, Tenex) are in the category of alpha-2 agonists; both were introduced as drugs for lowering blood pressure. Clonidine is the shorter-acting of the two. Sometimes it is used in low doses as a sleeping pill, because one of its side effects is sedation. It can also help to reduce the symptoms of hyperactivity. While some practitioners champion the use of clonidine, few studies have been done on the effectiveness of clonidine to treat ADD; it remains a second- or third-choice medication. Its best use may be as an adjunct to help reduce hyperactivity or induce sleep. It can also be used to treat aggression in children and adults.

Three cases of sudden death have been reported when clonidine was used in conjunction with Ritalin. Obviously, this is a combination to be avoided.

Tenex acts like clonidine, but it lasts longer, which is both good and bad. It may be too sedating over a longer period. For that reason, it is often used just at night, especially in combination with other medications to treat extreme hyperactivity or explosive behavior.

Beta-blockers

The beta-blockers—propranolol, nadolol, atenolol, and others—represent a relatively new class of medications introduced originally to lower blood pressure and improve cardiac function in general. Psychiatrists have adopted them because they are good medications for anxiety, tantrums, and rage. In the 1980s John Ratey did extensive research on using beta-blockers to treat chronic aggression and impulsivity. He also has pioneered their use in combination with the stimulants and antidepressants to treat impulsivity, tantrums, and anxiety, finding that the beta-blockers decrease feelings of inner tenseness, anger, and general body "noise," which often plagues people who have ADD.

Tricyclics

The tricyclic antidepressants, such as desipramine, nortriptyline, and amitriptyline were originally used to treat depression. They can be used to treat ADD, although their side effects take them to the bottom of the list of choices. When they first appeared several decades ago, they opened up a whole new realm of treating melancholy with medication. The very idea of doing that outraged certain experts and philosophers who believed that misery was best endured and talked through. Mercifully, that spartan point of view has lost out as depression took its rightful place among medical diseases amenable to medical therapies.

The tricyclics found other uses in medicine and psychiatry, including the treatment of bed-wetting, various headache syndromes, insomnia, and ADD. John Ratey pioneered the use of very low doses of tricyclics, especially desipramine, to treat ADD. John found that 10 mg of desipramine per day, as opposed to the usual therapeutic dose of 150 to 300 mg per day, could relieve the symptoms of ADD and not produce side effects.

Avoiding side effects is key, because the side effects of tricyclics can be extremely bothersome: dry mouth, constipation, skin eruptions, dizziness, urinary hesitation or retention, and drowsiness. Rarely, the tricyclics can also induce heart arrhythmias, which can lead to the worst of all "side effects," namely, death. For that reason, many doctors have abandoned the use of tricyclics except in low doses. But for someone who has ADD and also wets the bed, low-dose tricyclics can be the perfect choice. Just be sure to get an electrocardiogram (EKG) before starting the medication, and have your doctor monitor side effects carefully.

If you do take higher doses of tricyclics, it is also a good idea for your doctor to check blood levels of the medication to make sure the concentration does not rise too high.

In addition to the medications we have discussed, there are a host of medications that can be used to treat conditions that commonly co-exist with ADD.

For example, depression commonly accompanies ADD. I suggest treating the ADD with a stimulant first, before adding a medication for the depression, because often the depression lifts as the symptoms of ADD improve. Often the depression develops in reaction to the feelings of failure and frustration from untreated ADD.

However, sometimes a true, biologically based depression en-shrouds the symptoms of ADD. Stimulant medication makes the de-pression even worse, because now the person focuses only too well on how bad he thinks life is. This person needs an antidepressant with the stimulant medication. We suggest using one of the selective serotonin reuptake inhibitors (SSRIs), like Celexa, Zoloft, or Prozac. If you want to combine a stimulating effect with an antidepressant effect you can try Effexor XR. The XR stands for "extended release." Don't use regu-lar Effexor, as its side effects can be severe.

If anxiety complicates the picture, and the nonmedication ap-proaches to reducing anxiety don't help, then an SSRI might help here as well. Or one of the benzodiazepines, like clonazepam (Klonopin) might be useful.

If agitation, irritability, or euphoria raise the possibility of bi-polar disorder coexisting with ADD, a mood stabilizer or an atypical antipsychotic, rather than a stimulant, could be the first choice. The mood stabilizers—like Depakote, Tegretol, and lithium—or the atypi-cal antipsychotics—like Zyprexa, Risperdal, or Abilify—may work bet-ter than a stimulant if ADD and bipolar disorder coexist. On the other hand, you and your doctor may try using both a stimulant and an antipsychotic.

There is widespread fear about inducing a manic episode by using stimulants in a person who is trying medication for the first time. Research shows that this fear is exaggerated; however, one may still choose to start with a mood stabilizer or an atypical antipsychotic medication to avoid inducing mania.

CHAPTER 32

DON'T SPIN

I often compare the ADD mind to Niagara Falls, both wonders of gargantuan movement and energy. The trick to making use of the energy in Niagara Falls, and to doing well in life with ADD, is building a hydroelectric plant. You need to hook up the energy to some contraption that can turn it into a useful product.

When treatment begins, you are on your way to building that plant. Treating ADD may seem as difficult as building a hydroelectric plant—but it can be just as successful. You need to know some of the major pitfalls. This chapter and the next address two of the most common.

After an initial burst of improvement at the beginning of treatment of ADD, there is usually a leveling off. This may be followed by long, frustrating periods during which the person with ADD—or the entire family—feels stuck, as if they are simply spinning their wheels instead of making the kind of progress they should be making. Such spinning happens in people of all ages, but it is especially a problem in older adolescents and adults. With children, the natural forces of development, coupled with the influence of parents and school, usually prevail and the child progresses.

However, when the diagnosis is not made until late adolescence or adulthood, prolonged periods of going nowhere can stultify treatment. As one woman wrote to me, "I know you know this already, but there are some people who stubbornly resist help, who are caught in patterns too deeply rooted in the subconscious to be freed from. Sometimes I wonder if I am one of those. So don't bet your money on this horse. Remember, you can't save everyone, kid."

I call these periods of being stuck "spinning," based on an acronym, SPIN. The term sums up the usual causes of getting stuck:

S stands for shame.
P stands for pessimism and negativity.
I stands for isolation.
N stands for no creative, productive outlet.

Getting unstuck often depends on reversing the influence of some or all of the components of SPIN. You can do this with a therapist, a coach, a spouse, a support group, a friend, a pastor, a relative, or all of the above. Let me offer some suggestions on each element of SPIN.

Shame

The older you get, the more shame you are apt to feel if your ADD is undiagnosed. You feel ashamed of what a mess your pocketbook is always in. You feel ashamed of how late you usually are, no matter how hard you try not to be. You feel ashamed that you haven't made more use of the abilities you were born with.

The shame may penetrate to deeper levels. You may feel ashamed of your thoughts, desires, and predilections. You may feel that the only way you can be accepted is by putting on a mask, and that the real you is fundamentally flawed.

Such shame is toxic. It is also traumatic. It raises your stress-hormone levels and eventually corrodes your memory and executive functions. While your fifth-grade schoolteacher may have planted the roots of that shame, you are now the one who intensifies it. You imagine harsh judges everywhere, as if the world were swarming with strict fifth-grade schoolteachers. You project the harsh judgments you are making of yourself onto everyone you meet. Soon the world becomes like a huge set of judgmental eyes, looming down on you, and your only option is to hide.

With a therapist, with a friend, with a spouse—with someone, because it is all but impossible to do this alone—you need to talk through or "confess" what you take to be your sins. As you do this, you will discover that they are not nearly as bad in the eyes of others as they are in your eyes. It is all right that you have messes. People enjoy your unpredictable remarks, and those who don't can look elsewhere for friends. It is all right that you are late. Sure, it would be good to try to be on time, but as long as people know you are not just blowing them off, they can forgive lateness. If they can't, you don't need them as friends, either. How boring it would be if everyone were "normal." Where would Monty Python or Mel Brooks have come from? Remember, what is strange today becomes truth or art tomorrow.

Not only does shame hurt, it also is the chief cause of a huge problem in adults who have ADD, namely, the inability to feel good about their achievements. It is common for ADD adults to be all but impervious to positive remarks. Whatever they have legitimately achieved they feel must have been done by someone else, or by accident.

One of the main reasons adults with ADD can't take pleasure in their own successes and creations is, simply, shame. They feel too ashamed to feel good. They feel too defective to feel nourished. They feel it is practically *immoral* to feel proud of themselves. Healthy pride is such an alien emotion that they have to look back into the dim recesses of their childhoods to find the last time they felt proud of themselves, if they can find an instance even then.

Shame prevents you from allowing your best self to emerge. Shame gets in the way of every forward step you try to take. You call a business, and instead of asking to speak to the president or person in charge, you figure you're too small potatoes for them, so you speak to an underling who can do nothing for you. You apply for a job, but instead of making a strong case for what you can do for the company, you present a self-effacing persona that is charming but uninspiring. You go shopping for clothes and pick out outfits that allow you to recede into the background as much as possible. You shake hands, but have trouble making strong eye contact. You want to ask a question at a lecture, but you fear that your question is a stupid one. You have a bright idea, but you don't do anything with it because you figure it must not be that good if you thought of it. You do all the work on a project, then don't speak up when someone else gets credit for what you've done. When someone doesn't call you back, you assume it was because they found you lacking in some way. And on, and on.

Try as best as you can to override your feelings of shame. When you shake hands, make eye contact and give a strong handshake, even if you feel second-rate. When someone doesn't call you back, assume they're simply too busy and give them another call. If, indeed, they do find you lacking and reject you, don't internalize their judgment. Look elsewhere. You don't want someone who rejects you, anyway. And remember, rejection in one place is just the first step on the way to acceptance somewhere else, unless you let that first rejection stop you.

It is heartbreaking to watch an adult contribute wonderfully to the world, only to feel every day as if he hadn't. It is painful to watch an adult work hard and do much good, only to feel as if someone else had done it.

To allow the adult who has ADD to take deserved pleasure and pride in what he has done, he needs to detoxify the shame that has plagued him for years.

To detoxify his shame, he needs to engage in a deliberate, prolonged process. It will take some time. But it can and should be done. As long as he feels intense shame, he will never feel the kind of joy in life that he has every right to feel. He will stay stuck in a painful place. Instead, with someone else's help, he can work toward accepting and enjoying his true self.

If you struggle with this issue, you should try to get rid of the people in your life who disapprove of you or don't like or love you for who you are. Get rid of or avoid the people who are overly critical of you rather than accepting of you. Get rid of the harsh fifth-grade schoolteachers in your life—and within yourself.

Getting rid of that witch within you will be a lot easier if you get rid of the ones who surround you. Your shame has allowed them to stay. You have felt that's what you need—daily reprimands, daily belittlements, daily control. But that's the opposite of what you need. It's your shame that has let those people into your life. Your determination not to be ruled by shame any longer will send them away.

You need acceptance. You need people who see the best in you and want to help you develop that. As you surround yourself more and more with people who see more good in you than you see in yourself, the frightened, ashamed you will start to feel less afraid, less ashamed, and you will dare to feel proud, a little bit at a time.

Pessimism and Negativity

Pessimism and negative thinking create a roadblock that conscious intent can actually dislodge like a battering ram if properly aimed. Pessimism and negativity—which may be boulder-sized due to years of failure and frustration—block your growth at every turn. If every time you have a new idea or go to meet a new person or begin to play a game you feel, "Why bother? This won't work out well," you constantly reduce the chances that anything will work out well.

One remedy for pessimism is to achieve some successes, but in order to gain those successes you may need to overcome your pessimism. Sounds like a catch-22, doesn't it? But there is a way out of the catch-22. You can control what you think, to a certain degree. You need to work on dismantling your pessimism. That does not mean you should become a foolish, empty-headed Pollyanna. However, it does mean you should escape the embrace of Cassandra, the doomsayer inside of you.

Controlling what you think is the domain of what is currently called cognitive therapy. Aaron Beck and his student David Burns have written superb, practical manuals on how to break the shackles of negative thinking. Also, Martin Seligman describes a method for achieving optimism in his book *Learned Optimism*.

My favorite book on this topic for the ADD audience is *The Art of Living*, by the Roman philosopher Epictetus, as translated and put into a modern idiom by Sharon Lebell. One reason I like to recommend it to people who have ADD is that it is *short*—fewer than one hundred pages. Another reason is that it has stood the test of time, and then some. Epictetus lived more than two thousand years ago. He is the true father of cognitive therapy. His basic, guiding principle is that a person should determine what he can control and what he can't and then work on what he can control—similar to the serenity prayer used in Alcoholics Anonymous.

One element of life we can control, at least somewhat, is how we think. Epictetus began his life as a slave. Ordered around every day, poorly fed, beaten, and abused as a slave, he evolved a way of thinking that refused to intensify his suffering by adding to it with wretched thoughts. He was so persuasive in teaching others his methods that he was released from slavery and became renowned as a great philosopher. His words were written down by his students and compiled into one of the first and best "self-help" books ever, a book that was so useful in dealing with difficult situations that Roman soldiers often carried copies of it with them as they marched off into battle.

It worked for Roman soldiers, and it can work today. I highly recommend this slim volume if you suffer from excessive pessimism or persistently negative thinking.

Isolation

Isolation is often the by-product of shame, pessimism, and negativity. It intensifies the shame and negativity, and can lead to depression, toxic anxiety, drug and alcohol abuse, and generally poor performance in all aspects of life.

Staying connected with others is the most important lifeline any of us has. And yet, as naturally inclined to connect as most people with ADD are, their shame and negativity can grow so intense as to lead them to cut themselves off.

If you feel this happening to you, do all you can to counteract it. You may feel that all you want to do is hide. Try as hard as you can not to let yourself do that. Talk to a friend. Go see a therapist. Pick up the telephone and call someone you trust.

Isolation develops gradually, almost imperceptibly, and you justify it to yourself as it happens: "Those people are just a bunch of hypocrites"; "They don't really want me there"; "I'm too tired"; "I just want to stay at home and relax"; "I need my down time"; "My doctor told me to avoid stressful situations."

Of course, isolation is better than the company of nasty, disapproving, shame-inducing witches and warlocks. So, as you try to reconnect, do so judiciously. One friend makes for a good start. Have a regular lunch date. Or a weekly squash game!

No Creative, Productive Outlet

All of us do better when we are creatively and productively engaged in some activity. It doesn't have to be overtly creative, like writing a poem or painting a portrait. Almost any activity can become a productive outlet that you feel good about. Cooking a meal certainly can be. Even doing laundry can be.

How can doing laundry be fulfilling? By turning it into a form of play, by turning it into a game. Children show us how to do this all the time. My eight-year-old son, Tucker, turns his bath into a creative activity every time he takes one. He adds a few action figures and the game is on.

If you are willing to be a little silly and let yourself go, you can turn doing your laundry—or anything else, for that matter—into a playful, creative activity.

The more you can do that, the more likely the activity will turn into flow, a psychological term invented by the great pioneer of the psychology of happiness, Mihaly Csikszentmihalyi. Flow is the state of mind in which you lose awareness of time, of place, even of yourself, and you become one with what you're doing. In these states we are at our happiest as well as at our most effective.

The doorway to flow is play. You can play at *anything* you do. If you have ADD, play comes naturally to you. So do it!

Play is deep. Play changes the world. Play can turn the most mundane of tasks into an activity you lose yourself in. Play is not a silly, superficial activity. By play, I mean creative engagement with whatever it is you are doing. The opposite of play is doing exactly what you are told to do, which is the refuge of people who have attention surplus disorder. For people who have ADD, play should come easily. You just have to get shame, pessimism, and negativity out of the way and make sure you're not so isolated that you get too depressed to play.

To get out of SPIN, play. As you play, you will find something you like to play at over and over again. With any luck, it will have value to others. That is called a great career: some form of play that someone else is willing to pay you to do.

At its core, being stuck means not having a creative, productive outlet. If you hook up to a creative outlet you can't stay stuck. Oh, sure, you can get blocked. You can have periods of inactivity or frustration. But then you will start to fiddle around—to play—and you will dislodge the block.

Adults with ADD who stagnate after starting treatment need to find some creative outlet to get going again. Everyone does better with such outlets, but for people with ADD they are essential for a fulfilling life.

Once you find a creative outlet, or several, you will be much more able to hook up your waterfall to a hydroelectric plant. Don't say you can't find it. That's negativity speaking. Get with someone who believes in you, or listen to the part of yourself that believes in you. Brainstorm. Try this. Try that. You'll find your hydroelectric plant.

CHAPTER 33

AND DON'T SLIDE

If you have ADD, you can chart a fabulous course, have the ability you need to reach your goal, but trip over one obstacle after another as you try to get there. I pointed out one of the major obstacles, which I call SPIN, in the previous chapter. Now let me warn you about its cousin, SLIDE. If you can cease to SPIN and SLIDE, you will get to where you want to go.

When we wrote *Driven to Distraction* we didn't fully appreciate how arduous life with ADD can be, even with the best treatment and under ideal conditions. Many people who read *Driven to Distraction* felt disappointed that they didn't get the great results some of the people we profiled in that book got.

That's because we emphasized the beginning of treatment, the phase in which you usually see the most dramatic improvement, especially if a medication works. We hadn't followed enough adults long enough to realize that most of them encounter periods during which they get stuck, wheels spinning, or even slide backward.

If you slide back, don't despair. It does not mean that you're one of the unlucky ones or that there is no hope. All it means is that you are going through a normal and predictable period of difficulty. If you are in such a period, it is a good time to go back to the person who diagnosed you, or to seek help from some other specialist you trust.

You may be caught in the process of SLIDE. Here is what each letter stands for:

S stands for self-attack.
L stands for life-attack.
I stands for imagining the worst.
D stands for dread.
E stands for escape.

SLIDE-ing is common in the world of ADD (as well as elsewhere in life). Here's how it goes:

Self-Attack

Something bad happens. You feel disappointed and frustrated. For example, a proposal you make gets turned down, or someone you hoped to hear from doesn't call. What happens may even be trivial, like your hair not falling into place when you brush it.

Instead of taking the event in stride, you go nuts inside. You attack yourself. You call yourself all sorts of bad names, like incompetent, stupid, ugly, or a loser. This is self-attack. It makes a hissing sound in your soul.

Life-Attack

As you attack yourself, you seek relief by turning your rage outward onto life. This is life-attack. You take refuge in a gloomy place where you condemn life as a rotten state that is at best a mild form of torture.

Imagining the Worst

Collecting evidence for your condemnation of life, you summon into your imagination everything that has ever happened to you. This is the imagining the worst. You race through time, collecting every horror and misery you can find, as you fortify your belief in doom.

Dread

Your imagining the worst naturally leads you into a state of dread. You feel depleted, dejected, and defeated. Your usual spunky self has met its antiself and dissolved. You are now sliding into what John Bunyan so aptly named in *Pilgrim's Progress* "the slough of despond."

Escape

Once dread drops you down into the slough of despond, you feel such pain that you yearn to escape. You don't care how. Your search for escape leads you to bad decisions. You get drunk, you take drugs, you go to bed with someone you shouldn't, you make foolish business decisions, you say things you regret, you anger people you don't mean to, you turn on people who love you, you sabotage good friendships, you drive recklessly, you squander money—and you don't care. All you want to do is escape. But all you achieve is further sliding, deeper down into the slough of despond.

The trick to stopping the SLIDE is to intercept it at step 1 or step 2. You should try to stop the process before you hit step 3, imagining the worst, because people with ADD have powerful imaginations. This is one of our assets, except when we turn our imaginations against life and ourselves. Then imagination becomes an inner monster, hungry to feed on us and destroy all that supports us. Once imagination begins its feast, it is difficult to stop it before it wreaks a lot of damage.

Try to train yourself to recognize the trigger points in steps 1 and 2, the points when some negative stimulus leads you to react by attacking yourself or attacking life.

It usually happens in a blur, quickly. To slow it down you have to practice how in advance. You have to have deciphered the code beforehand, identified your usual triggers (standing on the scale? reading the newspaper? having a conversation with a certain poisonous person?), and rehearsed inside how you will counteract steps 1 and 2.

For example, if every time you talk to a certain "friend," you come away feeling demoralized, resentful, or envious, it would be best either to avoid that friend or to have a preset method of detoxifying yourself after you see that person (a few words about how nasty that person can be? a brisk walk? a phone call? shopping?). Or, if every time you make a presentation to a group you routinely fixate on the few negative reviews and then go into a tailspin imagining the worst, it would be best to have a preset method for preventing the tailspin (immediate reassurance from someone you trust? reminding yourself that this is just your crazy side coming out?).

Let me take you through a possible scenario to show you how you might do it. Let's say one of your triggers is stepping on your bathroom scale. One day you get on the scale and the number you see glaring up at you is higher than ever. You have about five seconds to take action before you hit step 3 and start to recklessly imagine the worst.

Your mind recoils in horror, you look down at your naked body and instantly fixate on an area you consider fat. You now *hate* that area—your thighs? your stomach?—and you hate yourself for allowing it to have grown to be what it is. *Now you've got to think fast.* Have a phrase on ready-alert to deal with this crisis. Or an image. Or an action.

Standing on the scale is, in fact, one of my triggers. I resort to a physical activity if I see a number I don't like. I start to furiously brush my teeth immediately. Sounds ineffective and innocuous, I know, but this buys me a few more seconds, as it focuses my mind, at least for an instant, on the toothbrush and the feeling of the vibrating bristles on my teeth and gums. Then I deliberately put the image of my kids into my mind, or some activity I am looking forward to, or something I have done well at lately. These images serve as kryptonite, repelling my monstrously rapacious imagination.

Oh, sure, I'll have some more painful pangs, and I'll resolve to eat less that day, and I will entertain a few lingering negative thoughts about my body, but the crisis of SLIDE has been averted.

You should make up your own kryptonite. Try this, try that. But it is best to be active, not passive, in these precarious moments.

Sometimes, the SLIDE will last for days, even weeks or months. If this happens, consult a specialist. Don't wait until you lose your job or lose your marriage or lose a friend. Don't fall into one of the greatest traps of all and say to yourself, "Well, I'm right. Life is awful."

Keep your kryptonite handy. Maybe it is religious belief. Maybe it is the image of someone you love or someone who loves you. Maybe it is the memory of the day your team won the championship, or maybe it is the hole in one you shot. Maybe it is a piece of music you can turn on, even in your mind if need be. Maybe it is a piece of literature, a part of a poem you can recite to yourself. Maybe it is a favorite store where you can go shopping, or a favorite friend you can call up.

Create your kryptonite in advance. Do it when you are feeling good. Then you can keep it available in your mind so that when you do start to SLIDE, you can stop.

CHAPTER 34

THE BIG STRUGGLE REVISITED:

ADD IN FAMILIES

S tephen, a twelfth-grader who has ADD, sits in my office. On the couch next to him sit his parents, and in a chair across the room sits his sister, Ellen, a junior in college. I am meeting with them for a follow-up session. I diagnosed Stephen with ADD six months ago, at the start of the school year. Since then, with the help of medication, he has done well in school, but he has not done well in getting along with his family. Actually, he would say that his family has not done well in getting along with him, and he would have a point. There is no good guy in what I call "the big struggle," just many people who feel hurt.

The big struggle develops in most families where there is ADD, with almost the same inevitability as tomorrow following today.

"What's our agenda?" I ask the assembled group. I always like to know what people are looking for at the outset of a family session.

"We need to bring some peace to this family," Mom says with a long sigh.

"We need a game plan," Dad adds. "Things just can't keep going as they're going."

"I'm away at college, so I don't know all the details," Ellen adds. "But I do know life is pretty crazy at home these days. Stephen is very unpredictable."

Stephen is slouched down into the most comfortable chair in the room, his hat turned around on his head and his legs stretched out, crossed at the ankles. He looks at me and in a monotone declares, "They are about to tell you what a rotten, irresponsible person I am. I could write the script. Do you really need me here? Why don't I just leave and let them all talk about me without having me here to listen?"

I can almost see Dad's tongue being bitten. Mom readjusts her glasses with thumb and forefinger of her right hand, raises her eyebrows, looks at Stephen, but, like her husband, suppresses her words.

Ellen, however, takes her brother's bait. "Stephen, don't be such a jerk. You may be able to push Mom and Dad around like a bully, but you can't do it to me. I don't know where the cute little brother I used to have has gone to. But I do know the one sitting over there is a royal pain in the butt."

Stephen raises a forefinger and makes a circular motion with it, taunting his sister. Ellen in turn shows him her middle finger, in a barely camouflaged version of the familiar vulgar gesture.

Suddenly Mom heaves a sob and reaches into her purse desperately. "There's a Kleenex right next to you on the table," I volunteer. Dad puts his arm around her and with his free hand takes one of her hands.

Ellen looks to them and says, "Don't let him do this to you."

"How can we stop him?" Dad asks, as Mom sobs.

"Well, I guess that's our agenda," I say. "What can be done to stop the struggle that's gripping your family?"

They all look at me, even Stephen. They think I have an answer to that question. I don't. There is no one answer.

I have many suggestions, and can offer various approaches that often work. We specialists in human nature must content ourselves with sidling up to problems, getting close to them without spooking them, and then hoping some suggestions we make will help. Over the years, we develop many approaches to problems—any one of which might work in a given situation. We are so far from having the great puzzle of life all figured out that the best of us remain humble. But we do learn from experience, and we do develop techniques worth writing about.

In the case of what I call the big struggle, you first need to recognize how common and understandable and unworthy of blame the big struggle is in families, especially in families where one or more members have ADD. Then you need to understand some of the psychology behind the big struggle. This helps you sidle up to it without spooking it. Finally—and most important—you need some practical approaches for dismantling it.

Since the big struggle develops in almost every family where there is ADD, if you are dealing with such a struggle in your family, don't feel alone or ashamed. It comes about as naturally as fire does if a lit match is put to kerosene.

Just look at the volatile, flammable mixture ADD brings into a family: enormous, sometimes uncontrollable energy; a love of high stimulation and conflict; poor impulse control; creativity; tenacity and stubbornness; a hatred of being told what to do; a maverick nature; a dislike of conformity and rules; difficulty in letting go of an argument, or any other kind of conflict; tremendous drive; and poor powers of self-observation. When you look at all those ingredients, it is a wonder families with ADD don't blow themselves to smithereens.

They sometimes come close. I was once awakened in the middle of the night by a telephone call from a mom who sounded aghast. "Dr. Hallowell? You must help!"

"How?" I said groggily, as I tried to place the terrified voice on the other end of the line.

"John has a baseball bat and he's chasing Tom around the house." Now I knew the family. John was the dad, a fortyish banker. Tom was the son, a teen with ADD.

"Tell John I said to put the bat down right now," I said, gathering my thoughts, hoping John's trust in me might carry some weight.

"Wait a minute, Dr. Hallowell. Oh, no, now Tom has picked up a hockey stick and he is chasing John. John did put the bat down, though."

"Tell Tom I said to put down the hockey stick. I am going to call 911 for you on my other phone. What is your address?"

She told me her address, then I heard her scream. "Louise!" I asked. "What is it? What happened?"

"The cat jumped onto my back and its claws dug in. Oh, that hurts!"

"Has Tom put down the hockey stick?"

"No. He is holding his father at bay by brandishing the hockey stick at him. They're both standing there, staring at each other, panting. What should I do?"

"Ask Tom if he'll speak to me on the telephone. I'll hold off calling the police for a minute. But you call right away if anything happens."

Tom got on the line. "He is so stupid. I hate him. I can't believe he is my father. I want to kill him."

"Hi, Tom. Listen, are you still holding that hockey stick?"

"Yes," he said.

"How can you hold the hockey stick and the telephone at the same time?" I asked.

"You know me. I can multitask," Tom replied.

Humor. I see hope. "You sure can," I said. "Do you think the hockey stick is helping the situation right now?"

"I want him to feel as bad as he makes me feel. He is such a loser."

"Does it help you when he makes you feel bad?" I asked.

"No," Tom replied glumly, picking up on my drift.

"Maybe there is a better way to solve this problem than with a hockey stick and a baseball bat?"

Tom grunted.

"Have you put down the stick?"

"Yeah."

"I'm glad to hear that. What do I say now, Tom? Help me here."

"Don't worry, Dr. Hallowell, I'll chill. I wasn't going to hurt him. He is just such a loser."

"And how about your dad? Is he sitting down?"

"My mother is sitting with him. She got him a glass of water. He looks wiped."

"I can imagine," I said. "Well, why don't you put your mom back on the line? Go to bed, okay?"

Louise got back on the phone. "Thanks," she said.

"We have to stop meeting like this," I said.

"I know," she said.

"Hockey sticks and baseball bats at three A.M. A second longer and I was calling 911. Do you think they're safe now?" I asked.

"Yes. But I'll call you if anything erupts, okay?"

"Oh, yes, for sure. And don't forget about 911."

That phone call—and many others like it that I have fielded over the years—epitomizes the big struggle run amok. Sometimes it gets worse. People get hurt. People go to hospitals or to jail.

Usually, it doesn't reach such crisis levels. Usually the conflict smolders, erupting in blazes now and then, but not burning down the house. Still, it does a lot of damage until it is doused.

If dousing it begins by recognizing how common it is and by appreciating how inevitable it is given the flammable elements of ADD, what's next?

I am a big advocate of preventive maintenance. The best way to prevent the big struggle from blazing out of control is to bolster what I call connectedness in your family. Connectedness is the word I use to refer to a feeling of belonging. It is a feeling that no matter what, you are welcomed, wanted, cared for, and loved. It is a feeling of being understood, even if not agreed with; of being respected, even if required to do things you don't want to do; of being valued for who you are, even if who you are is quite different from other members of the family.

You can bolster connectedness in many ways. Eating dinner together as a family on a regular basis bolsters connectedness. Reading aloud to your children bolsters connectedness. Going for walks together does too, or going to ball games, or eating popcorn together while watching a movie on TV, or staying up late into the night to hash out a problem (without the use of baseball bats or hockey sticks). Showing up for your kids' games or other special events bolsters connectedness. Requiring that your kids do certain chores bolsters connectedness. (It makes them feel that they contribute, even if they protest doing so.) Making sure your kids get to know your friends and making sure you get to know their friends bolsters connectedness and bridges generations.

As you start to think about it, you can develop your own list of ways to bolster connectedness in your family. If you want scores of practical suggestions, I refer you to two of my books: *Connect: 12 Vital Ties That Lengthen Your Life, Open Your Heart, and Deepen Your Soul* and *The Childhood Roots of Adult Happiness: Five Steps to Help Kids Create and Sustain Lifelong Joy.*

I can't overstate the value of connectedness. It is the key to emotional well-being. But by connectedness I do not mean enmeshment, the kind of sticky, stultifying overinvolvement that masquerades as connectedness. Enmeshment is as dangerous as disconnection. Members of a family need independence, privacy, and the freedom to make decisions on their own.

These days, however, disconnection is far more common than enmeshment. Both represent failures to connect properly. Establishing proper and healthy connectedness in a family is the top priority in preventing the big struggle from blazing out of control.

Caught up in a pattern of struggle with a young child, a parent will often ask me for advice on how to get her child to do what she wants him to. I always say that I will give advice on that, but first I offer the following suggestion: "Why don't you set aside twenty minutes of special time once a week, time when you and your child do exactly what he [or she] wants to, as long as it is safe and it is legal? Just twenty minutes. But during that time you take no phone calls, speak to no neighbors, run no errands, and take no bathroom breaks. You just spend the time with your child. And you let him know that this is going to happen every week from now on at the same time, barring disaster, and that if there is a disaster you will reschedule as soon as possible. Then keep your promise."

It is amazing how much good those twenty minutes a week can do. My friend, Dr. Peter Metz, taught me this technique. Peter is one of the most skilled child psychiatrists I have ever met. Ever since he suggested the twenty-minutes idea to me, I have seen remarkable results from parents who follow through. It bolsters connectedness in a major way. Just twenty minutes. And it goes far to reducing the risk of a big emotional blaze at home.

However, prevention is not enough. You need a method to deal with the conflicts when they occur. You need a method to deal with Stephen in my office, or Tom and John at home.

The best method I have found was developed by Ross Greene, a psychologist at Harvard and Massachusetts General Hospital.

Ross calls his method collaborative problem solving, or CPS. He and his associates train parents and professionals in this method at their institute in Boston, the CPS Institute.

His method is based on the idea that in the long run children (and adults) do better by learning how to negotiate than merely to obey.

The old, time-honored model of parenting stressed obedience. Children, like dogs, were trained to do what they were told, be seen but not heard, and behave politely at all times. As a parent, that sounds divine to me!

However, it did not produce the best results, especially with kids who had the symptoms of ADD. (Years ago no one was diagnosed with ADD, but just as many kids had the symptoms of it.) Children who did not obey—the difficult children, the slow children, the hyperactive children—received the time-honored treatment for disobedience. They received a beating. I am not referring to an occasional spanking. I am referring to severe beatings, administered daily. Beating upon beating produced obdurate, bitter, or broken children, soon to become marginal, miserable adults.

It is a part of human history we rarely speak of, the battering of children throughout the ages. I can think of nothing we humans have ever done that is more shameful and detestable than the sanctioned torture of children—and unequivocally, that's precisely what it was. The only grace that saves us, perhaps, is that people didn't know better. Indeed, they thought such beatings would produce actual *benefit*. They thought beatings would build character and instill discipline. They even invoked Scripture, using the name of God to justify the torture of children. They did it in schools. They did it at home. They—we humans—did it everywhere. Now it should end.

The obvious moral reasons aside, it should end because it doesn't work. It didn't work for centuries—people did it mainly to please themselves. Is that more than you are prepared to swallow—beating children pleased those who did it? And yet, it is true. Speak to a sleep-deprived parent who is frustrated by a screaming child or a teacher who has a class full of rude and obstreperous, unmotivated students and you will hear how pleasing it would feel to beat a child. When people beat them they gave in to their understandable temptation to exert their physical power over them.

But it did not help. All manner of data have shown that physical punishments don't help, and they open the door to abominable harm.

We need to find another way. We need to live up to the awesome responsibility given to us as parents, teachers, coaches, and others entrusted with the care of children. We need to control our primitive urges and employ our thinking brains to develop methods that work. We need to not give vent to our own frustration and take advantage of our temporarily superior strength.

We ought to approach the problem of children's disobedience and disruptive behavior with the same imagination, intellect, and patience that we use, say, to close a business deal, find a cure for cancer, or land on Mars. We shouldn't reserve for our children our least creative, least intelligent, and least controlled methods for solving problems. Any fool can stomp around the house, tyrannizing all who are smaller in size. We owe our children—and ourselves—a better way than that.

The "better ways" that you usually read about now encourage time-outs instead of beatings. That is a step in the right direction. However, time-outs alone are not enough.

You will also read about behavioral plans that involve rewards and consequences, sometimes point systems with chips, tokens, or coins. These work well for some families, but I, myself, find them to be impossible to stick to and hopelessly demoralizing. I couldn't monitor one of those programs for more than an hour, let alone months on end. Certainly if a parent has ADD, keeping track of points, rewards, and the rest of the elaborate system that is usually required is beyond absurd. It would be easier to learn Chinese than to follow such a plan.

Instead, I want a method I can use. Something that makes sense, is logical, and does not have to be memorized or rigged up like a three-masted schooner.

I developed such a method with my wife. We have always encouraged our children to negotiate because negotiating is a major life skill. I have always told my kids, "If you can talk me into letting you stay up all night, good for you. That skill will serve you well when you grow up." So far, they have not been able to talk me into it, but they have learned valuable skills in trying.

Of course, there are moments when negotiation won't fly. When it is in fact time to go to bed, we can't conduct a negotiation to extend bedtime. There are times when no negotiation is allowed, and when what Sue or I say goes. If what we say doesn't go, there will be a consequence (not a beating), such as a loss of TV time the next day.

Ross Greene took the method that Sue and I—and millions of other parents—had intuitively developed, refined it, gave it an understandable vocabulary, tested it, refined it some more, tested it some more, wrote about it, got feedback, refined it some more, and now presents it to the public in a comprehensive and practical way.

Instead of helping parents get better at making their children obey, Greene's method helps parents and children get better at solving problems together. What a huge advance this represents! As much as we might ruefully wish for an obedient automaton at times, most parents would prefer to teach skills of negotiation and problem solving over "skills" of blind obedience.

Greene suggests that parents divide points of conflict into three categories, or baskets. In basket A, you put those moments when you must demand obedience; for example, your child is running out into the street and you call him to come back. There is no room for negotiation. In basket B, you put those moments when you are willing to negotiate and explore possible options. And in basket C, you put those moments when you don't really care what happens, so you let the conflict drop altogether.

With imagination, intelligence, and patience, parents (and teachers, coaches, and others) can learn how to move most decisions and conflicts into basket B.

If you want to learn the technique, go to Ross Greene's book, *The Explosive Child*. Don't be put off by the title. The book is not just about explosive children but all children. The method is not geared to out-of-control families but all families.

If you look back at the examples I started this chapter with, you can see I applied a bit of Ross Greene's method of collaborative problem solving on the telephone with Louise and Tom. I used some of basket A, saying I was about to call 911 and asking Louise to tell John that I said put down the baseball bat, but most of what I did was from basket B.

I used humor as a means of getting into basket B with Tom, and then the process proceeded quite naturally.

It can be tougher than that. You might need to call 911. Doing that is not failing, it is protecting people. But the more you practice moving conflict from basket A to basket B as a family, the more you will develop a collaborative style, which, as I have stressed, is a major life skill in its own right.

And what about Stephen? What did I do with him and his family that day? I can't recall the exact script, but here's the gist of it:

Where we left off, Stephen, his parents, and his sister, Ellen, were looking at me for a response to my rhetorical question, "How can we undo the struggle that is gripping this family?"

No one replied. When it became clear that none of them was going to volunteer an idea, I offered some of my own. "I think you all have unintentionally conspired to create a drama. What none of you realizes, including you, Stephen, is how much Stephen loves drama and conflict. Conflict is so much more interesting than just getting along, taking out the rubbish, making your bed, and being polite. When you all rise to the bait, Stephen wakes up and becomes engaged. So, he keeps baiting the hook. That makes life so much more interesting. This love of conflict is one of the main reasons families struggle so much. It's fun!"

"It's not fun!" Louise lamented.

"I was using the word facetiously. But it is gripping, more gripping than harmony. Have you ever read a novel or watched a movie where everyone got along? Of course not. That would be boring! So, what you need to do as a family is find ways of staying engaged and interested in life without fighting with one another as a means of doing so!"

"And how might we do that?" Stephen inquired, as if out of a stupor.

"Well, there is a technique called collaborative problem solving," I replied. "Practicing it is interesting. It can be even more interesting than fighting. Instead of using defiance as a means of making life interesting and getting what you want, try thinking. Use the higher parts of your brain. The object of the game is to find solutions to conflicts that will leave everyone more or less satisfied."

"That sounds impossible," Dad countered. "If people could do that we'd have solved the problems in the Middle East and everywhere else."

"Good point," I admitted. "In some ways I actually believe the future of the world depends upon people learning this skill. But, that aside, you have to keep in mind that there are differences between your family and the people in the Middle East. For example, there are not as many of you."

"But my family is just as stubborn," Stephen said.

"Does accusing your family of being stubborn advance your cause?" I asked young Stephen.

"Depends what my cause is," he replied with a slight grin.

"You do get it, don't you, Stephen?" I proclaimed with delight. "You are exactly correct! If your cause is to perpetuate the big struggle, then accusing your family of being as stubborn as the warring factions in the Middle East does indeed advance your cause."

"But if his cause is to make peace, then it doesn't!" Ellen interjected. Middle fingers protruded now from Ellen and Stephen.

"This is hopeless," Louise said.

"It truly is not," I protested. "Families much, much more stuck than yours have learned how to switch from struggling to problem solving. Please, just give it a chance."

They did, and life improved. They still struggle, but not nearly as much as they used to. They can monitor themselves, and when the old pattern creeps back in they can see it and even laugh at it.

If you are struggling in your family, please don't give up hope. Try the approaches I have offered in this chapter, and if they don't help, see a good therapist. It is often difficult for families to help themselves without the aid of a professional who can act as coach and referee.

CHAPTER 35

LIVING THROUGH THE PAIN OF ADD

The feelings of futility I am about to describe need not plague a person who has ADD. If you get the right kind of help, your life will certainly improve. How much varies from person to person, but life with ADD can always get better. Never give up. There is *always* hope.

The dark side of ADD can lead you to feel absolutely hopeless, unable to find any seed of success despite trying as hard as you possibly can. You can feel stuck in a pointless Sisyphean struggle, doing your best to carry on, but gradually losing faith that you will ever make lasting progress. You don't want to burden your friends, so you keep your misery to yourself. You can't afford therapy, but you doubt it would help even if you could afford it, as you have tried it in the past and received no benefit, even though the therapist seemed to be a good one. You use every ounce of your energy to meet your responsibilities, but the piles of stuff that surround you keep growing as your ability to manage your life fails to keep pace with the demands that increase day by day.

Here's an e-mail I received that describes what I mean:

Dear Dr. Hallowell,

I am 39 years old. Recently divorced. The mother of 3 kids, ages 12 (w/ADD), 8, and 5. I stayed in an abusive marriage for

13 years, knowing this day would come if I ever left. Now chaos reigns. I'm drowning—sinking—buried and feeling hopeless. I cannot keep up with the demands of 3 kids . . . schoolwork, matching socks. What's for dinner? Did you sign my permission slip? I need a pencil. Checking accounts, yard work, and flat tires. The power bill was due when? My house is a disaster, my car is a mobile dumpster. My checking account has a negative balance, my gas was turned off last week, phone this week, and if I don't remember to pay the power bill by tomorrow, that will be next. My 12-year-old son just got his progress report . . . A, B, B, D, F, F. The other kids still don't have all their school supplies. We ate dinner tonight at 8:30pm—30 minutes AFTER my 5 year old should be in bed. The dirty dishes are still on the table. My driver's license is expired, so is my car insurance . . . and so is my tag. If I get all 3 kids to school on time in the morning, I feel like I'm doing well . . . and I'm exhausted when I drop them off at 8:00 a.m. I spend the time they're at school trying to decide what to do . . . but the list is so long . . . and I don't know where to start . . . so I do nothing. I am losing hope that I will ever be able to get my act together. And I'm realizing that I cannot take care of the kids . . . can't give them the life they need . . . not the way I am right now.

I was diagnosed with ADD about 6 years ago, by my son's behavioral pediatrician. I have tried to get help . . . the first physician I went to suggested diet pills—said they were easier to get and would do the same thing as ADD medication. I've tried a church counselor, and also a pastor, neither of whom could understand the depth of my problems. *"Just try harder. Make lists, put a key hook by the front door, and give yourself more time to get ready . . ."*

I am at the end of my rope. I have to find someone who really understands and knows how to help me, or I'll have to give the kids to their Dad. As bad as he is, he can give them a better life than I can right now. I have no insurance, and no money . . . what do I do?

Do you know where I can get help? I would travel anywhere, if it meant becoming the kind of Mom my kids deserve. Please, if you have any information that could help, let me know!

This woman, whom I will call Leslie, describes the dilemma of ADD so well. As is typical of people with ADD, her intelligence, creativity, and energy sparkle through the darkness of her desperate words. Even though she is hanging on by her fingernails, she can still find the strength to write a lengthy e-mail to me, she can still find the creativity to write it vividly, and she can still find the courage to keep trying.

But you can feel her desperation. Each day imposes a new ordeal. The people she turns to for help just don't get it. They offer reasonable advice, like putting a hook up next to the door for keys, making lists, and allowing more time to get ready. But they add the one phrase that shows how profoundly they misunderstand: *try harder.* Leslie is *already* trying as hard as she can. She is trying as hard as a dozen people could. The pastor who advised her to try harder wanted to help her and believed he was helping her, but in fact his advice cut her down, undermining her efforts even further. *I can't try any harder,* was all Leslie could think. *So does that mean there really is no hope?*

Day after day she tackles what may feel like an impossible task to the millions of adults who have ADD: meeting the everyday demands of everyday life. It is not laziness that makes these "simple" demands lead Leslie to despair; it is that, for Leslie, these demands seem insurmountable.

Like most adults who have ADD, Leslie is brave and tenacious. She also adores her children and does not want to give them back to her abusive ex-husband. So she squints, even though she can't see. She drives in heavy traffic, even though she can't truly focus. She pays bills she can't read, keeps track of schedules she can't follow, but tells others she's just fine, even though she walks into walls all the time.

In spite of her frustration, a voice somewhere deep within her says, *Don't give up. A better day will come.* Who knows where that voice comes from? Who knows how long it will last?

Some days, she can barely hear the voice. Some days she even thinks of suicide, but she puts the idea out of her mind because of her kids. So she's trapped. She has to live, but she can't live the way she knows she ought to, the way she wants to. She knows what she ought to do—put the hook up next to the door, make the lists, allow more time before she leaves, and a zillion other tricks that would help—but she *can't* do those things even though she knows they would make her life much easier.

Notice I say she can't. Why can't she invoke the Nike solution and *just do it*? The same reason fish can't fly.

That's why frustration and despair so often permeate life with ADD. Good people trying as hard as they possibly can but getting nowhere. Or getting somewhere, but only with colossal, unsustainable effort.

Proper treatment will help, but it never solves everything. Even with proper treatment, there usually remains a residue of frustration, an echo of despair.

Driven to Distraction gave some readers the impression that proper treatment always leads to miraculous improvement. Sometimes it does. And it will lead to some improvement for everyone. But, for most people, significant problems will persist. The problems simply become less damaging. Nonetheless, the dark side of ADD can crop up over and over again.

This is particularly true in adults because so much damage was done to them while they were growing up. It can also be true in children. Diagnosis and treatment help enormously, but they do not cure ADD. It is still difficult to get organized. Procrastination remains an exasperating problem. Inconsistency remains a problem. Moods can still veer toward the downcast, if not depressed, and confidence still lags.

These are parts of the dark side of ADD. As in all of life, no one has it made in the world of ADD. Everybody has problems, even after treatment has been going on for years.

The problems are, first of all, the same problems that have caused trouble all along. Whatever your brand of ADD might be, even after you get it diagnosed and treated, you will likely find that the symptoms still bother you, only less severely than before.

Beyond those issues, there are peculiarities to the dark side of ADD that defy reason, especially in adults. They derive from the residue that remains, even after the bowl has been scoured clean.

For those whose ADD was not diagnosed and treated until they became grown-ups, the magnetism of past experience keeps bringing them back to old habits and old states of mind, even if they have received the best treatment available. They are haunted by fears of failure, even if they have succeeded many times. They are still tormented by feelings of insecurity, even if they are objectively as secure as any human can be. They can't believe they have achieved what they've achieved, which means they can't fully own it, enjoy it, and feel nourished by it.

Of course, their life is not all bad. Many times, diagnosis and treatment leads to such improvement that the dark side seems minor or insignificant. And even when the dark side is still severe, the bright side can grow, thrive, and predominate.

But don't feel alone or ripped off if, even after diagnosis and treatment, you still struggle in your life, you still fight back gloomy states of mind, you backslide into old habits, or you persist in having trouble feeling good about who you are.

If there is such a thing as "the ADD condition," there certainly is this dark side to it, at least for most adults who have ADD. (Early diagnosis and treatment in children can spare the development of this dark side.) It is composed of pessimism, frustration, moments of despair, surges of self-contempt as well as baseless rage at others, unpredictability, lapses into addictive behaviors and substance abuse, ongoing struggles to get organized, feelings of being ineffectual and feckless no matter how successful the person becomes, and periods of being remote, cut off, and impossible to reach.

Dealing with this dark side is like dealing with your teeth and gums. You must work on it every day—brush and floss and rinse—but not be surprised if inflammation still sets in. I realize that this is a homely comparison, even vulgar. I intend it that way. It is best to approach this dark side in as practical and irreverent a way as possible.

All the tips and principles of treatment that have been mentioned in this book apply here. But a few deserve special emphasis:

1. Above all, make sure you have an ally—spouse, friend, doctor, therapist, hairdresser, anybody!—who knows you well enough to point out to you what's good about you and your life when you start to feel in the grip of what's bad. This is crucial. People with ADD typically lack the ability to reassure themselves. They quickly get overwhelmed by feelings of frustration, pessimism, and all the rest. They need some trusted ally, someone who really loves them for who they are, so they can turn to that person and get a shot of encouragement when they need it.

2. Don't be surprised when you get visits from what Winston Churchill called "the black dog." Expect that you will go through dark, depressed periods. Don't feel that all is lost when this happens. Just connect with someone else. Get help.

3. When it does happen—and it will—turn immediately to that trusted other. Don't isolate yourself. Short of killing yourself, isolating yourself is the greatest mistake you can possibly make. Instead, hook up with a person you like, a source of positive energy.

4. Make sure you have an ongoing relationship with a good doctor who can make adjustments to your treatment plan—medication, diet, supplements, and whatever else is germane—if dark periods persist.

5. Use physical exercise, play, fellowship, or creative work as your mood changers, not food, alcohol, or some other potentially harmful agent.

6. Know that however bad the dark period is, it will pass. And if it comes back, it will pass once again. It always has passed, and it always will.

7. So make sure you have a plan to get through the time of crisis, before the dark period has passed. The core of this plan should be to connect with human, positive energy in whatever way you can.

8. When you are feeling good, write a letter to yourself to read when you are feeling bad. Even though you may not be able to reassure yourself when you are in the grip of the dark side of ADD, you may be able to be reassured by words you wrote when you were not.

9. Don't make big decisions during these dark periods. Every adult who has ADD lives through these dark times. You just want to make sure that during one of these periods you don't make bad decisions that you can't undo.

10. When you feel that all else has failed, when you feel that nothing will help, when you feel that everything is bad and that there is no hope, *you are wrong*. Don't listen to yourself. You are in the grip of a poisonous state of mind. Get yourself into the company of another person, or get someone on the telephone, or watch mindless TV to distract yourself. Just don't believe what you're telling yourself. It is all subjective. It will change. Give it time.

11. Live through the pain. Make sure you are in touch with someone

else. Make sure you do not isolate yourself. Get whatever treatment your trusted expert recommends. Then live through the pain. You can do it. You may learn something from it; you may not. But in living through the pain you will go on, and when it's done you will be there for the people who love you and the part of you that loves to live.

CHAPTER 36

HOW TO GET RID OF PILES:

THE KUDZU OF ADD

A dults who have ADD tend to "organize" by putting things into piles. Piles, which may seem innocuous to someone who doesn't have ADD, can become the stuff of nightmares in life with ADD. They take on angulated, monstrous proportions, and leave the ADD adult feeling defeated, dispirited, and inept. Of all the problems I help adults with ADD to overcome, this one, which sounds insignificant and even funny, can be one of the worst. So, take it seriously.

One good way to begin to take it seriously is, actually, to laugh at it. If you can laugh at your piles, you are regaining control. And, for those of you who feel utterly defeated and see not an iota of humor in this hell, let me urge you to take heart. You can defeat your piles. You may not be able to laugh yet, but you can be laughing soon.

It takes a while for the piles to become the malignant problem that they can become. The piles start small, as little stacks of paper or a dishful of lost staples, clips, coins, stray baubles, and other bits of debris. But they grow and proliferate like the dreaded weed called kudzu.

What were mere stacks soon become gangling piles of papers, magazines, books, and old laundry, precariously tilting like so many leaning towers of self-esteem. The piles invade every horizontal surface they can find—not just desks, but tables, stairs, chairs and couches, countertops, car seats, dressing tables, the lids of toilet tanks, and, of course, floors. Not just office floors and basement floors and attic floors, but living room floors, kitchen floors, even bathroom floors. What was once a quaint dishful of coins and whatnot spills over and splays into amoeboid blotches of bric-a-brac, which gradually grow into piles of junk, overflowing from room to room, down the stairs, all over the house.

This is no way to live. So, take a deep breath and attack your piles. You need to get into battle gear, or at least battle mood. You need to acknowledge that you are up against a formidable foe, but a foe that you can defeat. You created this adversary. You can uncreate and deconstruct it.

Give yourself a pep talk. Get out of the defeatist attitude the mess has hexed you with. Shame and blame only make the problem worse. Think of yourself as a gardener who has neglected the weeds for too long and let the kudzu run wild. You have work to do, but it is good work, and you can do it. Others have done it. You can too. Pulling out weeds does not require special skill or extraordinary talent. All it takes is time. Do it little by little so you won't feel overwhelmed. Each bit you clear will make you feel better and better.

One good way to start is to create a filing system. But you must take care to keep it simple. Otherwise, you will soon create new piles devoted to paraphernalia you've purchased to create your filing system.

First, pick a place to put your files. Next, get a supply of folders and plastic label holders. Then get a Brother label maker; it costs under twenty dollars, but its value is priceless. Now you're making progress.

To attack your piles, you need to get your hands into them. You need to dislodge the piles from where they sit, stuck like barnacles to all manner of surfaces. But don't worry, they can't cut you as barnacles can. Pry them loose and then triumphantly pick them up. Feel control flowing back into your blood as you do this. It will create an endorphin rush if you relish the moment and exult in your triumph over those nasty, parasitic piles.

Next, move the piles, one at a time, to the dining room or kitchen table or some other place that is not cluttered, or take a pile to the library in a box. Or even to the dump. Move each pile to where it isn't embedded in your memory, or in the great dump that used to be your office, if not your entire house.

The novelty of doing this—setting up boundaries around your own places and spaces—is exciting and refreshing. Soon you will have the exhilarating experience of walking into a nearly empty room. You will feel a sense of *ahhhhhhhhh*.

Pile by pile you pick away at what *used to be* a total mess. From the brain's perspective, this grand transport extracts the piles from all the mental associations that the original mess conjured up. If you don't do it, the defeatist memories may overrun your mind and make the frustration too much to bear.

Chucking the piles, one by one, makes it clear who owns what. You own the piles, they don't own you. You win, they lose.

If you travel a lot, you can attack your piles by taking one pile with you on each trip. When you have a free night in the hotel room or dead time on the plane or train, you can bring the pile out of your briefcase or suitcase and dismantle it on the spot. You return home only with things that are important. Do this a pile at a time and watch them gradually disappear.

Once you have disposed of your piles—once you have rooted out the kudzu—you must set up a program of pile-control. You need to develop habits of weeding that will keep your garden healthy.

One of the best ways of doing this I learned from a former patient of mine. He suggested the acronym OHIO. It stands for Only Handle It Once. Whether it is a letter, a magazine, a bill, a memo, or anything else, try to get in the habit of either acting on it right away—i.e., answering the letter or paying the bill—or putting it into one of the labeled files you have created, or throwing it away.

Once you develop these new habits, piles will return, but not as the metastatic malignancy they used to be.

CHAPTER 37

WORRY AND ADD

Having ADD myself, I write books about ADD. In 1997 I wrote a book called *Worry: Controlling It and Using It Wisely.* I wrote it because I am a big-time worrier, of course! One of my friends asked me, "Ned, when are you going to run out of personal problems you can write books about?" I told him not to worry. The store is endless.

One of the rewards of writing *Worry* was finding out firsthand that there are a lot of remedies for toxic worry that actually work, and that excessive worrying really can be brought under control most of the time for most people. This is important news, news most people do not yet know about. The goal in dealing with worry is not to get rid of it entirely—indeed, the absence of worry is a dangerous state itself, called denial. The goal is to get rid of unnecessary, corrosive worry. Worry is like blood pressure: you need some to survive. Too much, however, is toxic. It can make you sick, shorten your life, even drop you where you stand. More than a few heart attacks have been brought on by worry.

People with ADD worry more than other people. Part of the reason is that ADD-ers tend to be smart and imaginative, and smart and imaginative people worry a lot. This is because it takes a sharp, creative mind to think up all the negative possibilities we worriers invent every day!

But there are other reasons why worry tends to sink its tentacles into the ADD brain more often than the non-ADD brain. ADD leaves us facing potential danger, if not disaster, all the time. We are always wondering: What did we forget? What might we say wrong? What didn't we do right lately? What did we not hear at the key business meeting we just attended? What bills have been left unpaid? How much longer can we put off taking care of the backyard, our dentist appointment, and so on?

Those of us who have ADD inevitably have a lot to worry about, at least until we learn how to manage our ADD effectively. (It can be done, but don't feel badly, no one does it perfectly or without sweat.) Indeed, one of the keys to managing ADD well is learning how to worry wisely. The wise worrier uses worry as a danger signal that leads to constructive action, as opposed to letting it paralyze her. Learning to worry wisely is really a key to success in life for everyone. As Andrew Grove, the former head of Intel Corporation said, "Only the paranoid survive!"

You need not be paranoid to worry wisely, just vigilant. Watch out for danger signals, and when you see them, take corrective action. Don't brood. Take steps to correct the problem. If the steps fail, you can make a new plan. Life is all about revising plans that haven't worked. Don't think so much that you get lost in what I call "the infinite web of what-if" as you contemplate the ominous core of life. Your mind will play tricks on you, your imagination will lead you into dark places, and you will get lost in worry after worry.

There's a special trap for people with ADD. We often use worry as a kind of entertainment or stimulation. Contentment, however pleasant it may be, is just too bland. But worry offers pain, which is stimulating—unpleasant, but stimulating. So the person with ADD is drawn to worry the way other people can be drawn to terrifying roller coasters or horror movies.

If you have ADD, consider how often you might inadvertently be drumming up topics to worry about as a means of focusing your mind to entertain yourself. After all, no one is riveted by contentment. But worry? Yes, you can be riveted by toxic worry, even if it's unpleasant, counterproductive, and bad for you.

So what are you to do about it?

These are my six major keys to combating toxic worry and finding the way to good, productive worrying:

1. *Never worry alone.* This is by far the most important principle. Talk to someone when you feel worried. Don't worry in solitude. Don't give in to the temptation of telling everyone to go away so you can sit alone and brood over your problem. You will lose perspective, get depressed, and make bad decisions. Instead, connect with someone you like and trust.

2. *Get the facts.* Toxic worry is usually based on lack of information or wrong information. You may not be able to get all the relevant facts, but get as many as you can. If you have a medical worry, see a doctor. If you have a business worry, consult an expert. If you are worried that a friend is upset with you, try to talk to the friend or someone who knows both of you. In any case, try to get the facts.

3. *Make a plan.* Once you have the facts, take action. Make a plan to fix the situation, whatever it might be. Even if the plan fails, you will feel better being active rather than passive. Toxic worry loves passive victims. As long as you stay active, toxic worry will leave you alone.

4. *Change your physical state.* Walk around. Run up and down stairs. Do some jumping jacks. Go out for a run. Play tennis. Any change in your physical state, especially that brought on by exercise, will change your brain's chemistry. It is like pushing the reset button on your brain.

5. *Let it go.* This is the difficult one. For worriers, letting go of worry can feel dangerous. We worriers feel safer worrying than not worrying, as if our worrying somehow protects us. We need to practice letting go of worry. Even if we never fully achieve the goal, at least we can head in that direction.

6. *Consult a professional.* If your worrying persists, go see a worry expert, like a psychologist or a psychiatrist or a social worker or other

kind of therapist. There are many kinds of toxic worry that most people do not know about, just as they didn't know about ADD a decade ago. Consult a professional to see if you have one of these. They are all treatable. Take advantage of what medical science has learned about worry.

CHAPTER 38

SEX AND ADD

Practically no one writes about sex and ADD, and yet almost every adult I have ever treated reports certain sexual problems that are related to ADD. They usually don't know that the problem is related to ADD, so they don't bring it up unless I ask.

It is important for the person who evaluates an adult to ask about sexual experiences. Sometimes this seems intrusive or inappropriate. However, if you don't bring up the topic, it is likely that it won't come up, as most people do not think of ADD and sex as being related at all. Let me review for you the sexual problems that I have seen most often in adults who have ADD.

DIFFICULTY LINGERING

One of the most common problems is lack of sexual intimacy in a couple, not due to conflicts around sex but to the inability of the partner who has ADD to linger over anything at all, even sex. This partner is usually male, but not always.

Except when it's done on the fly, making love requires that both partners settle down, relax, focus, and play. They need to be able to forget about the cell phone, e-mail, and Blackberry. To make love, you need to be able to forget about where else you might be long enough to be where you are. For most people, the prospect of getting naked with another person and stimulating each other's erotic zones is quite enough to rivet their minds.

Not so for the person who has ADD. He (or she, but, again, this is usually a he) can be in the midst of making love with someone he feels attracted to, and at the same time be thinking about his e-mail. He is all but incapable of being anywhere without simultaneously thinking about being somewhere else.

The inability to linger can ruin a romance. People with ADD are bottom-liners. They are impatient. They want to get to the meat of the matter and move on. In business meetings this can be a great advantage. But in romance, it backfires. Can't you just hear the impatient man with ADD whispering to his girlfriend as they look at each other in a dimly lit restaurant, "Okay, so you love me, now, what's your next point?"

That may sound extreme, but it captures the essence of the problem. People with ADD hop from stimulation to stimulation, and they don't want to wait. They don't want to linger over anything. Savoring the moment is a skill that does not come naturally to the person with ADD. Thrill must lead to thrill, whether it is in business or in golf or in conversation or in romance. Once the thrill of a relationship has settled into something a bit more mature, the person with ADD may simply go back to his regular habit of living off high stimulation.

Unless he learns about ADD and his attendant troubles with pausing, lingering, and listening, he may lose his chance at sexual intimacy with anyone. He may be a lot of fun to be with, a great date, even great in bed a few times, but as time goes by, he gets bored and moves on, or his partner gives up on him because he is so distractible and dumps him.

This problem is common and devastating. The person with ADD just can't seem to get as interested in lovemaking as in, for example, working on the computer, making business deals, or even watching TV or playing golf. (Those last two combine stimulation and novelty with autonomy and structure, a perfect recipe for focus.)

Many men, and a few women, like this have spent years in psychotherapy trying unsuccessfully to work through their unconscious conflicts around intimacy, when all they needed was to get the correct diagnosis—ADD—and the correct treatment.

The treatment begins with education. This person needs to learn about his brain. He needs to understand that his problem is not emotional as much as it is neurological. He needs to learn how to put on the brakes. He needs to learn how to linger. Lingering can be learned, but you have to be deliberate about it.

I will tell you how I learned to linger. First of all, I did not set my sights too high. I know I will never be a master lingerer, as, for example, my wife is. She can roam around in a museum for hours and hours, while I get stir-crazy after twenty minutes. I will never be an Olympian lingerer like her. It has helped me become better at lingering by not carrying the burden of believing that I should become a master of it.

Second, it helps tremendously that my wife understands my limitations and doesn't demand that I become a master lingerer, like her. She understands ADD, and she knows that I will never relish museums—or coffee after dinner, or sunsets, or long walks, or long novels—as much as she does. However, she asked me if I could get better at lingering than I was when we first met.

This is a realistic goal. The way I improved was first of all by not feeling that I had to be perfect. I had permission to leave the museum, or its equivalent, whenever I wanted to. Having that permission helped me to stay longer and longer.

Gradually, I started to enjoy lingering. I compare it to running a distance long enough that you reach the point where you feel the "runner's high." Endorphins kick in. I don't know what the chemistry is of the "lingerer's high," but I do believe there is one. If I sit long enough in front of a great painting, or pause long enough observing a sunset, or read far enough into a long novel, or walk far enough into a long walk, I reach a point where I don't want to stop. I become entranced, enchanted, captivated. I feel removed from the humdrum world, transported to a serene and pleasure-filled place, a place reached by lingering.

The same can happen in the bedroom. I urge my patients who have this problem of being unable to linger during lovemaking to practice lingering in other situations first. Once you learn to linger in one

arena, you can soon do it in other places. Since sex sometimes pro-
vokes anxiety or the memory of past conflicts, it can be easier to learn
to linger elsewhere first.

Medication can also help. Indeed, it can make a world of difference in helping someone with ADD to linger in the moment, and to
focus. We have treated many women who experienced their first orgasm after taking stimulant medication. It allowed them to focus for
an extended time during lovemaking, a prerequisite for orgasm, particularly in women.

But even if medication does not work, just reframing the problem
as a neurological one and then working on it from that standpoint can
improve the situation immensely.

PARENT-CHILD DYNAMICS

At a deeper level, the lack of sexual intimacy in a couple where one
partner has ADD may be due to an unacknowledged power struggle.
Without meaning to, the non-ADD partner becomes the one in control because she is the one handling the responsibilities, which leaves
the ADD partner feeling more like a child than a lover.

After a while, what began as a highly charged erotic relationship
settles into a mildly charged not-so-erotic relationship, and from there
eases into an only remotely erotic friendship, held together by shared
interests or children or financial convenience or simply inertia.

The non-ADD member of the couple feels frustrated, lonely, sexu-
ally unfulfilled (to put it mildly), and often self-doubting, wondering if
it is her fault that her husband is hardly ever her lover.

At this juncture, if the diagnosis of ADD does not get made, a low-
level depression engulfs the union. Both partners begin to feel that the
pizzazz is gone. I have seen marriages break up because of this, but
the more common result is simply chronic anger and dissatisfaction on
the part of the non-ADD partner. "What's your problem?" she understandably demands.

"I don't see that there is a problem," may be the reply. "I love you.
I am just so busy."

"No, you're more than busy. You are avoiding me. You don't ever
touch me. Are you still even attracted to me?"

"Of course I'm attracted to you. I love you."

"Then, why don't you show it? Why don't we ever, you know, do what we used to do?"

"We do now and then," he replies, a little defensively.

"Oh, really? Can you remember the last time? Because I can. It was over six months ago. I can't stand this. Do you think I'm ugly? Tell me, please. I can take it. Do you think I need to lose weight? Don't you like my bottom anymore? You used to love it. Now you don't even look at it, let alone pat it and kiss it the way you used to."

The man looks away. He too feels upset over the loss of the passion in their relationship. He also feels guilty; he knows she is trying her best to keep the passion alive and he has done nothing to help. He doesn't know what to say because he doesn't know what is going on.

"Honey, what can I tell you? I love you. I am attracted to you."

"Then, why don't you show it? I could walk right past you when you are on that computer and I could be wearing the sexiest bit of nothing you've ever seen and I could lean over and put my hands in your pants and you wouldn't react at all. You'd kiss my cheek and say 'I love you, honey,' and go right back to your e-mail!"

The man looks down, recognizing the truth in her words, but not knowing what to say or what to do. "I have failed you."

"Stop it!" she says. "I don't want that stupid, defeatist attitude. You haven't failed *me*! You've failed *us*! You're missing out on something that used to be good and fun and the best damn sex either one of us had ever had. Why did you let that go? Was it all just the thrill of the chase?"

That was part of it. The chase keeps all men focused, even those who have ADD. But once the chase ends, most men can maintain interest, even see it deepen. The man (again, or woman) who has ADD often sees the interest wane. The novelty is gone.

But it is other issues that really have killed the sex. Other issues crept in without being identified. Before the lack of sexual intimacy developed, a pattern developed outside the bedroom in which the non-ADD spouse had to do a lot of organizing, reminding, coaxing, even goading the ADD spouse. The two developed a parent-child relationship without meaning to and without seeing what was happening.

Parent-child feelings are antierotic. You don't want to have sex with your demanding, controlling parent. So, unwittingly, you begin to lose the enthusiasm, playfulness, vulnerability, and aggression that combine to create passion. You become interested elsewhere, you become more evasive and passive, and you fill your time with other matters. While you still love your partner, you no longer feel like making love with her. The magic is gone.

It doesn't have to stay gone forever. You can solve the problem by diagnosing the ADD, treating it, helping the non-ADD spouse begin to share the responsibility and work of organization, time management, money management, child care, and so forth. Gradually, as pent-up anger from both members of the couple comes out, romance can reawaken.

This takes time. A good therapist can help. Remember, there is a lot more to treating this problem than merely prescribing medication for ADD. Each member of the couple must have a chance to articulate what has been going on, get angry about it, then understand it, and figure out new ways of living together.

Then together they need to rebalance the workload and rebalance who takes on responsibility. Both partners should share the work equally, and share the responsibilities equally. No one should take on the role of parent, and no one should take on the role of child—unless it is part of some erotic game you both enjoy!

TIME MANAGEMENT

Another common problem is the couple who complain of lack of sexual intimacy, but here the problem is not primarily due to conflicts about sex or an inability to linger. In this pattern, the lack of sex is due to another symptom in the ADD group of symptoms: poor time management. The problem is so severe that this couple makes love rarely, if at all.

Lacking any other explanation, they usually conclude that their problem must be due to a conflict in their relationship, or their conflicts around sex. Sometimes both of these *are* significant factors. But in this pattern, they are not the most important factor.

The most important factor is a *scheduling problem.* The two people are almost never both awake and ready for sex at the same time. One is always at a desk online or doing something else. One patient of mine even calls her husband's computer his "plastic mistress."

If you think about it, this pattern makes perfect sense. One of the core problems in ADD is time management and scheduling. If it's true that scheduling problems get in the way of keeping up with friends or meeting deadlines, why wouldn't it be true about making love? "But I would think he would look forward to sex and make time for it," a wife will complain. "Doesn't he like sex with me? Am I doing something wrong?"

"No, you're not doing anything wrong," I reply. "And in all likelihood, he does like making love with you, but that isn't what's on his mind in a given moment. Remember, in ADD it's now or never, or maybe later. The trick is to work not on his emotions but on his schedule."

"But that's so unromantic. I don't want to feel like he's setting aside time for sex like he was taking his car for a lube job!" the wife will reply.

"It's your emotions you need to work on here. He doesn't mean it personally, so you shouldn't take it personally. When he is with you making love, he will love doing it. He will love the moment. I'm pretty sure that's not how he feels when he takes his car in for a lube job. You just need to understand that he is kind of strange this way. Many husbands stand panting next to the bed, ready to jump in at any time. But not your guy. However, that does not mean he isn't turned on by you or excited to be close to you. All it means is he has to be prompted and organized in order to do anything, even make love."

"So what am I supposed to do, wear a whistle around my neck and blow it when it's time for sex?" the wife will ask, exasperated.

"No, not unless that becomes part of an erotic game. But simple agreements, like, 'Let's meet in bed at ten P.M. Tuesday and see what happens,' followed up by a casual reminder or two as Tuesday draws near and ten P.M. draws closer, can make a world of difference. And this is lot cheaper than therapy!"

CAN'T GET ENOUGH

A fourth problem I have often seen reverses the previous one. One of the traits commonly associated with ADD is what medical people call hypersexuality, or an unusually intense desire for frequent lovemaking: some folks just can't get enough.

Sometimes the person with ADD takes care of this by having many affairs. However, what happens more often is that the ADD member of the couple drives the other member crazy with constant requests for lovemaking. If he does not get his requisite amount of sex (sometimes as much as four or five encounters a day), he becomes angry, resentful, and generally impossible to be with. Obviously, this does not lead to an increase in lovemaking, but rather a decrease.

If both members of the couple feel hypersexual, there's no problem—just a lot of lovemaking. But most of the time the situation is not balanced so nicely.

When there is an imbalance, the best solution I have found is some kind of compromise. The person who wants sex less often needs to reassure her partner that she does like sex with him, just not every hour. She needs to make it clear how often she likes to make love and offer reassurances that the lovemaking will truly happen. On the other hand, the person who wants sex more frequently needs to find substitutes, other activities—not other women—he can engage in when his partner is not in the mood to make love.

Having an affair is not a good substitute for obvious reasons. But other substitutes can work well. Some of these include masturbation, if you feel comfortable doing that and it does not bother your partner; exercise (yes, it can be almost as good as sex); and getting involved in an activity you really like, whatever that might be.

Indeed, this last suggestion, getting involved in an activity you really like, may point up where your extraordinary desire for sex came from. It was the one activity you could find that you really liked! Well, other activities can become so much fun and be so totally engrossing that they also set off the endorphins and other pleasure hormones that the body and brain put out in states of deep enjoyment.

It is a matter of searching, experimenting, and realizing that it is just not fair to expect another human being to want to make love five times a day simply because you do. If you force the issue, you risk losing your partner altogether.

SEX AS SELF-MEDICATION

Another common problem is a variation on the previous one. This is the man (or woman, but it is most often a man) who has ADD and uses sex as a form of medication. He flirts constantly, oversteps physical boundaries, and may have multiple affairs. However, even if he never has affairs, he is always looking for erotic contact in a way that risks offending others and getting him into trouble.

Usually if such a person seeks help for the problem, he seeks it from specialists in addictions, relationships, or sex. That's why it is so important for those specialists to understand ADD. What is needed here is for the diagnosis of ADD to be made and treatment to be initiated.

When such a man gets on the right medication, usually stimulant medication or Strattera, then he finds he can give up the wrong medication, i.e., excessive sexualizing of all human contact. Erotic feelings focus the mind, but so does stimulant medication. Essentially, this person has been using sex the way other people with ADD might use coffee, or driving fast, or gambling—as a form of self-medication.

CHAPTER 39

HALLOWELL & RATEY'S

TOP TIPS FOR ADULT ADD

Over the years John Ratey and I have collected various tips and tricks from people of all ages on how to live happily and successfully with ADD. We have also discovered and invented many of our own. You will not find all of these useful, and you may already use many of them. Just make note of the new ones that ring true to you, and try to put them into use in your life, or ask someone else to help you do this.

Some of these tips will seem trivial while others will seem too important or broad to include in a list of tips. However, it makes sense—at least to us—to include in one chapter in as brief a format as possible the major and minor bits of advice we have offered most often to our patients (and to each other) over the past twenty years. These are the nuggets of hard-won clinical wisdom that don't always make it into textbooks, practical bits of simple and succinct advice.

Most of these tips pertain to ADD in adults more than in children. However, many can easily be transposed into the life of a child, by changing the particulars. For example, instead of always putting your car keys in a basket next to the front door, a child might always try to put her book bag on her desk the minute she gets home.

1. Marry the right person: someone who loves you for who you are.
2. Find the right job. These first two bits of advice are keys to happiness for just about everyone, whether or not they have ADD. As Freud said, if you can find happiness in love and in work, you will be a happy person. The only reason it is worth mentioning such an obvious fact is that people who have ADD so often err in both decisions. They marry and work for controlling, demeaning people who constantly reprimand them for their shortcomings while not even noticing their talents and strengths.

    What you should do instead is find a mate who loves you for the best in you and can put up with your downside without a lot of complaining about it. And you should find a boss who does the same.

    The reason adults with ADD don't do this is because they think they aren't worth it. They think they need to be scolded and reprimanded at home and at work because that's what they've experienced their whole lives.

    How can an adult reverse a lifelong trend of selling herself short? How can an adult go into a job interview feeling confident or go on a date and expect to be treated well? This is where the work of diagnosis, education, and therapy can make such a big difference.

    You need help in getting to know the best you that lives within, a person you have never met. Making the diagnosis of ADD begins the process, learning about ADD continues it, spending some time in psychotherapy deepens it, and then acting differently in the world solidifies it.
3. Keep a basket next to the front door where you always put your car keys. When I give this kind of advice some of my adult patients tune out, as if this were too trivial to warrant their attention. But, for the want of a nail the kingdom can be lost, and for the want of car keys a job can be lost or a romance can end.

    The devil *does* reside in the details in the land of ADD. Most adults with ADD know what they want to do; they just don't do it. Nine times out of ten this is because of a slipup with details. They forgot the day of the big meeting and showed up at the wrong time. They forgot the place. They forgot to bring the slides or the DVD for the presentation. They lost the tickets. They forgot to make the call. They thought they had done whatever it was that was supposed to be done, but they hadn't in fact done it.

That's why several tips in this list relate to details. Please don't make the big mistake so many adults who have ADD make: because they are bored by details, they skip over suggestions on how to manage them. That is like driving through a stop sign because you are bored by traffic regulations. You can get killed.

4. Don't expect perfection. You may have to retrain yourself here. I am not suggesting that you endorse mediocrity, just that you realize that mistakes are part of every success. You may be so fed up with all your mistakes that you have become too harsh on yourself for each and every mistake made.

5. Attack your piles.

6. Buy lots of wastebaskets and trash cans. Use them frequently and empty them often. Don't have so few trash cans that you end up stuffing them all to overflowing. This is unsightly and depressing. Have wastebaskets galore throughout your house and office. Throw away as much as you can. It is a skill required in the modern world to be ruthless as you say to a piece of paper or a magazine, "I don't need you," and then to throw it away. Don't save stuff for "someday." The stuff will soon hold you hostage, and someday will never come. If you are famous and want to save everything for your biographers, even your old copies of *Time* magazine, build your own library, or rent space in a storage warehouse. But, for heaven's sake, don't save them around the house.

7. Do what you are good at. Don't spend your adulthood trying to get good at what you are bad at. In school and in childhood, you had plenty of time to find out what you were good at, and also to try to get good at what you were bad at. Since kids are usually bad at something the first few times they try it, it is right for kids to be asked to try to get good at what they're bad at.

8. Pay attention to your diet. We spell this out elsewhere in the book, but to reiterate: don't self-medicate with drugs or carbohydrates; eat a balanced diet; don't skip breakfast and be sure to include some protein in your breakfast; take a daily supplement of omega-3 fatty acids (we recommend Barry Sears's preparation, available through his website, www.drsears.com); and take supplemental multivitamins.

9. People with ADD need to remember that they might need a "closer," just as professional baseball teams have a closer—someone who can finish off the game. Many projects get started and some get to the sixth or seventh inning, but, for want of a middle reliever, the projects get stalled or forgotten and end up as fodder for more piles. Anybody can be your closer, even you. But if you have found over and over again that you can't do it for yourself, it's time to look for someone else to help, like your administrative assistant, a friend, or a coach whom you might hire.

10. Find a good accountant, a good lawyer, and other advisers to help with the details and the worries. Work with someone who is more time-conscious and detail-oriented than you are so that those concerns will not be left for your spouse to take care of. Many divorces begin because this kind of work was not delegated to a hired adviser.

11. DELEGATE! Write it in large letters above the mirror in your bathroom.

12. Don't stop doing what worked before and got you the successes you do have. You may have achieved your success on guts and determination, but don't get lazy. You need to throw the luggage around with the baggage handlers, like David Neeleman, CEO of JetBlue Airways does.

13. Don't repeat the same failed strategy. This is the reverse of number 12. One definition of insanity is doing the same deed over and over again, hoping for a different outcome. Instead of taking the same kind of job over and over, and quitting or getting fired each time, try a new field. Or instead of dating or marrying the same kind of person over and over, and breaking up or getting divorced each time, try going out with someone totally different. Or instead of inviting the same friend or relative into your life over and over, only to have him hurt and disappoint you over and over, try saying no the next time, or at least changing the terms of your invitation.

14. Find someone you can trust and *listen to that person*. People with ADD love being their own bosses, which is great, but, taken too far, you can isolate yourself. You can develop the habit of doing everything yourself and not listening to anyone else, ever. As brilliant and intuitive a strategist as you might be, this is a recipe for

disaster. It's only a matter of when. So, find an old friend, someone who knows you and knows your life, and listen to her advice. Often.

15. Don't trust everybody. This is the reverse of number 14. Sometimes people with ADD are so enthusiastic, open, and ready to act that they believe everything and trust everyone. What then happens is that you get burned one too many times and you flip-flop, becoming downright paranoid. Try to keep a reasonable middle ground. I know, I know, the middle ground is not where people with ADD like to be, but sometimes—like in this matter of trust—they really ought to bolt themselves to the middle ground.

16. For the ADD sleep pattern of staying up too late and then being unarousable in the morning, try a new device, the dawning alarm clock. This is a great invention. For those who have "sleep inertia," the dreamy types who typically have their circadian rhythm set so that they get up at noon and go to sleep at four A.M., the dawning alarm transforms the room gradually from darkness to daylight, and so wakes the sleeper naturally. You can find these on the Internet.

17. Give yourself permission to watch mindless TV. It can be a good way to recharge your batteries.

18. Beware of letdowns after finishing a big project or completing a mission. It happens to everyone, but to people with ADD it can precipitate horrible depression, which in turn can lead to binge drinking or drug use, or other self-destructive behavior. The best way to deal with the problem is to know that it might happen and make sure you keep in close contact with other people during the period of letdown. Also, get physical exercise.

19. Learn to listen to books on tape while driving. It keeps you off your cell phone and keeps your mind churning.

20. Get regular physical exercise. This has been mentioned before, but it is exceedingly important. Exercise promotes a boost in dopamine, norepinephrine, and serotonin. It's like taking a little bit of Prozac and a little bit of Ritalin holistically.

21. Celebrate victories. Adults with ADD typically move right along to the next task after a success or a victory. It is important to take some time to relish the good thing you have done. You don't need

to gloat or make a public display. However, it is important to allow the victorious moments to get into your system so that they can sustain and nourish you.

22. Set up reminders throughout your physical world. They may be visual, like a calendar or a sign above your desk or the proverbial string around your finger; they may be auditory, like a wristwatch alarm or a tone on a Palm Pilot or cell phone or a musical tone that announces it is time to leave; they may even be tactile, like a pebble you put in your shoe to remind you to do something in the morning right after you put on your shoes. As for olfactory reminders, these are usually inadvertent, like the piece of stinking old cheese that reminds you that you forgot to unpack the cooler when you got home from the picnic last month.

23. Set up reminders for your internal system too. You need to remind yourself that you are an okay person. So you might post in your closet a complimentary letter you received, so that you'll see it every morning; or you might put a photograph of your kids onto a keychain, so you'll have it readily available all day; or you might hang a photograph of a person who inspires you near your desk or your bed.

24. Get a fidget toy. They can work miracles. Here is how one creative man explained to me how he uses his:

As a medical student, I spend a lot of time in lectures, studying, and talking to patients. So with all the listening I do, I need something to fidget with. My solution is Silly Putty.

I have three eggs of Silly Putty. One egg lives in my book bag, so I can use it when I am in a lecture. One egg lives in the left pocket of my white coat, so I can reach in with my left hand and play with it while I am talking to a patient and still have my right hand free to take notes, and one egg lives at home on my desk where I can play with it when I am studying.

Silly Putty is great. It is easy to unstick from almost any surface, including most fabrics; it's fun to play with; and it's cheap, so if I lose an egg, it's just a dollar or so to replace it. And because it's roughly the same color as my skin, it's unobtrusive. Silly Putty must have been made for ADD-ers.

25. Most important: Know thyself. Know that you have foibles and

gifts and that you need to engineer the environment to promote what's best in you. And you have to work at remembering what you know about yourself, and continue to use it. Ironically, due to your ADD, you can learn but then forget the very knowledge that will help you the most, the knowledge of who you are.

CHAPTER 40

WHAT KIND OF MATE IS BEST

IF YOU HAVE ADD?

In a way, it's ridiculous to ask what kind of mate is best if you have ADD. After all, there isn't a catalog of romantic partners through which you can thumb, choosing among various types. Furthermore, ADD does not define you as a person. The best way to find a mate is to find someone you enjoy being with so much that you're willing to put up with the hassles of cohabitation.

On the other hand, I have seen adults with ADD make the same mistakes over and over again in love and romance. The most common mistake is one I have mentioned elsewhere in this book: they fall in love with, live with, or marry someone who resembles a caricature of a bad fifth-grade schoolteacher—someone who is controlling, demeaning, belittling, and very well organized. They fall for such a person because earlier in life they got the idea that that's what they needed.

Of course, what they really need is someone who sees the best in them and helps to bring it out. They need someone who sees more positive in them than they might see in themselves. They need someone who loves them for who they are.

It helps if the person is organized, but that isn't essential. What's essential is that your mate respects and loves you for who you are, not who she can turn you into. A love like that naturally improves both of the people involved.

The fundamental obstacle that people who have ADD put in their way is their own fear. They fear that they can't do life without a supervisor to look over them and correct their mistakes. They fear that they will fall flat if they give themselves the chance to be true to who they actually are. They fear that who they are just doesn't work in this world. They fear that they are such losers, no one could possibly love them. So they let themselves become ensnared with manipulative, controlling, demeaning people, both in love and in work.

Adults with ADD often see themselves as ugly ducklings. Not physically, necessarily, but in every other way. Impaired. Inept. Incompetent. What they need is what they have always needed, even—especially—back in the fifth grade. They need someone to see something good in them. But by the time you get to be an adult, you can't always make that happen. You can't just say, "Gee, today I think I'll go find someone who finds something good in me."

However, you can and you should try to get yourself into a frame of mind that allows precisely that to happen. You can do it by removing as many obstacles to its happening as possible. For example:

1. Don't associate with people who put you down on a regular basis.
2. If a person usually makes you feel bad when you see him, don't continue the relationship.
3. Some difficult relationships you can't avoid; for example, you can't choose your mother or father. But you *can* be selective about relationships outside the family. Use your free will!
4. Don't assume that if someone treats you well, she must have bad judgment or just want something from you.
5. Don't put on an act for anybody. If someone is going to fall in love with you, you don't want him to be falling in love with an act.
6. What? Nobody will fall in love with you *unless* you put on an act? You are wrong. Just give it a try. Try letting other people see who you really are.

7. Vulnerability is good. Vulnerability is what leads to the deepest, best kind of love. Don't hide your vulnerability; let it show.
8. Think of a relative who really, really loves you for who you are. Try to keep that person in mind wherever you go, whatever you do.
9. Don't go out with people you don't respect.
10. Think of the person you'd really like to see yourself with. Then ask her out. What's the worst that can happen? You get rejected. So what? Remember, no is just the first step on the way to yes.

So what kind of mate is best if you have ADD? Someone who loves you for who you are. Someone who gets a kick out of you. Someone whose voice lifts when he hears it is you on the other end of the line.

It is helpful if the mate can educate herself about ADD and not take the blunders that the ADD mate makes personally or as if they were done on purpose. ADD is not an excuse, but it is a powerful explanation.

This person may or may not have ADD; may be blond, brunette, have red hair, or no hair; may be organized or disorganized; may be rich or poor; may like sports or hate sports; may share interests with you or have little in common; may speak your language or not.

A woman who has ADD sent me the following poem, which she wrote. I think it tells well what real love can do.

TREASURED FRIEND

BY CHERIE DAWN MILLS

You are my hope.
You meet me where I am, and love me there—
not pushing, nor blaming, but only rejoicing
with me, or lending me your handkerchief.
You gently hold me earthbound in the blackness
of my fears, or during my endangerment from
flights of fantasy.
You do not fear the depths of my weakness,
nor the heights of my strength.

You ever see in me the wondrous possibilities
    that my sins and sorrows and daily concerns
    have caused me to forget.
Your love empowers me to give my love to others—
    to mold the dirty clay of my feet into
    sparkling angel wings.

CHAPTER 41

WHAT CAN YOU DO IF

YOUR MATE HAS ADD?

If you are married to or are romantically involved with someone who has ADD, some people would say you should run for cover. However, don't despair. There is hope.

In *Driven to Distraction*, we made a number of suggestions about how to deal with ADD in couples. Those suggestions still stand, but in this chapter I would simply like to add the most pithy and practical tips we have learned since then.

First of all, get the diagnosis. Many couples are near the breaking point simply because one member of the pair has ADD but doesn't know it. Undiagnosed ADD can put any couple over the brink. Here are some typical signs of distress in a couple where one member has ADD but doesn't know about it:

- The division of labor is wildly uneven. The non-ADD member does almost all of the "scut work"—the picking up, the organizing, the reminding, the cleaning, the planning—what psychologists call the executive functions.
- Lovemaking is infrequent due to built-up anger on the part of the non-ADD spouse.

- The non-ADD member of the couple carries a huge amount of pent-up resentment, but he is afraid to show it for fear the whole house might come falling down.
- The ADD member of the couple is forever making promises, but not keeping them.
- The ADD member of the couple gets most of the attention.
- Finances are constantly in a precarious state.
- The ADD member of the couple feels misunderstood and judged.
- The non-ADD member of the couple feels that she is more a parent than a peer.

If you find yourself in such a situation, get help. The diagnosis of ADD can save your relationship. It is more likely that you will solve the problem if you get outside help, as you really need a referee.

Here is an example of a couple who came to see me for help. The husband had ADD; the wife was going crazy. Let me name them Jim and Hope. They worked together in the same home-based business, which only intensified their conflicts. Although Jim had been dagnosed with ADD years before, and took Ritalin for it, many problems persisted. Here is a note Hope had prepared before coming to our first appointment. She handed it to me as she walked in.

Why we are here:
   Most of the time I don't feel like a wife, I feel like the single mother (or nanny) of a spoiled six-year-old child who is

- self-centered
- wants everything he sees
- loves teasing me and yanking my chain
- has very little patience, gets mad easily, and will occasionally smash objects that frustrate him
- thinks it's very funny when he gets away with behaving badly (he denies this but the smirk on his face tells the tale)
- shifts most of the responsibility for everything, big and small, onto me

He gets more work done than he did before Ritalin, but he

- works on what he feels like working on, not what needs to get done first
- has poor organizational skills and ignores to-do lists even though he asks for them
- finds that Ritalin gives him better focus, but he is just as likely to put time into researching his next vehicle purchase as getting his work done
- finds that Ritalin does help control impulsive behavior but not enough
- finds that while taking it he's less cranky than usual but it seems to get stored up and then he's more cranky than usual when he's not taking it
- is bored with the work we're doing and constantly looking for a distraction, a road trip or something else to do, but the business needs him
- says I don't give him credit for what he does do, which is probably true, but I see a lot of non-work stuff going on and he won't give status or track hours so I have no way of knowing

I think a relationship is about teamwork, working together toward common goals and helping each other. But

- he has a knee-jerk reaction to being asked to do something, no matter what it is—first reaction is usually to get out of it (which means get me to do it)
- he will say yes if he can't think of a good excuse but will then delay until I either do it myself or nag him into it
- he wants to control where we go and what we do—if he agrees to do something he doesn't really want to do, I pay for it with major attitude and don't get to enjoy it anyway
- to give him credit, he is pretty good about doing the tasks he chooses for himself—it's the things I have asked him to do that he can't be depended on to do. Unfortunately, that's most things

Miscellaneous

- he's trying to buy happiness
- his mother taught him to beg for things (the only thing he actually works hard at)

- he sees the world in black and white—always the extreme view
- he does not compromise well, and is immediately belligerent when discussing any disagreement
- he does not take responsibility for his behavior and doesn't even remember his behavior very well, so he does the same things over and over
- he does not admit to making mistakes or behaving badly—tries to find a way to blame me instead, or point out something I've done which he thinks is similar

Bottom Line—I'm tired of

- asking him to do things knowing full well that they won't get done without so much nagging on my part that I might as well just do it myself
- trying to ignore the crankiness, the personal comments, the constant complaining, and still enjoy being with him (gets harder all the time)
- constantly having to restrain him from buying one or more expensive items that he often doesn't really need and we can't afford, but he thinks he must have
- watching the expensive item he "had" to have sit unused because he lost interest in it after two days, and is now chasing something else
- trying to keep up with him in conversation while he jumps around from making plans for things he doesn't really intend to do, to plotting how to buy something we can't afford. Most of our conversation is about things he wants to buy, now or in the future; it's aggravating and seems like a lot of wasted effort
- watching him waste huge amounts of time plotting purchases and watching bad TV, then listening to him complain about how he never gets to do anything he wants to do
- getting him to take his Ritalin, which he would prefer not to do, without coming out and saying "I don't really like to be around you when you're not taking it, you're too obnoxious"
- feeling guilty every time I buy something for myself because he has already spent so much
- feeling like I go through life with a ball and chain instead of a partner
- feeling alone much of the time
- stress!!!! Living with him is incredibly stressful

Why did I decide to get help? Because

- I have tried to discuss all these issues but mostly just get denial, or he turns the discussion around on me
- each time we talk I have to start all over—he acts like he's never heard any of it before
- when we do manage to have a decent talk he always says he's willing to change and will do anything to save our relationship—so here's his chance
- I realized we have a huge mismatch in how we view this relationship when he mentioned the "only" time he's ever considered leaving. I think about it often
- I am beginning to feel like a candidate for Prozac myself; the daily aggravation is really wearing me down

So why haven't I just given up?

- there has been improvement over the years—teeny, tiny baby steps that aren't nearly enough but it's there, so I know the situation is not entirely hopeless
- none of the above happens 100% of the time; he behaves properly just often enough to prove he can (though this can make it all the more maddening when he doesn't)
- our skills complement each other nicely (when he chooses to use his) and we want basically the same things out of life
- I do love him—I'm not exactly sure why sometimes, but I do

What am I hoping to accomplish? I don't really know how much improvement is possible, so I am trying not to set any impossible goals; however, ideally . . .

- he will learn to act like an adult, to take responsibility for his actions and to focus on something more constructive than buy, buy, buy
- he'll learn to gain some satisfaction from doing something, even if it's not the most fun task on the list, and will start actually doing the things he agrees to do
- he'll learn to manage time so that the important things get done first, and there is time left over to do the fun things he wants to do
- he'll stop focusing on the equipment he doesn't have and

all the problems with what he does have, and learn to \work around the limitations so he can actually enjoy his hobbies

- unless/until he develops some responsibility with money, he'll leave the decisions to me with no whining, begging or complaining when he doesn't get what he wants
- he will learn to look at us as a team, and be willing to do things to help out his team member that he would not necessarily choose to do on his own
- we will learn to discuss things effectively when there is a problem
- he will learn how to be supportive without being flip, sarcastic, and blaming
- I will learn to be more tolerant of the things he can't change, whatever they turn out to be

That is one of the best and most succinct descriptions of how hard it is to be married to someone who has ADD that I have ever read. Time will tell if I will be able to help Hope and Jim. There is a lot of love between them, and with a change in medication and some coaching from someone other than his wife, Jim will do better.

Hope understands ADD; she is the spouse Jim needs and he is lucky to have found her. But now he needs to work on the issues, and he needs to accept help to make the relationship survive.

Hope even outlined a treatment plan, a list of dos and don'ts, which contains within it superb suggestions for all couples in which there is ADD. It also is laced with the bittersweet humor and irony that the non-ADD spouse in such a couple usually develops over the years.

DO:

- behave like an adult!
- learn that instant gratification often costs more than it's worth.
- read the e-mails I send you. I don't cc you gratuitously. I send you stuff because I actually want you to read it.
- take responsibility for your tasks and make sure everything gets done, not just the minimum.
- say no in the first place if you don't want to do something. Once you say yes, follow through with a smile.
- clearly state when a discussion is a "thought experiment," or

when you're talking about something you want to do far in the future.

- make sure the things you buy get entered in QuickBooks.
- learn to do time and task management—things should not sit until I have to remind you, regardless of whether it's something you like doing or not.
- get into better shape.
- dress a little nicer, and occasionally take me out on a date.
- ask me what's wrong if I appear to be upset, even if you already know it was something you did (or didn't do).
- figure out how to motivate yourself so more effort goes into our business than into surfing, watching TV, and plotting the next trip or illicit purchase.
- go through the exercises in the Harville Hendrix book with me and actually try to take it seriously.
- give compliments occasionally.
- make suggestions for improvement instead of just complaining about something and waiting for me to fix it for you.
- be romantic and affectionate occasionally, even when there's no foreplay involved.
- give me some advance warning when you're going to want me to do something or go somewhere.
- approach everyday life with a "how can I help" attitude instead of a "how can I get out of this" one.
- say what you think/feel directly, instead of hinting around or making pointed "jokes."

DON'T:

- try to turn the issue around when defensive and make it my problem instead of yours.
- announce reforms, like not drinking soda, unless you actually intend to follow through.
- buy things without consulting me—big things, anyway.
- do things you know you shouldn't, or not do things you know you should, simply out of laziness and/or hoping I'll do it for you.
- smirk and act pleased with yourself when caught doing something "wrong."
- spend so much time discussing things you want to buy, especially trucks.

- say and do things you know will bug me, just to yank my chain.
- spend all your time focused on the next road trip. It's insulting and unfair to me, and it's futile. You've rarely had one of those trips go the way you wanted it to, and you can't drive your way to happiness any more than you can buy it.
- ignore me when I ask you to not feed the dogs, and not tease them.
- snap at me and/or act like I'm being stupid.
- talk to me when I'm working, unless it's important! You often start talking again less than 5 minutes after I asked you to stop.
- do a half-assed job of something just because it's boring, or you're hoping I'll do it next time.
- ask me "what stinks" when I'm cooking—you don't have to eat it!
- act like it's a problem if I dress up or wear makeup. It's hard enough for me to make the effort as it is and knowing you'll complain just makes it harder.
- leave a mess wherever you go (in the house, that is).
- complain if you talk to me while I'm working and I don't pay close attention. You've wanted me to learn to tune out distractions for years!
- blame me for things that aren't really my fault, even as a joke (it's usually not "really" a joke).

Hope is acutely tuned in to what Jim needs help with—and what Hope needs help with as well. With such a concrete game plan, the chances are good that Hope and Jim will develop a better way for themselves.

In general, once the diagnosis of ADD is made, the next step is to sit down with each other, and with a couples therapist if possible, and see what's been going on through the lens of ADD, as opposed to the lens of judgment and blame. Once you understand what's been happening in terms of neurology instead of morality, forgiveness will come more easily.

But, at the same time, the anger does need to come out. You don't have to land punches, but the non-ADD spouse does need his anger to land. The non-ADD spouse needs to be able to tell his mate what a pain in the butt it has been to live with her. This anger really needs to be heard, and not be explained away. ADD is not an excuse for all the bad stuff that's happened. It is an explanation—a partial explanation—and a powerful one. But it does not excuse all the broken promises, undone dishes, laundry tossed under the bed, missed appointments and lost jobs, no-shows, and the host of other mishaps the ADD member of the couple has been responsible for. It is not healthy for the non-ADD spouse to stifle that anger.

As it comes out, understanding moves in to take its place, and with understanding comes forgiveness. You can fall in love again.

Before you think I am singing "Tra-la, tra-la," and imagining you dancing off into ecstasy, let me assure you that I know how arduous this process is, and how impermanent. It takes work. And for some couples, divorce truly may be the best option. On the other hand, I have seen couples who were on the brink of divorce create a better relationship than they ever had before once the diagnosis of ADD was made.

Then, with any luck, you can move on. It is good to make some plans and add some structure at this point. For example, you might schedule a regular date night, when you are sure to see each other in a relaxed setting. You might decide on a division of labor, so that it is clear who is supposed to take out the trash, do the dishes, make the bed, do the laundry, go to the dry cleaner, and so on. You might set aside a regular time for lovemaking; as unromantic as this sounds, it is better than not making love at all.

Also, make sure the ADD is getting properly treated. Make sure both members of the couple understand what ADD is. Make sure you are moving from the shame-and-blame game of the prediagnosis relationship into the mutual understanding of the new relationship.

Don't expect to go from a struggling relationship to perfect bliss. People who have ADD tend to be difficult and erratic, even after diagnosis and treatment. Each couple finds their own way of dealing with the difficult moments and difficult days. Here are some tips for those times:

- Give each other some space. Walk away. Don't storm out, slamming the door behind you. Just say something like, "I think we both need some time and space to cool down. I'll be back in a while." Then leave. Go upstairs, or go for a walk or a drive in your car.

- Look for humor, if you possibly can. Humor is a great diffuser of anger. I was on the phone the other day trying to order a product. I was in the midst of one of those infernal computer-voice decision trees. *If you want this, then push that,* and so forth. I was becoming irate. Finally I barked into the telephone, "I want to speak to a human being." The computer mechanically replied, "Sorry, we are out of that product."
- Remember ADD. In the heat of an argument it is easy to forget. While ADD is not an excuse, it is an explanation that opens the door to understanding rather than blame.
- Avoid the hook of the sadomasochistic struggle. Couples can get so accustomed to fighting that they unwittingly start to take strange delight in it and find ways to perpetuate it.
- Avoid the trap of the parent-child model. Often the non-ADD spouse takes the role of parent, and the ADD spouse takes the role of child.
- Get help sooner rather than later. You don't want your couples counselor to take on the role of simply being the last obligatory stop on the way to divorce.

While it can be hell to be married to someone who has ADD, it can also be heaven. Marriage is difficult for all. There's no way around that fact, at least no way that I have ever discovered. However, with persistence, and with a foundation of respect and attraction, couples can not only make it, they can thrive.

Don't let ADD split you up. If you are to split up, let it be for some other reason. ADD is too treatable for you to let it end what could be a great marriage.

CHAPTER 42

GETTING *WELL ENOUGH* ORGANIZED:

THE HALLOWELL APPROACH

Everyone else seems to have a method for getting organized; why shouldn't I? I did a Google search on the topic "Getting organized," and was given 2,740,000 sites I could visit. Then I went to www.amazon.com and searched the topic "How to get organized," specifying only books, nothing else. I got 64,732 titles. Some of the titles didn't quite seem to fit the topic, like the story of Shackleton's trip to Antarctica, but, then, he must have been one very organized man.

There seem to be as many methods for getting organized as there are ways to get disorganized. Maybe nature eternally ebbs and flows, from organization to disorganization and back again. I know my desk does.

Indeed, one of the fundamental laws of thermodynamics is the rule of entropy, the tendency of all matter to drift toward disorder and chaos. Certainly all matter in my life obeys that law!

Humorous as it can be, disorganization can plague your soul. It is one of the great bugaboos in the life of someone who has ADD. We have trouble organizing *things*. We have trouble organizing *time*. We have trouble organizing *thoughts*. We have trouble organizing *data*. We put things into piles. We put time into limbo as we procrastinate. We allow our thoughts to run around like puppies, playful, undisciplined, and nipping at all they can find. We let data accrue in cyberspace or on to-do lists like kudzu. As inevitably as a match burning out, we fall behind. Then, one unsuspecting day, we walk into our disorganized office and see that it looks like a dumpster was emptied in it, and we fall to our knees and cry. We feel overwhelmed and inept. Incompetent. Lost. And so sad.

When we appeal to others for help, as much as they might offer practical advice, as much as they might try to be patient and listen to our lengthy lament, as much as they might want to help us and not dismiss us, we sense that their basic solution is the one that Nike promotes: *Just do it.*

After all, isn't that what everybody else does? Isn't getting organized something that you *just do,* like making your bed or brushing your teeth? Ah, but I can tell you of many people who never make their beds, and a select few who never even brush their teeth. Lots of people—not just people who have ADD—can't get organized these days. So many that 64,732 books and 2,740,000 websites stand ready to tell you there is much more to getting organized than the Nike solution. They will tell you that they can help you. A growth industry of professional organizers and coaches crowds the Internet. Some are excellent; many are not. But there wouldn't be so awfully many of them if there weren't some powerful need they were trying to address, a need that didn't exist twenty-five years ago. The organizational demands of modern life exceed those of any prior point in human—or unhuman—history. Entropy reigns.

So what's a body to do? Especially an ADD body? After all the claims and extravagant promises of help, when you come right down to it, no matter how vast the chaos or how deep the mess, isn't the solution to disorganization, well, organization? If you look at all those books and all those websites, will you find something better than common sense parsed into myriad bits of obvious advice? Are these experts really doing anything more than borrowing your watch and telling you what time it is?

Most aren't, but some of them are. You see, some people have an astonishing gift for organization. I know a woman, for example, who can organize basements and attics. She is a savant at this. She has no other extraordinary talents, but she can go into the most jumbled attic or a dumpster-depot of a basement and render it shipshape in an afternoon. Her talent is like none I have ever seen in anyone else.

Some other people have a gift for teaching. This gift is more common than the organizational gift. And some very few combine the two: they are gifted teachers of organization.

One of the best is a woman I have never met. Her name is Liz Franklin and she wrote my favorite book on getting organized. It is called *How to Get Organized Without Resorting to Arson: A Step-by-Step Guide to Clearing Your Desk Without Panic or the Use of Open Flame.* She combines humor with practical advice in this brilliant book. She also recognizes an obvious fact that most books on getting organized overlook: people are different. What works for you may not work for me. You need to adapt your organizational techniques to your personal style of disorganization.

For people who have ADD, the problem with any book on how to get organized is, first of all, that it is a book. (That's also the problem with this book; it's a book!) Many people with ADD just don't read.

So they need messengers. Other people who do read can take the message of the book and try to feed it to the person who has ADD in a form he can take in. But even then, if the methods gain access to the brain of the disorganized person, the methods may not get applied.

There are some books on getting organized written specifically for people who have ADD. A good one is *ADD-Friendly Ways to Organize Your Life,* by Judith Kolberg and Kathleen Nadeau. It has many specific tips and methods that will help people who have ADD.

But often it is not so much methods that these people need as it is attitudes and companionship—someone to join them in their efforts. They need to start thinking in ways that work well for them, and they need someone to be there now and then to help them get through the onerous task of picking up.

I have looked at the best general books on getting organized— outstanding books, like Marilyn Paul's *It's Hard to Make a Difference When You Can't Find Your Keys* and Julie Morgenstern's *Organizing from the Inside Out*—and found that while they do contain novel and effective suggestions, they also provide a caring presence in the midst of the mess, at least as much as a book can do. They do not mock or ridicule disorganization. They understand and they empathize.

People who have ADD often feel so ashamed of their piles and messes that they get bogged down in negative energy and never feel the pick-me-up a person needs to undertake a difficult, hateful task—like straightening up a big mess of a room. Instead, shame sets in like a fog, and the mess continues to spread its tentacles of paper, magazines, books, loose envelopes, and Post-its.

My friend Sharon Wohlmuth told me of an open house she held to raise funds for a community organization. Sharon is a Pulitzer Prize–winning journalist and photographer, and a best-selling author. Among her books are *Sisters, Mothers and Daughters* and *Best Friends*. She also has ADD. Her office, which is in her home, usually looks like some desperate criminal just ransacked it looking for a tiny piece of paper.

On the day of the open house, Sharon had a decision to make. Should she leave the door to her office open, in which case all the visitors could see her mess, or should she close the door? She chose to leave it open. She watched and wondered what people thought as they peered into the maelstrom of her work space.

The next day the people who had arranged the open house told Sharon how many people had commented on her bravery in leaving that door open. They knew she had the option of closing it. Many people said that her willingness to show how she really worked gave them courage not to feel ashamed of how disorganized their own work space was—and these people did not even have ADD (as far as we know).

Knowing Sharon as well as I do, I know what an ongoing struggle organization has been for her. We have had telephone calls in which she broke down in tears, despairing over her inability to keep her office in proper shape.

It has caused her a lot of pain, but she keeps attacking the problem. She keeps trying. She has hired coaches and organizational consultants, who have helped her. She has read some books, and tried to follow the books' advice. She has listened to suggestions from anyone who had a good suggestion to make. She has tried various medications and psychotherapy.

What remains is an intermittent mess. Sharon straightens up her office only to see the mess return. Then she determinedly straightens it up again, but—like the demon it is—the mess returns. She has not been able to develop a system that will keep her office in a constant state of organization. She has hired people to set up such systems, which they have done, but she has been unable to stick to any one system. They all make sense; she just can't follow them.

But she is tough. She never gives up at anything. When she was a reporter for *The Philadelphia Inquirer,* she went into the most dangerous parts of Philadelphia to interview people and connect with the heart of her stories. She went to Africa and lived amid severe poverty and disease. She has been mugged in the city; she has been parched in the desert. She can handle pretty much anything that gets in her way.

And she is handling disorganization. Not easily. Not logically. But she is handling it. She would not get an A in neatness and organization from a fifth-grade schoolteacher. She would get a D or maybe an F, with a comment that she really ought to try harder. Her parents would be asked to come in to help motivate her. She would receive lectures on the importance of neatness and organization and the need to take responsibility for one's life. She would be made to feel shame for her shortcoming.

But now, as an adult, let me please give her the A she deserves, and the thousands of others like her out there who manage to stay organized well enough to, say, win a Pulitzer Prize, like Sharon, or be CEO of a huge company, like David Neeleman at JetBlue.

Sharon deserves an A because she gets something done well enough not to let her lack of skill in this one area destroy her. She knows that organization is not her strength, nor will it ever be. But she is smart enough not to waste too much time or mental energy trying to make it into a strength.

She has tried all the logical remedies. She has done what she can do. None of those remedies work. She doesn't blame the remedies. She knows that the problem is within. But instead of packing it in and giving up on her dreams, Sharon said to herself, "I can find a way to succeed in spite of all my disorganization." She looks around her and cries now and then at the mess she sees, but the tears don't last long. She gets the tears out, then finds what she needs to do her next job.

And what jobs she has done! Her photography—which is mostly black and white—is beautiful. Her eye for detail is uncanny, and her ability to cue in instantly on a moment of strong emotion, even if it is at the end of a day or a shoot, surpasses almost anyone I know. Her lens, so to speak, is always focused and ready.

She relies on various strategies to keep her well enough organized, whatever strategy has struck her fancy of late. There isn't one prevailing strategy that she has used for years, other than persistence.

And humor. She laughs at the problem most of the time. She doesn't ignore it or trivialize it with humor; she plucks its fangs with humor.

She also knows that a certain degree of disorganization is common among creative people. She doesn't like it, but she knows it usually comes with the territory of the kind of mind she's got. As one friend of hers put it, "In your office I can see your creativity in progress."

Life would be easier for her if she were a neat freak, but it's no big deal. She is *well enough* organized to fulfill her dreams. That's all she really needs.

And I think that is all any of us needs. We people who have ADD can spend too much time and money trying to become superorganized. That goal is not only out of our reach, it is not necessary. You simply need to become well enough organized to achieve your goals. There is a huge difference between the two.

Becoming well enough organized is a realistic goal for even the most disorganized ADD-er. I urge you to make this your goal, or your child's goal. I see people suffering and wasting time as they fruitlessly try to become someone they can't possibly become: a thoroughly organized person. Instead, I urge you to adopt my approach. Become well enough organized to reach your goals.

People often ask me how I managed to get through medical school having ADD. Other people ask me how, having ADD, I manage to juggle being a husband and father of three children, giving seventy-five to one hundred lectures every year, writing books (this is my twelfth), and maintaining an active private practice in psychiatry.

The answer to those questions is that I learned how to be well enough organized to reach my goals. I learned the basic tools of organization in fifth grade. I went to a highly structured school in West Newton, Massachusetts, called Fessenden. That school saved my life. One of the many ways in which it did this was by teaching me the basic tools of organization.

No one had taught me the basics at home. My family, God love them, was characterized by what I call the WASP triad: alcoholism, mental illness, and politeness. The adults in my family were usually drunk or crazy, but they were always polite. However, they were not interested in teaching me how to get organized. When I hit Fessenden I had a lot to learn.

My teachers taught me how to make lists. They taught me how to write down my assignment on a piece of paper and put it in a place where I wouldn't lose it. They made a game out of all this, so I felt motivated to learn how to do it. They taught me to pay attention to details, like not tearing the ring hole when taking a piece of paper from my three-ring binder. They taught me how to make flash cards if I needed to memorize names or dates or vocabulary words or anything at all. They equipped me with a set of organizational tricks I could use when I needed them.

I got through all the memorizing in medical school by making flash cards, a technique Mr. Magruder taught me in fifth grade. I get through each day now with what amounts to an assignment book, another technique Mr. Cook taught me in fifth grade.

I also rely heavily on a technique my teachers always stressed: ask for help when you need it. Since I need a lot of help in getting organized, I ask for that help. I am not ashamed that organization does not come as naturally to me as it does to others.

As an adult, I can also do something I couldn't do when I was in school: I delegate. I can hire assistants to help me with my organizational demands. And do they ever! I would be totally lost without them.

If you were to look at my office at home, where I do my writing, you would see that it resembles Sharon's. Even my fourteen-year-old daughter's bedroom is less cluttered than my home office. But I know where things are, and I can reach and get what I need.

Every so often an urge will hit me, like a kind of seizure, and I will spend three or four hours decluttering my office. I will straighten everything up. I will feel clean and smooth, as if my teeth had just been cleaned. And that feeling will last about as long as it does in my mouth. Soon the clutter returns. But I don't look at it as an enemy. It is the by-product of my work. It is the sign that I have been busy. I have picked up a book and put it down. I have read from a journal and tossed it aside. I have opened a letter and set it down. Someone else would have put the book back in the bookcase, or put the journal in a rack, or filed the letter. I am not such a person. I digest—and reading is somewhat like eating for me—a bit of material and then I want to do something with it, usually write something. I want to write something rather than get up and file the letter or put the book in the bookcase.

Over time, that makes me look disorganized. And I am. But I get done what I need to get done. I am well enough organized to reach my goals. That's what matters.

Most people will counsel you on how to get superorganized. I urge you to ignore that advice if you have ADD. It is just not in the cards for you. But it doesn't matter. Instead, put your energy into getting well enough organized to reach your dreams.

CHAPTER 43

WHAT THE BEST TREATMENT

MUST INCLUDE

Let me begin by describing what to avoid. It acts like a poisonous gas; no one sees it or smells it, but it destroys the treatment even before it begins. It is the poison of disconnection.

There are so many treatments for ADD available that it is impossible to say for sure which work and which don't. It is a safe bet that most treatments have helped at least a few people; otherwise the person offering the treatment would not have gone to the expense of setting up shop. But *all* treatments should include the vital force of the feeling of connection between patient and doctor, or client and provider, whatever the provider's discipline, guild, or system of belief.

Medication in combination with education, coaching, structure, and other lifestyle changes comprise the best-tested and most convincingly validated program for treating ADD. However, that does not mean that medication must be used in all treatments, or that a treatment that follows other paradigms will be ineffective. We live in the midst of exciting ongoing research; until every treatment has been evaluated we must acknowledge and contend with uncertainty.

My concern in this chapter is not about the specifics of the treatment regimen you follow: whether or not you use medication; whether or not you try nutritional supplements; whether or not your doctor urges you to exercise; whether or not you try cerebellar stimulation or any of the newer treatments available that I have mentioned in this book.

My concern is about the kind of doctor or other mental-health professional you go to see, and the kind of clinic. Whatever the treatment might be that you are offered, it is how you are offered it that I wish to discuss here.

Unfortunately, a large number of practitioners and clinics can't take the time to provide you with a proper diagnostic work-up, or develop a proper treatment plan. I don't just mean the complete and correct set of techniques, although they certainly matter.

When I say "proper," I am referring to the quality of the connection you feel with the person providing your treatment and the place where it is provided. You need to feel understood, heard, and known as you go through the process of diagnosis and treatment, however brief it may be. Perhaps the most common mistake a mental-health professional makes these days is leaping over the person as she tries to grab hold of the diagnosis and offer treatment. The person is left bewildered.

Above all else, you need to see a doctor who will naturally regard you as a person first, who can share a joke with you, laugh at himself, and get to know you a bit, maybe ask about details that have nothing to do with the matter that brought you to the office in the first place.

For various reasons, mostly economic and medicolegal, but also as a reaction to the ruling dogma of the previous generation, psychiatry is losing sight of the person in the patient. Our interventions are becoming far too cut-and-dried, often just a matter of diagnose-and-medicate. You can sometimes more easily get a smile or a joke out of someone who works at the Department of Motor Vehicles than certain mental-health practitioners. Practitioners have retreated behind an impersonal façade, avoiding emotional connection in the way the old-fashioned psychoanalyst once did. When it comes to treating the mind, this works about as well as treating a stomachache with a punch to the gut.

How did we get into this mess? Fifty years ago, orthodox psychoanalytic theory held mental-health practitioners and patients in a vise. So dogmatic and powerful was the ruling theory that neither patient nor doctor dared object to it, even when the theory bordered on the crackpot. The medicines we have today are indeed much better, but the process by which we dispense them is, if anything, much worse. We have replaced doctrinaire psychoanalysis with a process equally impersonal, unhearing, and demeaning.

Meanwhile, while no one was looking, psychoanalysis has evolved into an open-minded, vital, interactional process that may not get the attention or command the power it did in the 1950s and 1960s but helps people much more than it used to. Although I am not a psychoanalyst—I couldn't sit still long enough for the years of training it requires—I admire what psychoanalysis has become today. People outside the field don't know it, but psychoanalysis is perhaps the last spot left in all of medicine where understanding the patient as a person is the first task, if not the only task.

At the same time, modern psychiatry risks becoming merely a game of connect the dots. Patients arrive at the doorstep filled with pain and worry. After they fill out numerous forms, they get a quick visit with the doctor. In ten or fifteen minutes they are asked to list their symptoms, while the psychiatrist's mind whirs through the various patterns he has learned from the diagnostic manual, or DSM-IV. He often doesn't have the time or the training to look for the person inside the patient sitting before him. He is trying to match up a required number of symptoms with a given DSM-IV entry to make a diagnosis. Once the patient lists enough symptoms in a category, *Bingo!* You have a diagnosis. Maybe it's major depression. Maybe it's mania. Maybe it's generalized anxiety disorder. Maybe it's ADHD.

Once you name enough symptoms to reach a diagnosis, your doctor's mind now whirs through the medications that match the diagnosis, and she picks one to offer you. Sometimes she picks a few, and lets you join her in making the decision.

A few minutes later, you leave the office having been given a diagnosis and a medication. You feel confused, unheard, and unhelped. But, being in distress, you take what you've been given and hope the medication will be good enough to make up for what the process lacked in empathy.

The interaction with the doctor takes as little time as possible, because the insurance company is watching, and such time wasters as empathic conversation or humorous asides take minutes for which there will be no reimbursement.

This is a caricature, but, sadly, a caricature that comes close to the hurried reality of psychiatry today. We psychiatrists rightly boast that we are more evidence-based than we used to be, and that our diagnostic criteria are based upon objective symptoms and behaviors, not subjective intuitions. But while the science has progressed spectacularly, our implementation of it has grown so impersonal as to be frequently ham-handed and even rude. That's not a good way to heal emotional wounds.

Unfortunately, the diagnosis and treatment of ADD (or ADHD) lends itself all too easily to this mechanical model. The diagnosis depends upon identifying six or more symptoms in one or two lists of nine symptoms each. If you are a busy doctor and you have only a short time, either you have to give your patient a list to fill out in the waiting room or at home, or you have to read through the two lists of nine symptoms each and check them off as you do. Both alternatives can be mechanistic and off-putting. They are tolerable if you have more time to spend in conversation, but if you don't, the process can suffer in the ways I have mentioned. The patient may feel diagnosed, but neither welcomed nor understood.

To compound the problem, many people with ADD will tell the doctor exactly how they want it. They want to cut to the chase, hurry it up, get to the bottom line, get their prescription, and leave. The quicker the better!

So you need to see a doctor or other mental-health professional who can say, "Whoa! Slow down! Stay a moment. Talk to me!"

When you protest, and say you know everything he's going to ask anyway, and you already gave him all the answers in the forms you filled out or the letter you wrote or the e-mail you sent last week, you need a doctor who will say, "Well, I still need to get to know you a little better. Humor me. And it would be good if your wife could come in with you as well." In other words, you need to see someone who will not accept too many shortcuts. It doesn't need to be an agonizingly slow process, but it does need to be more than five minutes.

All of medicine has shifted toward the fast approach. Fast as well as defensive. Fast and defensive combine to create something strange. Have you ever talked to someone who has felt suicidal and gone to an emergency room, or, worse, a mental hospital for help? The "help" can be enough to make the jauntiest person suicidal. If you confess ever to having thought of suicide, for example, you may get committed to the hospital against your will. Most people have thought of suicide. Just don't make the mistake of telling that to a busy mental-health worker who has access to an inpatient unit, or you may spend the night there.

Here we glimpse another of the reasons my field risks becoming a travesty of what it ought to be. The threat of being sued occupies a primal spot in the minds of most doctors, especially psychiatrists, far more than it did a generation ago. The reason your confessing to ever having thought of suicide can get you locked up is not that the doctor really believes you might kill yourself, but because he wants to protect himself from a lawsuit, just in case. He will sleep better with you locked up.

When I began my training in 1979, the lawyer who consulted to the hospital where I trained met with all of us rookies and told us what we were up against. I'll never forget his closing words: "If I were in your shoes, I would never practice psychiatry. I'd look for a job in research or administration, as far removed from clinical responsibility as possible. This is because every word you speak with a patient, every note you write, or, more importantly, forget to write, every gesture you make, every medication you prescribe, in other words everything you do, can end you up on the losing end of a lawsuit or on the losing end of disciplinary action from the Board of Registration in Medicine."

We were all stunned. Here we were, just about to enter the field we had dreamed of and worked so hard to reach, only to find out that we were entering a minefield.

I still know that lawyer today. He is my go-to guy when I have a medicolegal question. He is a brilliant man and a really good man. In other words, he is not your stereotypical, overly cautious lawyer. What he told us that day more than two decades ago is even truer now that it was then. It points up one of the major reasons the field of mental health, not just psychiatry, has become so impersonal and defensive.

Fear permeates just about every word and gesture of many clinicians' work. I don't blame them, and I certainly confess that I am subject to those fears myself. I am simply describing why it is so difficult to find an open and honest human to turn to as your psychiatrist these days. The field is better suited to computers.

The whole process really does not require a human in the role of psychiatrist the way it's practiced today. A well-programmed Apple or

PC with some good graphics and sound could do it just as well, indeed better, since such human factors as fatigue, inconsistency, irritability, fading memory, or inattention would not get in the way.

Most psychiatrists—except those who don't like people—don't like what's happened to the field. Patients don't like it. No one closely involved in the process likes it. It doesn't have to be done that way, and it shouldn't be done that way.

Most mental-health professionals have found ways to preserve humanity in their work. They may have to work quickly, they may ask you to fill out various forms, and they may take copious notes, but you get the sense when you are with them that they care about you. They can laugh. They can listen. They make you feel comfortable, even if the time must be short. Make sure when you seek treatment that you find one of them.

Even if you are an impatient adult who has ADD, you owe yourself a visit with a doctor who can sit back and listen just a bit, or get you to talking more than just a bit. You have a lot to say. You ought to say it. You'd be amazed how much more wants to come out of your brain, more than you ever knew was there. Much more than a computer can draw forth.

Be sure you see a human. Whatever it is that gets people better, whether they have a cold, cancer, or ADD, the human relationship is at the core of it.

A COMPENDIUM OF RESOURCES

This section of the book was compiled by two women from the state of Washington, Kay Murray and Roxie Nickerson. I met them both at a lecture I was giving, and when they asked me if I intended to include a section in my new book devoted to helping people find help for ADD, I told them that I did intend to do so, but that I would need help. The next thing I knew, they had volunteered. Not only did they help; they did the whole job themselves.

Kay and Roxie, I am sure I speak for readers everywhere in saying we can't thank you enough.

SUPPORT, EDUCATION, AND ADVOCACY ORGANIZATIONS

The organizations listed below offer information and support to those in need. Call to locate an office or support group near you, as well as to obtain a list of their individual publications and membership information.

ADD Organizations

Attention Deficit Disorder Association (ADDA)
P.O. Box 543, Pottstown, PA 19464
484-945-2101

www.add.org

National clearinghouse for information, support, and advocacy for ADHD adults.

Attention Deficit Disorder Resources

223 Tacoma Avenue S #100, Tacoma, WA 98402

253-759-5085

www.addresources.org

Offers support, education, and resources for those with ADD. Website includes National ADHD Directory.

Children and Adults with Attention Deficit Disorder (CHADD)

8181 Professional Place, Suite 150, Landover, MD 20785

301-306-7070

www.chadd.org

Through family support and advocacy, public and professional education, and encouragement of scientific research, CHADD works to ensure that those with ADHD reach their inherent potential. Local chapters hold regular meetings providing support and information.

National Center for Gender Issues and ADHD

3268 Arcadia Place NW, Washington, DC 20015

888-238-8588

www.ncgiadd.org; e-mail: contact@ncgiadd.org

The National Center for Gender Issues and ADHD has been founded by Patricia Quinn, M.D., and Kathleen Nadeau, Ph.D., to promote awareness, advocacy, and research on ADHD in women and girls.

Learning Disabilities Organizations

Council for Exceptional Children (CEC), Division for Learning Disabilities (DLD)

1110 North Glebe Road, Suite 300, Arlington, VA 22201

703-620-3660

www.cec.sped.org, www.teachingld.org

A nonprofit organization with seventeen specialized divisions. DLD is the division dedicated to learning disabilities. It provides free information and holds conferences.

Council for Learning Disabilities

P.O. Box 4014, Leesburg, VA 20177

571-258-1010

www.cldinternational.org

An international organization concerned about issues related to
students with learning disabilities.

Educational Resources Information Center (ERIC)
2277 Research Boulevard, 6M, Rockville, MD 20850
301-519-5157, 800-538-3742
www.eric.ed.gov; e-mail: eric@ericit.syr.edu
National information system funded by the United States Deptartment
of Education.

International Dyslexia Association (formerly Orton Dyslexia Society)
Chester Building, Suite 382, 8600 LaSalle Road, Baltimore, MD
21286-2044
410-296-0232, 800-222-3123
www.interdys.org; e-mail: info@interdys.org
The most distinguished organization of its kind in the world. The society
has more than forty branches throughout the United States and
Canada which offer informational meetings and support groups.
Referrals are made for persons seeking resources. In addition, the
society publishes journals and publications regarding dyslexia.

Learning Disabilities Association of America (LDA)
4156 Library Road, Pittsburgh, PA 15234
412-341-1515
www.ldanatl.org; e-mail: info@ldaamerica.org
International organization of parents of learning-disabled children,
adults with learning disabilities, and professionals. Activities include
education, legislation, and research.

National Dissemination Center for Children with Disabilities (NICHY)
P.O. Box 1492, Washington, DC 20013
800-695-0285
www.nichcy.org; e-mail: nichcy@aed.org
Serves as a source of information on IDEA, No Child Left Behind, and
research-based information on effective educational practices.

National Institute for Learning Disabilities
107 Seekel Street, Norfolk, VA 23505
757-423-8646
www.nild.net
This organization has developed its own individualized educational

therapy, which includes a special form of tutoring combined with exercises that stimulate certain parts of the brain.

Organizations Devoted to Disorders Related to ADD

Child & Adolescent Bipolar Foundation
1187 Wilmette Avenue, P.M.B. #331, Wilmette, IL 60091
847-256-8525
www.bpkids.org
Support and education for families raising children with bipolar
    disorder.

The Juvenile Bipolar Research Foundation
49 S. Quaker Hill Road, Pawling, NY 12564
www.bpchildresearch.org; e-mail: info@bpchildresearch.org

MAAP Services for Autism and Asperger's Syndrome
P.O. Box 524, Crown Point, IN 46308
219-662-1311
www.maapservices.org; www.asperger.org
Provides information and advice to families of individuals with autism,
    Asperger's syndrome, and pervasive developmental disorder.

National Alliance for the Mentally Ill (NAMI)
200 N. Glebe Road, Suite 1015, Arlington, VA 22203-3754
703-524-7600, 800-950-NAMI
www.nami.org

National Depressive and Manic-Depressive Foundation (NDMDA)
730 N. Franklin Street, Suite 501, Chicago, IL 60610
800-82-NDMDA
www.ndmda.org

Tourette Syndrome Association, Inc.
42-40 Bell Boulevard, Bayside, NY 11361
718-224-2999
www.tsa-usa.org; e-mail: ts@tsa-usa.org
Website for education and advocacy.

Laws, Accommodations, and Employment

Association on Higher Education and Disability (AHEAD)
P.O. Box 540666, Waltham, MA 02454
781-788-0003

www.ahead.org; e-mail: ahead@ahead.org
International multicultural organization of professionals committed
to full participation in higher education for persons with
disabilities.

Council of Parent Attorneys and Advocates (COPAA)
1321 Pennsylvania Avenue SE, Washington, DC 20003-3027
202-544-2210
www.copaa.net; e-mail: copaa@copaa.net
COPAA is an independent nonprofit organization of attorneys,
advocates, and parents established to improve the quality and
quantity of legal assistance for parents of children with disabilities.

Equal Employment Opportunity Commission (EEOC)
1801 L Street NW, Washington, DC 20507
202-663-4900, 800-669-4000
www.eeoc.gov
Information on employment issues, federal laws, and discrimination.

Job Accommodation Network
P.O. Box 6080, Morgantown, WV 26506-6080
800-526-7234, 800-ADA-WORK
www.jan.wvu.edu; e-mail: jan@jan.wvu.edu
A free consulting service that provides information about job
accommodations, the Americans with Disabilities Act (ADA), and
the employability of people with disabilities.

Office for Civil Rights (United States Department of Education)
400 Maryland Avenue SW, Washington, DC 20202
800-USA-LEARN
www.ed.gov/about/offices/list/ocr/index.html;
e-mail: customerservice@inet.ed.gov
The mission of OCR is to ensure equal access to education and to
promote educational excellence throughout the nation through
enforcement of civil rights. Contact for Section 504 related issues.

Magazines and Newsletters

ADDitude magazine
Inquiries: 42 West 38th Street, New York, NY 10018
Subscriptions: P.O. Box 500, Missouri City, TX 77459
888-762-8475
www.additudemag.com; e-mail: additude@additudemag.com

National bimonthly magazine for the ADD community. Dr. Hallowell
writes a regular column for this magazine.

ADDult ADDvice newsletter
223 Tacoma Avenue S #100, Tacoma, WA 98402
253-759-5085
www.addresources.org
Published quarterly, this is available with ADD Resources membership.

ADDvance Magazine for Women
No longer in publication in print format. To receive ADDvance Online,
a new monthly electronic newsletter, go to www.ncgiadd.org
(website of the National Center for Gender Issues and ADHD).

ADHDNews.com by Brandi Valentine
www.adhdnews.com
Active website; sends out an e-mail newsletter.

The ADHD Report by Russell Barkley, Ph.D.
Guilford Press
800-365-7006
www.guilford.com
Bimonthly newsletter for practitioners, educators, teacher trainers,
scientists, and parents. It contains insights and cutting-edge
techniques of today's leading authorities on ADHD. Dr. Barkley is
one of the true pioneers in the field of ADHD.

Attention! magazine
Published quarterly, this is available with CHADD membership.

Focus
P.O. Box 543, Pottstown, PA 19464
484-945-2101
www.add.org; e-mail: mail@add.org
Newsletter available with ADDA membership.

Coaching Resources

ADDA Coach Register
www.add.org
Listing of ADD coaches throughout the United States, Canada, and
Puerto Rico.

ADD Consultants

www.addconsults.com

Provides private, personal ADD consultations, both nationally and internationally, via e-mail.

ADD Resources National ADHD Directory

253-759-5085

www.addresources.org

Listing of ADD coaches.

American Coaching Association

P.O. Box 353, Lafayette Hill, PA 19144

610-825-8572

www.americoach.org

ACA's mission is to link people who want coaching with people who do coaching, to acquaint the general public with the concept of coaching, and to provide coaches with training.

Nancy Ratey

www.nancyratey.com

Nancy Ratey (John's wife) is a teacher of coaches and can make referrals to coaches in various parts of the country. You can reach her via her website.

ADD Educational Materials

ADD Warehouse

800-233-9273

www.addwarehouse.com

Mail-order and online catalog of resources on ADHD, oppositional defiant disorder, Asperger's syndrome, autism, Tourette's syndrome, and learning problems. It offers a wide variety of books, videos, and other resource materials.

Additional Web Resources

ADD Consults

www.addconsults.com

Provides private, personal ADD consultations, both nationally and internationally, via e-mail.

ADDers.Org

www.adders.org

A site to learn about our friends in England. It has information on
support groups worldwide.

ADDResource.com

www.addresource.com

Web directory/resource exclusively about attention deficit disorder and
related learning disabilities.

ADDvance.com

www.addvance.com

www.ncgiadd.org

A resource for women and girls with attention deficit disorder.

ADHD of the Christian Kind

www.christianadhd.com

A website that offers articles, education, Bible studies, and many other
Christian-related resources.

All Kinds of Minds

www.allkindsofminds.com

A wealth of information about learning disabilities, including resources
for professional development, discussion groups, and information
about Dr. Mel Levine's All Kinds of Minds Institute. Dr. Levine is
one of the true innovative geniuses in this field.

Born to Explore

www.borntoexplore.org

A site that emphasizes the positive aspects of ADD.

LD Online

www.ldonline.org

A website on learning disabilities and resources, for parents, teachers,
and other professionals.

National Resource Center on ADHD

800-233-4050

www.help4adhd.org

National clearinghouse of information and resources. This is a program
of CHADD that was established with funding from the Centers for
Disease Control and Prevention.

BRIEF BIBLIOGRAPHY

For Children Who Have ADD

Dendy, Chris A. Zeigler, and Alex Zeigler, *A Bird's-Eye View of Life with ADD and ADHD: Advice from Young Survivors* (Cherish the Children, 2003).

Written for teens by twelve teens and a young adult.

Hallowell, Edward, M.D., *A Walk in the Rain with a Brain* (Regan Books/ HarperCollins, 2004).

An illustrated children's story (for ages four to twelve), the moral of which is that smart and stupid mean very little; what matters is finding what you love, then doing it. As Manfred the brain says in the story, "No brain is the same, no brain is the best, each brain finds its own special way."

Lowry, Mark, and Martha Bolton, *Piper's Night Before Christmas* (Howard Publishing Company, 1998).

This is the first in a series of four books; the others are *Nighttime Is Just Daytime with Your Eyes Closed* (1999), *Piper Steals the Show* (2000), and *Piper's Twisted Tale* (2001). Having grown up with ADHD, Mark Lowry readily identifies with the character in his books, Piper the Hyperactive Mouse. Mark is a multitalented artist who is a comedian, singer, and songwriter, as well as co-author of these children's books. Each book comes with a CD of Mark narrating the story.

Mooney, Jonathan, and David Cole, *Learning Outside the Lines* (Fireside Books, 2000).

Two Ivy League students with learning disabilities and ADHD give you the tools for academic success and educational revolution.

Moss, Deborah, *Shelley, the Hyperactive Turtle* (Woodbine House, 1989).

A delightful story of a bright young turtle who is not like all the other turtles. Shelley moves like a rocket, and is unable to sit still for even the shortest periods of time.

For Parents of Children Who Have ADD

Barkley, Russell, Ph.D., *Taking Charge of ADHD: The Complete Authority Guide for Parents* (The Guilford Press, 2000).

A parent resource incorporating the most current information on ADHD and its treatment.

Brooks, Robert, Ph.D., and Sam Goldstein, Ph.D., *Raising Resilient Children: Fostering Strength, Hope, and Optimism in Your Child* (McGraw-Hill/Contemporary Books, 2002).

This book explains how to help children become emotionally and mentally strong to face the challenges of modern life.

Greene, Ross, Ph.D., *The Explosive Child* (HarperCollins, 1998).

A practical approach to treating spirited children. Dr. Greene explains that the difficulties of these children stem from brain-based deficits in the ability to be flexible and to handle frustration.

Hallowell, Edward, M.D., *The Childhood Roots of Adult Happiness* (Ballantine, 2003).

Provides a succinct, practical, evidence-based guide for parents on how to raise children in a way that will maximize the chances of their becoming happy, successful adults, whether or not they have ADD.

Jensen, Peter S., M.D., *Making the System Work for Your Child with ADHD* (Guilford Press, 2004).

Silver, Larry, M.D., *Dr. Larry Silver's Advice to Parents on ADHD* (Three Rivers Press, 1999).

This resource addresses the subjects all parents wonder about when they suspect their child has ADHD: causes, signs to look for, getting an accurate diagnosis, latest information on medications and other treatments.

Wilens, Timothy E., M.D., *Straight Talk About Psychiatric Medications for Kids* (The Guilford Press, 2002).

With numerous real-life examples, answers to frequently asked questions, and helpful tables and charts, Harvard University researcher and practitioner Timothy Wilens explains which medications may be prescribed for children and why.

For Adults Who Have ADD

Hartmann, Thom, *Attention Deficit Disorder: A Different Perception* (Underwood Books, 1997).

Thom Hartmann explains some of the positive characteristics sometimes associated with ADD and provides an explanation of the disorder that can help adults at home, at work, and in school.

Kelly, Kate, and Peggy Ramundo, *You Mean I'm Not Lazy, Stupid, or Crazy?! A Self-Help Book for Adults with Attention Deficit Disorder* (Scribner, 1996).

Kolberg, Judith, and Kathleen Nadeau, Ph.D., *ADD-Friendly Ways to Organize Your Life* (Brunner-Routledge, 2002).

This collaboration brings together the best understanding of the disorder with the most effective and practical remedies from ADD experts in two important fields: professional organization and clinical psychology.

Novotni, Michele, Ph.D., *What Does Everybody Else Know That I Don't? Social Skills Help for Adults with Attention Deficit/Hyperactivity Disorder (AD/HD)* (Specialty Press, 1999).

Social skills help for ADD adults.

Solden, Sari, *Women with Attention Deficit Disorder* (Underwood Books, 1995).

Sari Solden combines real-life histories, treatment experiences, and recent clinical research to highlight the special challenges facing women with attention deficit disorder.

————, *Journeys Through ADDulthood* (Walker & Company, 2002).

Offers a wealth of wisdom, sound advice, reassuring experiences, and hope for adults with ADHD.

General Books on ADD

Amen, Daniel G., M.D., *Healing ADD* (Putnam, 2001).

Dr. Amen explains his theory of the six types of ADD and provides a comprehensive treatment program that can lead to a normal, peaceful, and fully functional life.

Hallowell, Edward M., M.D., and John J. Ratey, M.D., *Driven to Distraction: Recognizing and Coping with Attention Deficit Disorder from Childhood through Adulthood* (Pantheon, 1994).

————, *Answers to Distraction* (Bantam, 1996).

Jensen, Peter S., M.D., and James R. Cooper, M.D., editors, *Attention Deficit Hyperactivity Disorder: State of the Science, Best Practices* (Civic Research Institute, 2002).

This is the most up-to-date, comprehensive, authoritative academic volume on the topic available today. Jensen and Cooper bring together various points of view under one cover. A superb reference book.

SUPPORT AND EDUCATION GROUPS BY STATE AND CITY

The following was written by the women who compiled this list:

This is not an all-inclusive list of groups for ADD adults and parents of ADD children. Our goal is to offer a few resources in each state where you may call to obtain additional support information for your area. The national organizations listed above offer more comprehensive lists of support groups and resources; see the above websites for additional contact information.

We have tried to make this list as accurate and up-to-date as possible. We apologize if you find any contact details that are out of date, incorrect, or if there are other supports that we did not know about.

If you have any additions or corrections to this list, please let us know. Send information to Roxanne Nickerson, 1920 5th Street, Marysville, WA 98270, or, by e-mail, roxienickerson@yahoo.com. Those wishing to contact Lisa Poast of Bellingham, WA, who compiled the first listing of adult ADD support groups for *Driven to Distraction*, may do so by calling her at 360-647-6681.

Alabama

Montgomery

Learning Disabilities Association
  of Alabama
334-277-9151
www.ldaal.org
e-mail: alabama@ldaal.org

Alaska

Anchorage

Dr. William Larson
907-344-2707

PARENTS, Inc. (statewide
  support and education)
907-337-7678, 800-478-7678
www.parentsinc.org

Arizona

Ahwatukee

Jeri Goldstein, M.C., R.N.
Adult ADD Group
480-753-5045
e-mail: jeri123@aol.com

Prescott area

Adults & Families with ADD
  Groups
928-636-5160
e-mail: cbrehmer@northlink.com

Scottsdale

The Attention Deficit Disorder
  Clinic
480-424-7200
e-mail: add@addclinic-az-nm.com

Tempe

East Valley CHADD
480-706-1086
e-mail: eastvalleychadd@qwest.net

Tucson

Tucson CHADD (adult and
   parent support groups)
520-744-9493
e-mail: adsedw@aol.com

Yuma

ADD/ADHD Advocacy
928-344-1459

Arkansas

Jonesboro

Focus Inc. (statewide network for
   families of children with
   disabilities)
870-935-2750

California

*Alameda, Butte, Contra Costa,
   Humboldt, Lake, Marin,
   Mendocino, Monterey, Napa,
   Nevada, Sacramento, San Benito,
   San Francisco, San Joaquin, San
   Mateo, Santa Clara, Santa Cruz,
   Sonoma, and Yolo counties*

CHADD of Northern California
510-291-2950, 888-759-9758
www.chaddnorcal.org
e-mail: inquiries@chaddnorcal.org

Arcadia

Adult ADD Group
626-301-7977

Calabasas

Attention Management (adults
   and children)
818-878-9002
e-mail: ADDDepot@aol.com

Contra Costa County

Pat Churchill, M.A., M.F.T.
Monte Churchill (ADD adults
   and couples)
925-825-4938

Fresno

Changes: Center for Generational
   Change
559-438-3021
www.addpathfinders.com

Lafayette

Adult ADD Support Group
   and Individual ADD
   Counseling
925-284-9795
www.strategic-coaching-
   services.com

Long Beach

ADD Adults
562-438-7488

Adult ADD & Couples
   Groups
562-493-1496

Palo Alto

ADD Adult Group
650-949-5472

Kitty Petty ADD/LD Institute
   (adults)
650-329-9443
www.kpinst.org
e-mail: kitty@kpinst.org

San Diego

Learning Developmental Services (adults)
619-276-6912

San Francisco

San Francisco/North Peninsula CHADD Adults Group
415-771-5518

Simi Valley

Center for Attention Disorders
805-527-9414

Whittier

Southeast Los Angeles CHADD
562-946-8411

Wildomar/Riverside County

Temucula Valley CHADD Adult Group
909-678-7452

Colorado

Denver

ADD Women's Support Group
303-320-4425
e-mail: lol51@msn.com

CHADD of Colorado
303-646-5299

Denver Treatment Center for Adult ADD
303-322-1291
e-mail: lol51@msn.com

Fort Collins

ADD Adult Support
970-223-1338

Connecticut

Danbury

Greater Danbury CHADD
203-790-8654
e-mail: lorilu725@aol.com

Niantic

Connecticut Parent Advocacy Center (statewide advocacy and support)
860-739-3089, 800-445-2722
www.cpacinc.org
e-mail: cpac@cpacinc.org

Delaware

Newark

Greater Newark CHADD
302-737-5063
e-mail: newarkchadd@yahoo.com

Wilmington

Brandywine Valley CHADD (adults and parents)
302-376-0900
e-mail: brandyw_chadd@yahoo.com

Florida

Boca Raton

Adult ADD Group
561-706-1274
addadults.net
e-mail: leslie@addadults.net

Fort Lauderdale

Associates in Counseling and Mediation
954-474-1119

Fort Walton Beach

Fort Walton Beach CHADD
850-934-1178
www.geocities.com/bo91195
e-mail: pat.davis@mindspring.com

Gulf Breeze

Pensacola/Santa Rosa CHADD
850-934-1178

Miami

Center of Attention (Adults)
305-661-0373

Pembroke Pines

CHADD of South Broward and
North Dade counties
954-680-0799

Georgia

Decatur

Adults with Attention Deficit
(coed and women's groups)
404-378-6643
www.lullwaterschool.org

Douglasville

Parents Educating Parents &
Professionals for All Children
770-577-7771
www.peppinc.org
e-mail: peppinc@peppinc.org

Hawaii

Honolulu

AWARE
808-536-9684, 800-553-9684
e-mail: jschember-
lang@ldahawaii.org

Learning Disabilities Association
of Hawaii ADHD Support
Group
808-536-9684
www.ldahawaii.org
e-mail: ldah@ldahawaii.org

Idaho

Boise

Idaho Parents Unlimited, Inc.
(support, information, and
assistance to families)
208-342-5884, 800-242-4785
www.ipulidaho.org
e-mail: evelyn@ipulidaho.org

Twin Falls

Twin Falls CHADD
208-734-2854

Illinois

Chicago

Adult ADD Support Group with
Peter Jaksa, Ph.D.
312-372-4824
e-mail: drjaksa@aol.com

CHADD of Chicago Parent &
Adult Groups
773-250-3200
chaddofchicago.tripod.com
e-mail:
chaddofchicago@yahoo.com

Marion

Southern Illinois CHADD
618-542-5142, 618-996-2131
www.angelfire.com/il2/chadd/
index.html
e-mail: sichadd@yahoo.com

Peoria

Counseling Works
309-693-0038

Southwest Chicago area

ADAPPT (adults)
708-361-3387

Indiana

Bloomington

Abilities Unlimited (adults)
812-332-1620

Monroe County CHADD
812-334-1524
www.geocities.com/chaddmonroe
county
e-mail:
chaddmonroecounty@yahoo.com

Columbus

Bartholomew County CHADD
812-375-9573
e-mail: jemcountry@aol.com

Indianapolis

Education & Problem Solving
317-581-1779

Iowa

*Cedar Rapids, Des Moines,
Dubuque, Iowa City, Muscatine,
Quad Cities (Bettenford and
Davenport, Iowa, and Malone
and Rock Island, Illinois), and
Siouxland*

CHADD of Iowa
563-557-7529, 319-373-0255
e-mail:
chadd_of_iowa@mchsi.com

Des Moines

Access for Special Kids (resource
for children and adults with
disabilities)
515-243-1713, 800-450-8667
www.askresources.org
e-mail: ptiiowa@aol.com

Kansas

Wichita

Families Together, Inc. (family
information network)
316-945-7747, 888-815-6364
www.familiestogetherinc.org
e-mail:
connie@familiestogetherinc.org

Kentucky

Lexington

Bluegrass CHADD
859-219-2137
e-mail: kisenhou@cs.com

Louisville

FIND (family information
   network)
502-584-1239
www.findoflouisville.org
e-mail: find@councilonmr.org

Louisiana

Baton Rouge

Louisiana CHADD
225-261-0613
e-mail: lacachadd@hotmail.com

Covington

Center for Development and
   Learning
985-778-9334

Houma

Bayou Region CHADD
985-872-0945
e-mail: teva@cajun.net

Metairie

Families Helping Families
   (training and resources)
800-766-7736, 504-888-9111
www.projectprompt.com
e-mail: info@fhfgnoorg

New Orleans

New Orleans CHADD
504-468-5400
www.msnusers.com/
   chaddofneworleans
e-mail: chaddnola@msn.com

Maine

Augusta

Maine Parent Federation
   (advocacy, education, training)
207-623-2144
www.mpf.org
e-mail: parentconnect@mpf.org

Bangor

Bangor CHADD
207-990-1555

Maryland

*Anne Arundel County, Frederick
   Howard County, Harford County,
   Linthicum, Bethesda, Silver
   Spring, Timonium*

CHADD of Montgomery County
301-869-3628
www.chadd-mc.org
e-mail: volunteer@chadd-mc.org

Easton

The Learning Connections LLC
Beverly Rohman
410-763-7097
e-mail: info@
   thelearningconnections.net

Germantown

Living & Loving with AD/HD
   Adult Support Group
301-444-0394
www.sclifecoaching.com
e-mail: spclarke@prodigy.net

Massachusetts

Boston, Sudbury, Andover, and surrounding areas

The Hallowell Center for Cognitive and Emotional Health
142 North Road, Sudbury, MA 01776
978-287-0810
www.DrHallowell.com
This is Dr. Hallowell's private practice. The center has a staff of more than twenty clinicians who specialize in the treatment of ADD in children and adults. The center also offers referrals around the country for people who are having trouble finding adequate help in their area.

Lynn

North Shore ADD & LD Family Support Group (adult and child)
Mary Ann Murray, B.A.
781-599-6818

Wayland

Metro West CHADD
508-655-2590
e-mail:
metrowestchadd@verizon.net

Michigan

Big Rapids

CHADD of Big Rapids
231-796-4874
e-mail: chaddbr@tucker-usa.com

Birmingham

CHADD of Eastern Oakland County (adults and parents)
248-988-6716

Detroit

CHADD of Metro City
313-574-9090

Minnesota

Bloomington

Twin Cities CHADD
952-922-5761
e-mail: CHADD@gtd.org

Hopkins

Applied Behavioral Health Care, Adult & Family Support
952-933-3460

Minneapolis

Loring Family Clinic ADD Group (adults)
612-872-9072

Rochester

Rochester CHADD
507-280-6937
e-mail: misseward@home.com

Mississippi

Jackson

Parent Partners (training and information center for parents of children with disabilities)
601-354-3302, 800-366-5707
www.parentpartners.org
e-mail:
tburton@parentpartners.org

Missouri

Kansas City

Missouri Parents Act (statewide
  parent training and information
  center)
816-531-7070
www.ptimpact.com
e-mail: msavage@ptimpact.com

Greater Kansas City CHADD
816-537-7124
e-mail: laura.miller@
  mail.raytown.k12.mo.us

Livingston, Carroll, Saline County

Livingston, Carroll, Saline County
  CHADD #975
660-534-7737

Montana

Billings

Parents Let's Unite for Kids
  (statewide information, support,
  training)
406-255-0540, 800-222-7585
www.pluk.org
e-mail: plukinfo@pluk.org

Bozeman

Bozeman CHADD
406-587-7962

Kalispell

Flathead Valley CHADD
406-756-9359

Nebraska

Omaha

CHADD of Nebraska
402-734-0681

PTI Nebraska (statewide training
  and information for families
  with special needs)
402-346-0525, 800-284-8520
www.pti-nebraska.org
e-mail: info@pti-nebraska.org

Nevada

Las Vegas

Las Vegas CHADD
702-580-1955
Parents Encouraging Parents
702-388-8899, 800-216-5188
e-mail: pepinfo@nvpep.org

Reno

Reno-Sparks CHADD
775-626-6957
e-mail: renosparks@hotmail.com

New Hampshire

Southwest New Hampshire area

SW New Hampshire CHADD
603-357-0479

New Jersey

Long Beach

ADD Adult Support Group
  (adults and their significant
  others)
732-842-4553
www.drlopresti.com
e-mail: drlopresti@drlopresti.com

Morristown

Morris ADDult Support Group
973-361-5365, 973-971-8934
www.drrayprice.com
e-mail: ray.price@ahsys.org

Sommerville

Adult CHADD Group
908-647-3985
www.chaddofsomerset.com
e-mail: jkmorrow01@aol.com

Summit/Union County

Stepping Forward Counseling
Center
908-277-1727

New Mexico

Albuquerque

The Attention Deficit Disorder
Clinic (adult and child)
505-243-9600

Bernalillo

Abrazos (support, education,
information)
505-867-3396
www.swcr.org
e-mail: epicsproj@swcr.org

New York

Herkimer

Mohawk Valley CHADD
315-867-5730
e-mail: chaddofmv@aol.com

New York City

Manhattan Adult ADD Support
Group
Contact: Paul Jaffe
845-278-3022
www.maaddsg.org
e-mail: MAADDSG@aol.com

NYC Chapter of CHADD
212-721-0007
e-mail: chadd.ny@usa.com

Rochester

Greater Rochester Attention
Deficit Disorder Association
(adults)
585-251-2322
www.netacc.net/~gradda

North Carolina

Chapel Hill

All Kinds of Minds (Dr. Mel
Levine's clinic)
1450 Raleigh Road, Suite 100,
Chapel Hill, NC 27516
www.allkindsofminds.org

Charlotte

Mecklenburg County CHADD
704-551-9120
www.angelfire.com/nc2/
chadd4meck
e-mail:
chadd4meck@angelfire.com

Raleigh

Triangle Area CHADD
919-990-1032
www.wakechadd.org; e-mail:
van-wake@prontomail.com

Wilmington

Coastal Carolina CHADD
910-452-6042

Ohio

Akron

Adult Attention Deficit Support
  Group
330-344-7602
www.akrongeneral.org/add
e-mail: mromaniuk@agmc.org

Cleveland

Adults with ADD Living in
  Balance (ADDLIB) &
  Individualized ADHD
  Coaching
440-423-1787
e-mail: emc2org@aol.com

Columbus

ADDvance!
614-846-6513
addvancecolumbus@aol.com

Adult ADD Support Group
614-286-2018
e-mail: mad4annie@yahoo.com

Columbus Ohio CHADD
614-855-1114
e-mail:
  susanforchadd@insight.rr.com

Marion

Marion County CHADD
740-389-3606
e-mail:
  marionchadd@netscape.net

OCECD (Ohio Coalition for the
  Education of Children with
  Disabilities)
Parent Training and Information
  Center
740-382-5452, 800-374-2806
www.ocecd.org

Oklahoma

Oklahoma City

Central Oklahoma CHADD
405-722-1233

Oregon

Corvallis

Lorna Huddleston, M.A.
  (resource information, support)
541-754-3830

Eugene

Eugene Branch of Portland
  CHADD
541-344-2221
e-mail:
  eugeneadultadd@yujean.com

LaGrande

Union County CHADD
541-962-8853

North Bend

Coos Bay/North Bend CHADD
541-756-7763

Portland

Portland Metro CHADD (adults
  and parents)
503-294-9504

Pennsylvania

Delaware County

Main Line CHADD/Parents
  Supporting Parents
610-626-2998

Pittsburgh

Southwest Pennsylvania CHADD
  Network, Adult Support
412-563-6003

West Chester

Chester County CHADD
610-429-4060
www.geocities.com/chestercounty
  chadd

Rhode Island

Providence

Rhode Island Adult ADD Support
  Group
401-782-4286, 401-463-8778
  (hotline)
e-mail: members.aol.com/adon

Warwick

CHADD of Rhode Island
401-943-9399
www.chaddofri.org/pages/1/index.
  htm
e-mail: coordinator@chaddofri.org

South Carolina

Charleston

Life Management Center (adults,
  children, and families)
843-577-2277

Parent Training & Resource
  Center
843-792-3025
www.ptrc.org
e-mail: mccartyb@musc.edu

Columbia

Mental Health Association in
  Mid-Carolina Adult ADD
  Support Group
803-779-5364

PRO-PARENTS (support and
  education)
803-772-5688, 800-759-4776
www.proparents.org
e-mail: proparents@aol.com

South Dakota

Sioux Falls

South Dakota Parent Connection
  Training & Info Center
605-361-3171, 800-640-4553
www.sdparent.org
e-mail: lynnbf@sdparent.org

Tennessee

Chattanooga

Greater Chattanooga CHADD
423-876-1241
www.chattchadd.org
e-mail: info@chattchadd.org

Gallatin

Sumner County CHADD
615-644-2348
e-mail: chadd-of-
sumnercounty@juno.com

Nashville

ADD's UP (adults)
615-292-5947

Texas

Austin

Austin CHADD
512-292-1518
e-mail: dbutler1@austin.rr.com

Dallas

Dallas Chapter for ADD Adults
(ADDA)
972-458-9226

San Antonio

San Antonio CHADD
210-493-3974
e-mail: margohall3307@aol.com

Utah

*Farmington, North Logan, Provo,
Riverton, Salt Lake City, St.
George*

CHADD of Utah
801-295-5565
members.aol.com/chaddofutah
e-mail: chaddofutah@aol.com

Vermont

Burlington

Vermont Parent Information
Center (support, education,
information)
802-658-5315, 800-639-7170
www.vtpic.com
e-mail: vpic@vtpic.com

Virginia

Fairfax

Northern Virginia CHADD
703-641-5451
www.chaddofnova.homestead.com
/main.html
e-mail: nova_chadd@hotmail.com

Leesburg

Loudon County CHADD
703-771-3943
e-mail: coleslau6288@aol.com

Newport News

PADDA (People with Attentional
and Developmental Disabilities
Association)
757-591-9119
www.padda.org

Norfolk

Tidewater CHADD
757-479-9993
www.tidewaterchadd.org
e-mail: duzlaps@juno.com

Washington

Bellingham

Lisa Poast
Adult ADD Association
360-647-6681

Bothell (Eastside)

Nancy Crawford Holm, M.A.,
ADD Coach (knowledgeable
about resources and groups for
children and adults)
425-483-5811
e-mail: nancyholm@msn.com

*Federal Way, Lake Washington,
Seattle, Kitsap County, and
Snohomish County*

NW CHADD (Adults and
parents)
206-622-2127
www.nwchadd.org

Seattle

ADD Resources Seattle Adult
Support Group
206-617-6206
e-mail: don@donbakerma.com

Tacoma

Attention Deficit Disorder
Resources
253-759-5085
www.addresources.org

Washington, D.C.

Advocates for Justice and
Education (education and
support)
202-678-8060, 888-327-8060
www.aje-dc.org
e-mail: kim.jones@aje-dc.org

West Virginia

Clarksburg

Parent Training Information
Center (statewide support and
education)
304-624-1438, 800-281-1436
www.wvpti.org
e-mail: wvpti@aol.com

Morgantown

West Virginia CHADD
304-364-5305
www.citynet.net/wvchadd
e-mail: leab@citynet.net

Wisconsin

Green Bay

Northeast Wisconsin CHADD
920-494-9470
e-mail: brbjmb@yahoo.com

Waukesha

Adult Support Group
262-542-6694

Wyoming

Buffalo

Parent Information Center
  (statewide education and
  support)
307-684-2277, 800-660-9742
www.wpic.org
e-mail: tdawson@wpic.org,
  tdawsonpic@vcn.com

ADD RESOURCES AROUND THE WORLD

Canada

Chlliwack, British Columbia

Attention Deficit Disorder
  Support Association
  (ADDSA)
604-793-9311
e-mail: addsa@vcn.bc.ca

New Westminister, British Columbia

Attention Deficit Disorder
  Support Association
  (ADDSA)
604-524-9183
www.vcn.bc.ca/addsa
e-mail: addsa@vcn.bc.ca

Ottawa, Ontario

CHADD Canada
613-731-1209
www.chaddcanada.org
e-mail: info@chaddcanada.org

England

London

Attention Deficit Disorder
  Information and Support
  Services (ADDISA)
020 8906 9068
www.addiss.co.uk
e-mail: info@addiss.co.uk

Manchester

ADD/ADHD and Related
  Syndromes Family Support
  Centre
0161-790-1455
www.addfocus.co.uk
e-mail: info@addfocus.co.uk

Puerto Rico

Caguas

Caguas, Puerto Rico CHADD
787-743-7937
e-mail: caguasprchadd@
  centennialpr.net

Dorado

Dorado, Puerto Rico CHADD
787-278-2519
e-mail: chadd983@yahoo.com

Russia

Anatoly Chubukov, M.D.
Sakhalin region, Yuzhno-
Sakhalinsk city, Popovicha street
55-34, 693007

8(42422) 3-47-92, 8(4242)
402834
www.chubukov.snc.ru
e-mail: sakhdocs@snc.ru

Additional Worldwide Resources

www.adders.org
This website includes support resources for Argentina, Australia, Austria, Belgium, Brazil, Canada, Columbia, Costa Rica, Denmark, England, Estonia, Finland, France, Germany, Guernsey, Hong Kong, Iceland, India, Israel, Italy, Japan, Luxembourg, Malaysia, Malta, Mexico, Netherlands, New Zealand, Northern Ireland, Norway, Puerto Rico, Republic of Ireland, Romania, Scotland, South Africa, Spain, Sweden, Switzerland, the United States, and Wales.

INDEX

ABOUT THE AUTHORS

EDWARD M. HALLOWELL, M.D., was an instructor at Harvard Medical School for twenty years and is now director of the Hallowell Center for Cognitive and Emotional Health in Sudbury, Massachusetts. He is the co-author of *Driven to Distraction* and the author of *The Childhood Roots of Adult Happiness* and *Worry*, among other titles. He lives in Arlington, Massachusetts, with his wife and three children. He welcomes hearing from readers and can be reached through his website, www.DrHallowell.com.

JOHN J. RATEY, M.D., is an associate professor of psychiatry at Harvard Medical School and has a private practice in Cambridge, Massachusetts. He has lectured extensively and published many articles on the topic of treating ADD adults using psychoeducation and pharmacotherapy. His other major research interest is the treatment of aggressive behaviors across a range of diagnoses. Dr. Ratey has most recently published *A User's Guide to the Brain*. He has co-authored *Shadow Syndromes* (1997) with Catherine Johnson, Ph.D., and also co-authored *Driven to Distraction* (1994) and *Answers to Distraction* (1995) with Edward Hallowell, M.D. He has also edited several books, including *The Neuropsychiatry of Personality Disorders* (1994).